Discerning the Time by the Signs

Amazing Prophecies
Being Fulfilled Book 3

Herb Rogers

D1534098

PRESS

TABLE OF CONTENTS

In memory of Ernest Pickering

His leadership inspired me
He friendship encouraged me
His godliness challenged me
His mentoring changed me
His tact and gentle spirit built me up
His depth and simplicity of preaching was a model for me
His support gave me confidence

As a close friend for most of my adult life, he was a major factor
in the deepening of my relationship with the Lord. I will forever be
grateful that God brought him into my life.

INTRODUCTION

W hat a difference a day makes! One day all the preserving, healing and helping influence of Christians is being felt throughout the world. The next day all of the good influence of Christians will be entirely absent, gone from government, gone from business, gone from homes and gone from education.

One day, Christians are extending errands of mercy, acts of compassion and kindness and expressions of love. The next day, the needs of the world will be met with depraved indifference. One day, millions of tenderhearted believers are trying their best to lead people to Christ. The next day, a lost man will be saying, "No man cares for my soul."

The difference? The abrupt disappearance of all believers at an event called the Rapture. The word *rapture* means to remove away suddenly—a carrying away to sublime happiness. The word rapture, a word coined by believers, is not found in the Bible. It was coined to signify the incredible and sudden catching up of believers into heaven.

As sure as Philip was literally caught away from the Ethiopian eunuch in Acts 8:39, and the convert saw him no more, so will the church be caught away and they who are unsaved and left behind will see them no more. Listen to the Scriptures!

Acts 8 shares this concept in the following words: "And when they were come up out of the water, the Spirit of the Lord caught away Philip, that the eunuch saw him no more: and he went on his way rejoicing" (Acts 8:39).

In a different scripture, Paul declares, "Then we which are alive and remain shall be caught up together with them in the clouds, to meet the Lord in the air: and so shall we ever be with the Lord" (I Thessalonians 4:17).

It will happen in the twinkling of an eye. When it happens, there will be no warning. It will happen so suddenly there will be no time to prepare for it. Out of the blue, quickly, unexpectedly, all true believers will be gone. 1 Corinthians describes this for us: "In a moment, in the twinkling of an eye, at the last trumpet. For the trumpet will sound, and the dead will be raised incorruptible, and we shall be changed" (1Corinthians 15:52).

The Greek word translated by the English word *moment* here is where we get our English word atom. An atom of time is how rapidly the Rapture will happen. In other words, it will be over as soon as it starts.

Since some folks may not understand, Paul describes the length of time involved in the rapture of the true church with the words *in the twinkling of an eye.* Most people think when they read the statement, *in the twinkling of the eye,* it's the blinking or the winking of the eye. But that isn't what the Greek says at all. Winking takes 1/50th of a second.

If you look into a light, the pupil of your eye will twinkle. How long does that take? A twinkling is the length of time it takes a light beam to get to your eye. Light travels at 186,000 miles a second. In other words, that's how rapidly the Rapture will happen. It will happen so fast, there is no way to describe it.

Then we learn from I Thessalonians 4 that not only is the Rapture of the church a sure and sudden event, it's also a *silent* event. The insight from this scripture states, "For the Lord Himself will descend from heaven with a shout, with the voice of an archangel, and with the trumpet of God. And the dead in Christ will rise first" (1 Thessalonians 4:16).

This verse of Scripture makes it sound like the Rapture is a noisy event, but it's not. Sound is a relative thing that relates itself to certain objects.

These objects are related to sound in such a way that there are many sounds we do not hear. For example, if I blow an ultrasound whistle you will not hear a thing, but a dog down the street will hear it. While your ear cannot hear it, there are ears that can!

This is what I mean by saying that sound is relative. While an ultrasound whistle is not related to you, it *is* related to a dog.

If we had a radio and turned it on, we would pick up all sorts of sounds. Sounds of various radio stations are passing through a room constantly whether or not the radio is turned on. The sound is in the room even if there is no radio present. If the radio is not turned on, you can't hear it! WHY? It's because *that* sound is related to a certain receiver. To hear the sound, you must have a radio in your possession, and you must tune the radio to that station to hear it. Only true believers will have the spiritual ears to hear the sound of the voice of Jesus at the Rapture. No one else will hear a thing. When millions of people all over the world suddenly disappear, those left behind will not hear a thing. They will not have so much as a clue as to where all the missing people went. They will hear nothing, but those who know Jesus Christ as their own personal Savior will hear. We will simply vanish from this earth to be with our Lord forever.

1 Thessalonians 4:16 declares at the Rapture of the church, Christ will shout. Why is the Lord going to shout like a military officer? I believe John 5 shares the reason. He will shout to indicate which of the dead should come out of the grave.

When Jesus raised Lazarus, He shouted, "Lazarus, come forth." Had He not prefaced the words "come forth" with the name Lazarus, everyone in that cemetery would have been raised from the dead.

John 5 gives us the exact account of this amazing event regarding the raising of Lazarus from the dead. This scripture enlightens us regarding the meaning of Jesus' shout. It declares, "Do not marvel at this; for the hour is coming in which all who are in the graves will hear His voice and come forth; those who have done good, to the resurrection of life, and those who have done evil, to the resurrection of condemnation.

Here we learn there is more than one resurrection. At the Rapture of the church, only people who have received Jesus Christ as their own personal Savior during the church age will be raised from the dead. All others will remain in the grave. Those who have not received Jesus Christ as Savior will be resurrected at the Great White Throne Judgment (Revelation 20:11-15).

In conclusion, notice that according to John 5:28, *dead* people will hear His voice. That is truly amazing. But just as surely as Lazarus heard the voice of Jesus calling him back from the dead, so will all true believers in Jesus Christ hear that same voice calling them back from the dead. We will be called to life everlasting with Jesus Himself. What a day that will be!

One of the things that will cause the Rapture to be so horrible for those left behind is because true believers alone have been holding the line against absolute evil. When they are gone, the Bible declares that unprecedented evil will break out on this earth. It will be earth's darkest hour. Thank the Lord true believers will be gone before that event strikes the earth. It is after the Rapture that satanic power and evil will bring this world into an unimaginable, dreadful and shocking horror. There will be pandemonium, turmoil and anarchy.

Even though we can't know the exact time of this event, Matthew 24 gives a list of signs that will indicate the day is near. By comparing what Jesus said would be signs of the end time in Matthew 24 with today's newspaper headlines, we can know that the end is near.

Matthew 24:1-2 says, "Then Jesus went out and departed from the temple, and His disciples came up to show Him the buildings of the temple, and Jesus said to them, Do you not see all these things? Assuredly, I say to you, not one stone shall be left here upon another, that shall not be thrown down."

> In 70 AD when the Roman General Titus entered into Jerusalem, he gave orders not to destroy the Temple, as he wanted it to stand as a monument to the greatness of his victory. But during the battle, a fire started and the heat became so intense that the Temple was destroyed. But how did the prophecy of Jesus come about where He said, "Not one stone would be standing on another?" Well, the beams in the Temple were overlain with pure gold, and the intense heat of the fire caused the gold to melt. As the gold melted, it ran down the walls and in between the mortar that

held each stone to other stones. When the frenzied Roman army saw the gold for the taking, they were given permission to take it if they could get it. But to get the gold meant to take apart every stone in the temple area, as the gold which had melted hardened in every crack and in every stone in the building.[1]

This is how the prophecy of Matthew 24:1-2 was fulfilled. Note that it was *literally* fulfilled. All the signs that Jesus went on to give His disciples will be fulfilled just as literally as was this prophecy of the stones fulfilled.

It is worth noting that many of the signs of the times could not be understood until their fulfillment began to happen. The following insightful observation reports on this:

The Bible teaches that many of the end time prophecies will not be understood until the time of their fulfillment. And that is exactly what has been happening in the past 100 years. Historical developments and scientific inventions are now making it possible for us to understand end time prophecies that have never been understood before.[2]

When God revealed end time events to Daniel, Daniel did not understand the things he wrote about. Daniel 12:8 makes this very clear: "And I heard, but I understood not: then said I, O my Lord, what shall be the end of these things?" Then the Lord answered Daniel with these words: "And he (God) said, Go thy way, Daniel: for the words are closed up and sealed till the time of the end" (Daniel 12:9).

As an Example of this I shared a sign in my first book that predicted there would be airplanes in the end time. This prophecy could not be understood by anyone until God brought it to pass.

Through the prophet Isaiah, God foretold that in the last days people would fly to the holy land on airplanes. The prophet Isaiah stated it this way:

It shall come to pass in that day That the LORD shall set His hand again the second time To recover the remnant of His people who are left, From Assyria and Egypt, From Pathros and Cush, From Elam and Shinar, From Hamath and the islands of the sea. He will set up a banner for the nations, And will assemble the outcasts of Israel, And gather together the dispersed of Judah From the four corners of the earth. Also the envy of Ephraim shall depart, And the adversaries of Judah shall be cut off; Ephraim shall not envy Judah, And Judah shall not harass Ephraim. But they shall fly down upon the shoulder of the Philistines toward the west; Together, they shall plunder the people of the East; They shall lay their hand on Edom and Moab; And the people of Ammon shall obey them (Isaiah 11:11-14).

How could anyone in the day in which Isaiah wrote these words understand that human beings would fly in the sky like birds? That is a thing that could be understood only by those living in the days in which the prophecy was fulfilled.

This simple prophecy makes it obvious why the things spoken of back then could not be understood until they happened. If you wrote these prophecies several thousand years ago and tried to explain how people would fly in airplanes in the end time—how would you word your prophecy? Wouldn't you use terms that the people of that day were familiar with? Obviously, you could not use a word like airplane. Who would know what you were talking about? These prophecies could not be understood by people living when they were written. The reason we are able to understand these things today is because the reality of the prophecies exist in our time.

In Matthew 24, Jesus gave some startling signs of the times. He said that when these signs begin to be recognized, it would indicate the end is near. These signs are the main subject of this book and are explained in the order in which Jesus gave them.

CHAPTER 1

ABOUT MATTHEW 24

Before looking at any of the signs in Matthew 24, it is necessary to understand Matthew 24:7-8. This is where Jesus gave the key to understanding His prophetic words. Read carefully what He said. We are told that, "For nation will rise against nation, and kingdom against kingdom. And there will be famines, pestilences, and earthquakes in various places. All these are the beginning of sorrows".

I want to emphasize three words found in verse 8. First, note the word *all*. This means that each and every sign that Jesus gave in Matthew 24 is being spoken of in Matthew 24:8.

Second, note the word *beginning*. This means that when these things are initially observed. It does not denote that the end is here. Rather, it means that when these signs begin to happen, they will act as an indicator that the beginning point of the end time is at hand.

The third word we need to understand is the word *sorrows*. The Greek word translated *sorrows* here is the Greek word for birth pangs. Why would the Lord tell us that the end time signs are like the pangs that a woman has in giving birth? First of all, when these signs are completely fulfilled at the end of the seven-year Tribulation, a new age will be born. Second, the pains a woman in labor experiences increase both in intensity and frequency as the experience comes to its conclusion.

Derek Prince has written the following words, "Jesus says that once these birth pains start in human history, they will become more frequent and more intense. There is no way of reversing that process; the birth will occur." [1]

I hear many people say, "Although there are signs of the time that are presently in the world, events could cause a backing away from the signs and thus the end may not come for another 100 years." Nothing can be further from the truth. The picture is that once a woman is pregnant, it's irreversible — there is no going back or adding time to the normal process. The "beginning of the end," as Jesus calls it, is when signs appear on the earth they are not going to go away or pause or retreat. God makes that clear. Time is short, and things will only intensify and get worse.

I suppose the reason why people want to delay the coming of Christ is because they are afraid of it. They may be afraid because they are not saved or because they are not living a righteous life as a Christian, so, they are ashamed. Derek Prince has a word on that also. He says:

> Here is a question that represents one way we can test ourselves regarding end time prophecy: Do we want to stop the pain or do we want to have the baby? If we want to have the baby, we must have the birth pangs, for there is no way to give birth without them. If we say, "Oh, I can't stand all this! It's too terrible. I don't know why I'm living at this time," then we are not really excited about the baby. If we want the baby, we will welcome the birth pangs even if they are very painful.[2]

So it is, that while there have always been earthquakes, wars, famines, etc this sign does not tell us these things are new. They are *not* new. What is new and different from the wars, famines, etc. of the past, as compared with these things to be experienced in the end time is the increase in frequency and intensity of the Matthew 24 signs.

Why do you suppose that WW I was called World War I. It was because, never in human history has there ever been such a war. The same thing was true of WW II. The intensity of WW II was far greater than WW I. This helps us see why Jesus used the birth pangs of a woman in labor to explain how wars of the end time would be dramatically different from the wars fought throughout all of human history.

The identical thing can be said of the signs of Matthew 24 from the weird weather to the horrible pestilences like aids and other horrifying new diseases which presently exist in today's world.

So Jesus is saying, it's *not* that these things have never existed before, it's that they have never existed with the frequency and intensity they will have as the end draws near when our Lord gives birth to a new age. There is a verse in the Old Testament that tells us about exponential growth. Daniel 12:4 tells us, "But you, Daniel, shut up the words, and seal the book until the time of the end; many shall run to and fro, and knowledge shall increase." This verse will be fully explained later. I mention it now so that you might see the word *increase*. This is what God say would happen tgo knowledge in the ends time. What we are seeing in this regard since Israel became a nation?

Allow me to illustrate exponential growth for you. Suppose someone offered you a job for the month of January—a month with 31 days. The offer was that you had a choice of two pay possibilities. First, you could receive a lump sum of one million dollars for the months work or second, you could work the first day for 1 penny. Each day afterward your daily salary would double. Which would you accept? If you chose the million dollars, you fooled yourself, and you do not understand the principles of exponential growth. Below is a chart that will show you what your daily salary would be with running totals. Study it and discover how incredible exponential growth is.

WEEK # 1

DAY	PAYMENT	TOTAL
Jan. 1	$0.01	$0.01
Jan. 2	$0.02	$0.03
Jan. 3	$0.04	$0.07
Jan. 4	$0.08	$0.15
Jan. 5	$0.16	$0.31
Jan. 6	$0.32	$0.63
Jan. 7	$0.64	$1.27

WEEK # 2

Jan. 8	$1.28	$2.55
Jan. 9	$2.56	$5.11
Jan. 10	$5.12	$10.23
Jan. 11	$10.24	$20.47
Jan. 12	$20.48	$40.95
Jan. 13	$40.96	$81.91
Jan. 14	$81.92	$163.83

WEEK # 3

Jan. 15	$163.84	$327.67
Jan. 16	$327.68	$655.35
Jan. 17	$635.36	$1,310.71
Jan. 18	$1,310.72	$2,621.43
Jan. 19	$2,621.44	$5,242.87
Jan. 20	$5,242.88	$10,458.75
Jan. 21	$10,485.76	$20,971.51

WEEK # 4

Jan. 22	$20,971.52	$41,943.03
Jan. 23	$41,943.04	$83,886.07
Jan. 24	$83,886.08	$167,772.15

Jan. 25	$167,772.16	$335,544.31
Jan. 26	$335,544.32	$671,088.63
Jan. 27	$671,088.64	$1,343,177.27
Jan. 28	$1,343,177.28	$2,684,354.55

WEEK # 5

Jan. 29	$2,684,354.56	$5,368,709.11
Jan. 30	$5,368,709.11	$10,737,418.23
Jan. 31	$10,737,418.24	$21,474,836.47

That is exponential growth. This is exactly what the Bible says the end time will be like. That's why Jesus used the illustration of the signs of the end being like the birth pangs of a pregnant woman. Her pains increase in frequency and intensity as the time for the delivery nears.

The main thing I would like to address in this book is that in our lifetime there *are* things happening that have never happened in the entirety of world history. All of these things were predicted by our Lord.

CHAPTER 2

FALSE CHRISTS AND FALSE PROPHETS

SIGN # 1 FALSE CHRISTS

The first of these signs is shared in Matthew 24:5. There we are told: "For many will come in My name, saying, I am the Christ, and will deceive many." This verse deals with the deception of people who should know better. Today that lie is packaged and sold to us in the form of the New Age movement.

Notice carefully that the above scripture states that this sign is the rise of false christs not false prophets. Let me explain the difference between a false Christ and a false prophet. A false Christ is one who claims to be the Messiah, the actual Son of God. A false prophet claims to have the spiritual gift of being able to foretell the future, when, in fact, he does not possess such a gift from the Holy Spirit.

I will share what the Bible says about false prophets in the next sign so that we can have the benefit of comparing false Christs with false prophets to better understand them both.

But first, let's examine the sign Christ gave in Matthew 24:5 about false Christs.

As far back as the Feb. 20, 1989 issue of Time Magazine there was an ad in which two robots converse. This ad, placed by a major engineering firm, asks you to imagine a generation of robots that can learn from their experiences and make their own decisions.

It shows a robot father saying, "When I was your age, robots did what they were told." The son says, "But Dad my generation is different." It's now the talk of those involved with robotics to implant into these robots biological type material so that robots can begin to make decisions independent of the inventor. Some people are calling this the second genesis. They say we have now created a man. [1]

As a result of creating another being, they believe we have become gods ourselves. This is the thinking of the New Age. In the past fifty years, there have been over one thousand people claiming to be "the savior of the world." The thing that will make the world go after the real Antichrist, who will claim to be the world's savior, will be that they believe he is able to bring peace to this world. Already sovereign nations are willing to surrender their authority to the UN. But there will be no peace. 1 Thessalonians 5:3 clearly states: "For when they say, 'Peace and safety!' then sudden destruction comes upon them, as labor pains upon a pregnant woman. And they shall not escape."

Scripture gives us numerous characteristics as to what the Antichrist will be like. These characteristics, in themselves, become a sign of the time as they relate to Satan. The stage needs to be set for the Antichrist and his characteristics to take over the world. Therefore in the age in which he would be accepted for what he is, the world must find these characteristics to be acceptable and widespread. I will list as signs of the times several of these important characteristics.

Satan seeks by imitation to overthrow the purpose of God in this world. In every day, in every age, he has been consistently working to undermine the truth of God. In it's place he seeks to establish his lie and error. The apostle John in his writing in 1 John made this very plain when he writes:

Beloved, do not believe every spirit, but test the spirits, whether they are of God; because many false prophets have gone out into the world. By this you

know the Spirit of God: Every spirit that confesses
that Jesus Christ has come in the flesh is of God, and
every spirit that does not confess that Jesus Christ has
come in the flesh is not of God. And this is the spirit
of the Antichrist, which you have heard was coming,
and is now already in the world (1 John 4:1-3).

John is speaking of teachers who come to teach what purports to
be God's Word. Thus we are not to believe everything that a teacher
says because many false prophets are in the world. When John wrote
a generation after the ascension of Christ, he said there was already
present in his day *the spirit of the Antichrist.* This spirit of the Antichrist
is what this section of this book is addresses. I believe this spirit, which
was present then, will accelerate until it fills the earth and culminates
in the Antichrist. We must understand what 2 Thessalonians teaches if
we are to understand the trends in today's world:

Let no one deceive you by any means; for that Day
will not come unless the falling away comes first, and
the man of sin is revealed, the son of perdition, who
opposes and exalts himself above all that is called
God or that is worshiped, so that he sits as God in
the temple of God, showing himself that he is God.
Do you not remember that when I was still with you
I told you these things? And now you know what is
restraining, that he may be revealed in his own time.
For the mystery of lawlessness is already at work;
only He who now restrains will do so until He is
taken out of the way. And then the lawless one will
be revealed, whom the Lord will consume with the
breath of His mouth and destroy with the brightness
of His coming (2 Thessalonians 2:3-8).

If you were to catch a skunk and put it in a barrel and put a lid
on the barrel, the skunk would be confined and limited in its activity.
But everyone would still know that the black and white kitty was
still around. Even so, they do not know anything of what it will

22

be like when the lid is taken off the barrel and the skunk is turned loose. Today, Satan's system is being confined and limited in it's activity until the influence of the Holy Spirit is gone as a result of the Rapture. The Bible teaches that sometime after the Rapture there will be a second outpouring of the Holy Spirit.

Despite the fact that the spirit of the Antichrist is present, that present-day spirit is nothing compared to what is to come. The spirit of the Antichrist has so accelerated in our day that one wonders how much longer it can increase until it's in full bloom. The Bible thoroughly defines what the spirit of Antichrist is, and lists a number of things in various portions of the Word of God that explain this.

SIGN # 2 INSUBORDINATION

A re-read of 2 Thessalonians 2:4 is where we come to understand the situation. Of the Antichrist it reads: "Who opposes and exalts himself above all that is called God or that is worshiped, so that he sits as God in the temple of God, showing himself that he is God."

This insubordination is one of the identifying characteristics of the Antichrist. This is the very thing that caused Satan to fall from the high estate that he enjoyed at one time. In Isaiah 14 we read of him where he said: "For you have said in your heart: 'I will ascend into heaven, I will exalt my throne above the stars of God; I will also sit on the mount of the congregation On the farthest sides of the north;

I will ascend above the throne of God" (Isaiah 14:13-14). This statement characterizes all that is Satan. It is part of the spirit of the Antichrist.

Insubordination is seen in virtually all phases of our society today. It's presence, problem, and intensity certainly points to the fact that we are in the end time.

First, this insubordination can be seen in the relationship of children with their parents. The Bible points out that at the end of the age the insubordination of children to their parents would be one of many signs of the times that Timothy speaks of in 1 Timothy. In this important prophetic portion of Scripture Paul says, "But know this, that in the last days perilous times will come: For men will be lovers of themselves, lovers of money, boasters, proud, blasphemers, *disobedient to parents*, unthankful, unholy" (2 Timothy 3:1-2).

Since World War II juvenile delinquency has exceeded anything ever known in the history of civilization.

Then *second,* this spirit of insubordination can be further seen in the relationship of wives to their husbands. After God instituted marriage He had this to say in Gen 3:16, "To the woman He said: 'I will greatly multiply your sorrow and your conception; In pain you shall bring forth children; Your desire shall be for your husband, And he shall rule over you.'"

This verse does not mean that the woman is inferior to the man. It simply means that in God's ordained order in marriage, the husband would be in the position of leadership much like a CEO heads a company. The CEO is to put the company first and his decisions should be for the welfare of the company. Many Christian husbands abuse this verse by treating their wives as second-rate human beings, which is not at all what God said.

Third, we see this insubordination in the relationship of a man to his employer. God commands man to obey his employer and to give an honest days work. But what do we see today? We see strikes with unions telling the companies what to do. There is absolute chaos and insubordination in the business world. This is almost unknown in world history, but is a major problem in today's workplace.

Then *fourth*, we see insubordination of people in relationship to their government in Matthew 22:21 where Jesus set forth the command to be in subjection to government. "And He said to them, "Render therefore to Caesar the things that are Caesar's, and to God the things that are God's."

The apostle gives further instruction on this subject in Romans 13 where we read:

> Let every soul be subject to the governing authorities. For there is no authority except from God, and the authorities that exist are appointed by God. Therefore whoever resists the authority resists the ordinance of God, and those who resist will bring judgment on themselves. For rulers are not a terror to

good works, but to evil. Do you want to be unafraid of the authority? Do what is good, and you will have praise from the same. For he is God's minister to you for good. But if you do evil, be afraid; for he does not bear the sword in vain; for he is God's minister, an avenger to execute wrath on him who practices evil. Therefore you must be subject, not only because of wrath but also for conscience' sake (Romans 13:1-5).

In our lifetime we see draft dodgers, civil disobedience and all sorts of violent upheavals against ordained government. This is the spirit of the Antichrist.

The *fifth* way in which this spirit of insubordination is seen **is** in the relationship of students with their teachers. Students now go on strike and defy the ordained administrative powers. In a Chicago high school two boys took a sawed off shotgun out of a brief case and began killing students and teachers. The mass murder of people in our public schools is a matter of which everyone is all too familiar. We are living in a day in which teachers are physically attacked and raped by the students. Students take over colleges and burn the life work of their professors. This is the spirit of the antichrist and is exactly whar the Bible declared the end time would be like.

There is a *sixth* and final way in which we see this insubordination. It is seen in the church in its relationship to Christ. The dominant fact in all Christian experience is the Lordship of Christ. That is why Matthew 23:8 makes the following declaration: "But you, do not be called 'Rabbi'; for One is your Teacher, the Christ, and you are all brethren." Christians are cold in their attitudes to Christ's wooing and Lordship. They are insubordinate. This is the exact condition that our Lord said would exist in the end time. Matthew 24:12 says: "And because lawlessness will abound, the love of many will grow cold."

What we have seen in the paragraphs above is certainly the spirit of the antichrist, and it is evident on *every* hand today. But that's not all, note that the spirit of the Antichrist is visible not only in a spirit of insubordination but also in individualism, our next sign.

SIGN # 3 INDIVIDUALISM

Revelation 13:4 gives insight into this spirit of individualism that is an end-time sign. It says: "So they worshiped the dragon who gave authority to the beast; and they worshiped the beast, saying, "Who is like the beast? Who is able to make war with him?"

Progress in the fields of science, medicine and invention have inflated man's ego until he's mad with success. He has developed a spirit of independence, which has magnified his personality without dependence on God. God does not object to progress, but when, as a result man sets himself above and against God, then we have the spirit of the antichrist.

We see it in athletes, politicians and movie stars as well in other professions. Many people all but worship them as God. In the field of education, we see all that is anti-God thrives. Our children are not to bring their Bibles to school and we are not to pray in it's classrooms, but pornography is required reading. We can't sing Christmas carols, but communists can teach. It's the spirit of the Antichrist that is flaunted before our children. Each passing year this situation is increasing exponentially.

In religion, it is now taught that man is god and that Christ was a man just like us. Man has finally taken into his own hands the salvation of his own soul.

The spirit of the Antichrist can also be seen in the sensationalism of our day, as in the following sign.

SIGN # 4 SENSATIONALISM

This sign is announced in several New Testament verses where we are told the following.

"And he deceives those who dwell on the earth by those signs which he was granted to do in the sight of the beast, telling those who dwell on the earth to make an image to the beast who was wounded by the sword and lived" (Revelation 13:14).

"Let no one deceive you by any means; for that Day will not come unless the falling away comes first, and the man of sin is revealed, the son of perdition" (2 Thessalonians 2:3).

"The coming of the lawless one is according to the working of Satan, with all power, signs, and lying wonders, and with all unrighteous deception among those who perish, because they did not receive the love of the truth, that they might be saved" (2 Thessalonians 2:9-10).

The deception of the Antichrist will be in the sensational abilities that he will have. We are living in a sensational age with the emphasis on the spectacular. Each day the newspaper is almost a Ripley's Believe It or Not column.

For example, take the field of sports. We have produced a generation of supermen with records constantly being broken. Some years ago we questioned the possibility of the 19-second 100-yard dash, a 4 minute mile, a 7 foot high jump, a 27 foot broad jump. *Now* these things are considered common. Our athletes are so taken with convincing the world they are superhuman, they are filling their bodies with illegal drugs so their records will be the greatest ever.

We see sensationalism in the field of education, learning and discovery. Daniel 12:4 clearly declare this to be a sign of the time for it reads, "But you, Daniel, shut up the words, and seal the book until the time of the end; many shall run to and fro, and knowledge shall increase."

One hundred years ago the principle mode of transportation was the same as that used by Moses. Just a few decades ago, when the Spirit of St. Louis flew non-stop from New York to Paris, the world wondered how far it would all go. Today men have visited the moon. *That* is sensational.

Medicine is another area of spectacular achievements. We read of heart and liver transplants. We are stunned when we read of men changed to women and vice versa. One is almost fearful of going into a doctor's office for fear he will come out something different from what he was when he went in. We see the prediction of re-growing physical limbs. We hear about the possibility of deep-freezing our bodies for 100 years until a cure for the disease we have can be found. We see where they now successfully grow hair on bald heads. We read about a woman who is dead for twenty minutes and is revived and lives.

This is indeed an age of spectacular things. Still more spectacular though is the fact that there is so much sensationalism in religion. Emphasis is placed on little boy and women preachers. This is spectacular but unscriptural. And lastly, we see the spiritual glamorization of so-called saved ex-convicts and Hollywood Christians.

But there is more. The spirit of the Antichrist is also seen in the spirit of confusion as in sign # 5 that follows.

SIGN # 5 CONFUSION

The basic text for most of these "spirit of Antichrist" signs has been found in 2 Thessalonians. This sign is not an exception to that. Again 2 Thessalonians 2:3 tells us: "Let no one deceive you by any means; for that Day will not come unless the falling away comes first, and the man of sin is revealed, the son of perdition."

2 Thessalonians 2:10-11 said, "and with all unrighteous deception among those who perish, because they did not receive the love of the truth, that they might be saved. And for this reason God will send them strong delusion, that they should believe the lie."

This is the object of most of what Satan does. He deceives and confuses. It is a persistent destruction of truth—of accepting a lie in its place. This is *exactly* what is happening in our world today. Good is being called evil and evil is called good, exactly what Scripture predicted it would be like in the end time.

The world has never been in such a state of confusion. One leader says this—another leader says that. There is no answer to our present situation. If someone dare speak the truth about something that is happening, he is silenced. Is it any wonder that in Luke 21:25-26 it states that in the end time nations will be in a state of perplexity? The word perplexity means to be in a state of confusion with no answer.

Furthermore, the spirit of the Antichrist is expressed in lawlessness.

SIGN # 6 LAWLESSNESS

Again, I take you to 2 Thessalonians. Note in particular 2 Thessalonians 2:7-8: "For the mystery of *lawlessness* is already at work; only He who now restrains will do so until He is taken out of the way. And then the lawless one will be revealed, whom the Lord will consume with the breath of His mouth and destroy with the brightness of His coming."

Today, we see lawlessness in the home. God never intended that the child should rule the home, but how often do we see it? God seems to be permitting us to see the beginning of the lawlessness that will prevail in the Tribulation which follows the Rapture. Thus the lawless system is on display for all to see.

A good text to give understanding to what the end time will be like is 1 Timothy 3:1-5 which imparts a picture of that day for us: "But know this, that in the last days perilous times will come: For men will be lovers of themselves, lovers of money, boasters, proud, blasphemers, disobedient to parents, unthankful, unholy, unloving, unforgiving, slanderers, without self-control, brutal, despisers of good, traitors, headstrong, haughty, lovers of pleasure rather than lovers of God, having a form of godliness but denying its power. And from such people turn away!"

Note that throughout the time that society is in this state, they have a form of godliness. So what does this mean? Simply this, we are fast approaching a day when the Holy Spirit will remove restraints. The *only* thing that prevents absolute lawlessness is the presence of the church on earth.

In the last verse of the book of Judges we see a condition that is like our own day. It says, "In those days there was no king in Israel; everyone did what was right in his own eyes."

There was no king to curb lawlessness, and what was the result? It was anarchy. That is the condition in which the book of Judges concludes. Men could not indefinitely live in a state of anarchy; so, what did they do? They cried to God for a king. WHY? So that there would be one strong enough to curb and control lawlessness so they might live without fear.

We find this principle then: when men are lawless, they need strong authority to curb that lawlessness. When Israel went into lawlessness, their only recourse was to ask for a king that could control it. When you come to the New Testament, you see in Romans 13 that God has a plan to control lawlessness in society and that plan is governmental power. We learn that it's the job of government to punish those who are lawless and to reward those who are good.

As the age comes to a close, the Bible pictures government as unable to perform the function for which it was intended. It will fail to punish evildoers; thus, government will become ineffectual and anarchy will result.

What, for example, was the campus revolt of the `1960's and 70's but this philosophy—they wanted academic freedom and permissiveness without restraint. They wanted the privilege of living together without marriage, the privilege to use obscenities in the classroom, the right to drink and have co-ed dormitories. Because of this, we have a call for sweeping changes to do away with the rules and restraints that have always existed. The more we give in to this, the more they will want and the worse it will get. The spirit of lawlessness prevails on every hand. People are saying, "I don't have to obey laws that I feel are not right." We even have judges in this country who are giving rulings that are contrary to the clear directions of the Constitution of the United States. They say the Constitution is flawed. Yet, when they take office they are required to take an oath to uphold the Constitution!

It is my conviction that, in the light of the Scriptural teaching of lawlessness. we are all witnesses to this lawlessness in our generation. Lawlessness involves a revolution in the concepts and function of government. Government is no longer performing its intended function. Therefore the Supreme Court passes laws for the protection of criminal rights that have made it impossible to protect the rights of law-abiding citizens.

People who murder and rape serve a few years and are turned loose to do it again. It's not only a serious problem that he who breaks the law goes unpunished, but in so doing, the groundwork for lawlessness will eventually be made uncontrollable.

Remember in the book of Judges that anarchy and lawlessness existed and *then* the people cried out for a strong leader to control it all. They got Saul, but he was worse than nothing. Eventually God removed him and put His own choice of David in power. In that, God has given us a picture of the prophetic program. The lawlessness of the end time will continue and increase until government is completely impotent. Then the people will cry out for a strong man to control it all. At that time Satan will introduce his puppet to the world—the Antichrist.

He will be accepted on the same basis that Israel accepted Saul. Then God will have to remove that satanic impostor so that, as He in the past implanted David, He will implant Himself to rule this earth.

If you were to view this from one standpoint, you would say this is indeed a dark picture. There is not one line in Scripture that offers any hope at all for this age.

Another view is that of encouragement, because, before all this is consummated, we will be caught up in clouds to meet the Lord Jesus in the Rapture.

THE IDENTIFICATIOIN OF FALSE MESSIAHS

One of the principle end-time prophecies is found in I Timothy where we are told, "Now the Spirit expressly says that in latter times some will depart from the faith, giving heed to deceiving spirits and doctrines of demons" (1 Timothy 4:1).

In our lifetime we have seen the old denominations fall away from a Biblical position to accept the lies of doctrines of demons. These doctrines are based on lies and half-truths that contradict God's holy Word. Because of this, we see an ever-increasing horde of people who claim to be the Messiah.

As a result of the departure from the faith that has gained momentum in our day, it has left a vacuum that is being filled by false messiahs. Millions are following their teachings. Usually a false messiah is one who declares that he has a *new* word from God. Ed Hindson, a well-known Christian author, does a great job of identifying this for us. In an excellent message on the subject, he lists several who claim to be the Messiah. Then he reveals information from the writing of a few of these self-declared messiahs that prove they all claim to have a special revelation from God that makes only those of his or her group eligible for heaven. Below is a summary of his research on some of the blasphemous statements made by them.

Judge Rutherford (Jehovah's Witnesses): "Jesus Christ returned to earth in 1914 to establish the Theocratic Millennium Kingdom. The world is awaiting this revolution" (The Kingdom, 1933).

Father Divine (Peace Mission): "I am God Almighty. . .the Holy Spirit personified . . . the Prince of Peace" (New Day, July 16, 1949).

Elijah Muhammad (Black Muslims): "Wallace Farad (Muslim version of Father Divine) is God Himself. He is the one we have been looking for the last 2,000 years" (New York Herald Tribune, April 3, 1963).

Mother Baba (Sufism Reoriented). "I am Jesus Christ personified" (Parvardigar).

Sun Myung Moon (Unification Church): "Jesus Christ will return by being born in the flesh in Korea . . ." (Divine Principle, pp.501ff).

David Berg (Children of God): "Forget not thy king . . . forsake not his ways, for he hath the key, even the key of David! Therefore thou shalt kiss the mouth of David. For thou are enamored with my words and thou art in love with me, thy savior." (The Kingdom: A Prophecy, August 20, 1971, Lo. No. 94).

Herbert W. Armstrong (Worldwide Church of God): "We grow spiritually more and more like God, until at the time of the resurrection — we shall then be born of God—we shall then be God" (The U.S. And British Commonwealth, p. 9).

David Koresh (Branch Davidians): I am the Lamb of God" (People, March 15,1993, p.41). [2]

These false messiahs believe that they, and only they, have the truth of God and all others who do not accept that are destined to go to Hell. Hindson gives a few examples of this delusional belief with the following quotations:

Jehovah's Witnesses believe the church age ended in 1914 with the return of Christ to earth. Therefore, they do not meet in churches, but in Kingdom Halls. They say that only Jehovah's faithful witnesses (the 144,000) know and believe the truth—all others are lost.

Mormons believe they alone are the "latter-day saints" of God. Brigham Young said, "Every spirit that does not confess that God has sent Joseph Smith, and revealed the everlasting gospel to and through him, is of antichrist."

Christian Scientist founder Mary Baker Eddy said, "A Christian Scientist requires my work *Science and Health for* his textbook . . . because it is the voice of truth to this age . . . uncontaminated by human hypotheses.

The Unification Church (Moonies) teaches that Sun Myung Moon is the second messiah ("Lord of the Second Advent") sent to complete the work of salvation begun by Jesus Christ. Moon says of himself and the church, "No heroes in the past, no saints or holy men of the past, like Jesus or Confucius have

excelled us. We are the only people who truly understand the heart of Jesus and the hope of Jesus."[3].

SIGN # 7 FALSE PROPHETS

First we need to have an understanding of a false prophet and
what the Bible says about such a person.

We begin our discussion with 2 Thessalonians 2:6-7, which says,
"And now you know what is restraining, that he may be revealed in
his own time. For the mystery of lawlessness is already at work; only
He who now restrains will do so until He is taken out of the way."

These verses are saying that the Antichrist (called the lawless
one) will be restrained by the presence of certain things. We learn
that there is a thing and a person holding the Antichrist in check.
Verse 6 says, "you know *what* is restraining," while verse 7 declares,
"*He* who now restrains will do so until He is taken out of the way."
The word *what* of verse 6 is speaking of the church and the word *He*
of verse 7 is speaking of the Holy Spirit.

How does the church restrain the revealing of the Antichrist?
The true church is comprised of those who are born again through
the blood of the Lord Jesus Christ. In the book of Romans we are
clearly taught that a born again person is indwelt by the Holy Spirit.
"But you are not in the flesh but in the Spirit, if indeed the Spirit of
God dwells in you. Now if anyone does not have the Spirit of Christ,
he is not His" (Romans 8:9).

Another of the many verses that teach when one is born again
the Spirit of God literally indwells his human body is found in 1
Corinthians 3:16. It reads: "Do you not know that you are the temple
of God and that the Spirit of God dwells in you?"

With that truth clearly set in your mind, you can understand that
it is the Spirit of God in the born again child of God that acts as a
restraining influence on Satan and the coming Antichrist. Perhaps
that helps you understand why demons are more active in Africa
than America. There is a greater percentage of the population born
again in America than in Africa. Therefore, the restraining influence
will be greater.

However, the Bible indicates that in the last days demon activity will increase. The reason for this is that in the end time many Christians will not live godly lives. With this decay and decline of biblical Christianity their restraining influence is diminished. As the church goes apostate and as the population explosion continues, a smaller and smaller percentage of the total population constitutes born again people. Thus the influence of the Holy Spirit, who works through those whom He indwells, is less and less proportionately speaking. Thus, Satan moves in to fill the vacuum.

Does it not stand to reason that the fewer born again people through whom the Holy Spirit restrains from a percentage stand-point will also mean less restraining influence?

In 1850, 1 in 4 people in the world professed to be Christians. Now that number is less than 1 in 20. That is a startling change! Therefore, we find a rise in demon activity as the Bible predicted. This exhibits itself in many ways. The most obvious of all is found in 1 Timothy 4:1: "Now the Spirit expressly says that in latter times some will depart from the faith, giving heed to deceiving spirits and doctrines of demons." The world is literally filled with the doctrines of demons today. We see it in communism, modernism and ever-expanding numbers of cults, to name just a few.

ASTROLOGY AND HOROSCOPES

There are many ways in which false prophets speak in today's world. One of the foremost deceptions that proclaim false prophecy is found in horoscopes and astrology.

Astrology and fortune telling are definitely stated in God's Word to be sinful practices led by Satan and his hosts. Many are listening to doctrines of demons through horoscopes. It's estimated that 1,200 of the 1,700 daily newspapers in the U.S. print daily horoscopes. It's reported that at least five million Americans plan their lives by the horoscopes. No respectable newspaper is without a horoscope section.

According to the latest estimates, stargazers have about 18 million devotees. Besides that, another 30 million read the astrological columns in the daily newspapers. One leading astrologer proudly claims astrology is the key that opens the door to all occult knowledge.

It's not just the ignorant who are following astrology, but businessmen, presidents, and other highly educated people follow their horoscopes before making a decision about important issues in their lives. In the United States, about 100 movie stars consult their favorite astrologers before taking a new role.

Even stock market speculators look to astrology. Some will pay as much as $100 to consult their favorite astrologer. In India, most Hindu marriages are based on the horoscope.

One leading American astrologer said, "Most people won't admit that they believe in astrology, but most people know what sign they wore born under."

When an American girl got engaged to the crown prince of Sikkim, the marriage date was postponed for a year because it was at that time the prince's astrologer said would be best. In the East, astrologers determined not only the time but the precise direction of ceremonial marches. Palace walls are torn down so that a funeral or marriage procession can move in harmonious alignment with the planets.

Many became more interested in astrology after the flood. The Bible speaks in Genesis 10 of Nimrod, who was a mighty man. After his death, his wife Semarisas, attempted to hold his kingdom together by art and craft. She claimed that Nimrod had gone to heaven and was represented by the constellation Orion. This was the beginning of Babylonian astrology.

In the book of Daniel Nebuchadnezzar had a dream. Daniel 2:2 we tells us: "Then the king gave the command to call the magicians, the *astrologers*, the sorcerers, and the Chaldeans to tell the king his dreams. So they came and stood before the king."

Astrology is not a new thing. It's been going on since shortly after creation. What makes it different today is the fact that those dabbling in it have increased exponentially. This is exactly as the Bible predicted. The dramatic increase is no doubt due to the availability of newspapers and other publications that did not exist in ancient times.

Throughout the Bible we find this cult being practiced. To many Christians it doesn't seem to be something bad. But to God it is.

Search with me through the Scriptures. In Jeremiah 10:2 we read, "Thus says the LORD: Do not learn the way of the Gentiles; Do not be dismayed at the signs of heaven, for the Gentiles are dismayed at them."

Thus God says we are not to follow the teachings of astrology. God gives a warning about the false gods of astrology six verses later: "But they are altogether dull-hearted and foolish; A wooden idol is a worthless doctrine" (Jeremiah 10:8). Foolishness and vanity is what God calls the doctrine of astrology. Think for a moment how utterly absurd it is to believe   that chunks of rock. barely visible millions of miles away, can exercise influence on human lives. To think such things can determine whether a man should be a carpenter or a singer is incredible!

Even Israel fell to such worship in 2 Kings 17:16: "So they left all the commandments of the LORD their God, made for themselves a molded image and two calves, made a wooden image and worshiped all the host of heaven, and served Baal."

Sadly, history is repeating itself today. We are plunging into the same age-old satanic deception. Millions are being deluded as they follow their horoscopes religiously and daily. That this cult is a satanic deception is obvious from a thorough study of the Bible. It is Satan's objective to get humans to worship any kind of idol or thing to draw them away from the true God. The Bible gives repeated warnings about being involved with horoscopes and the stars.

Fortune tellers are here by the thousands. Even born again people are being sucked into spiritism through astrology.

Many today claim power to heal—actually heal. Multitudes are drawn into doctrines of demons through this method. I recently read where that there are now so-called healers who specialize in healing animals. Thus animal lovers, through this method, are getting involved. The various methods of occult are legion in number, each appealing to a different type of individual.

There is no present-day-phenomena more prominent than the rise of fortune tellers and prophets. That such things are the offshoot of pagan idolatries is indisputable from God's Word. Leviticus 19 makes it very plain. We are told: "Give no regard to mediums and familiar spirits; do not seek after them, to be defiled by them: I am the LORD your God" (Leviticus 19:31.

Witches, mediums and the like were considered by God to be such a serious sin that he commanded that they be put to death. Note how clearly God states this in Leviticus 20:27, "A man or a woman who is a medium, or who has familiar spirits, shall surely be put to death; they shall stone them with stones. Their blood shall be upon them."

Thus, in light of this, end time demon activity through fortune telling and so-called modern day prophets, we need to see what God's Word has to say about the same.

When the disciples asked Jesus what would be the signs of the end of the age. Jesus told them what to look for. He said in Matthew 24:24: "For false christs and false prophets will rise and show great signs and wonders to deceive, if possible, even the elect."

TRUE AND FALSE PROPHETS

The Bible teaches that not all prophets have their gifts from God. One of the great sources of confusion during Old Testament times was that there were many false prophets. Because of that, God spelled out certain rules to help us distinguish between the true prophet and the false prophet.

Rule number one was the test as to whether or not the prophecy came to pass. If it did not, it exposed the so-called prophet as a fraud. We find this rule revealed in Deuteronomy 18:21-22: "And if you say in your heart, 'How shall we know the word which the LORD has not spoken?' when a prophet speaks in the name of the LORD, if the thing does not happen or come to pass, that is the thing which the LORD has not spoken; the prophet has spoken it presumptuously; you shall not be afraid of him."

Thus God says that a true prophet *cannot* he wrong on his prediction of things to come. If one who claims to be a prophet of God makes a prediction that does not happen, you will know he is not a true prophet. Under the law he was to be killed.

Rule number two is also given in Deuteronomy where we are told: 'But the prophet who presumes to speak a word in My name, which I have not commanded him to speak, or who speaks in the name of other gods, that prophet shall die" (Deuteronomy 18:2),

This is very appropriate for today's prophets since they are right only part of the time—wrong *most* of the time. For that reason, we know such so-called prophets are not of God.

Rule number three: Scripture teaches that a false prophet *can* predict with accuracy part of the time. Such a prophet was found to be false, not on the ground that the prophecies did not come true, but on the teachings of the prophet. This test involves whether or not they practice the teaching of God's Word in their lives. Do they lead others to follow God's Word. Deuteronomy 13 makes this clear for it states:

> If there arises among you a prophet or a dreamer of dreams, and he gives you a sign or a wonder, and the sign or the wonder comes to pass, of which he spoke to you, saying, 'Let us go after other gods which you have not known; and let us serve them,' you shall not listen to the words of that prophet or that dreamer of dreams, for the LORD your God is testing you to know whether you love the LORD your God with all your heart and with all your soul (Deuteronomy 13:1-3).

Note in this passage that God is speaking about a false prophet with a real ability to foretell the future at times. When such a one claims to be speaking for God and encourages his hearers to participate in things that God condemns, the gift is not from God. It is from the forces of evil. Surely Isaiah 8 is clear enough in itself:

> Bind up the testimony, Seal the law among my disciples. And I will wait on the LORD, Who hides His face from the house of Jacob; And I will hope in Him. Here am I and the children whom the LORD has given me! We are for signs and wonders in Israel From the LORD of hosts, Who dwells in Mount Zion. And when they say to you, "Seek those who

are mediums and wizards, who whisper and mutter," should not a people seek their God? Should they seek the dead on behalf of the living? To the law and to the testimony! If they do not speak according to this word, it is because there is no light in them (Isaiah 8:16-20).

We are seeing a rise in false prophets in our day. God's Word says we can recognize them for what they are. Take Matthew 7 as an example: "Beware of false prophets, who come to you in sheep's clothing, but inwardly they are ravenous wolves" (Matthew 7:15).

Today's so-called prophets dabble in astrology, crystal balls and various forms of occultism. God's Word condemns this. Therefore, people who claim to be prophets from God and are involved in such practices are not of God. They are of the Devil.

What has happened to create such a widespread interest in these things in our day? *First,* we have mentioned that a decreasing percentage of this world's population is Christian.

Second, in the last days the Bible predicts demon activity will rise.

Third, the rise of interest in future events is that people sense there are profound changes on the horizon. They are wondering whether or not this world can survive the problems that exist. Therefore, they look to the so-called prophets of today for answers to their curiosity and concerns.

A *fourth* reason — and the most important of all — is there is widespread apostasy in the present day church that has left a colossal spiritual emptiness in the hearts of millions of people. As air rushes in to fill a vacuum, powerful forces are vying to occupy this void left in men's hearts by the abandonment of the Christian faith.

One of the most amazing aspects of Bible prophecy today is the beginning of the fulfillment of the prophecies that speak of the end time rise in demon activity. Unfortunately the warning of the danger of demonic activity is not being heeded. Satan and demons are as real to the believer in the occult as Christ is to the believer.

40

As God allowed the magicians of Egypt to exercise miraculous power in the day of Moses, we are seeing such things today. Certainly these things tell us that the end is near. Are you ready?

Now what about the false prophets of today? Are they not involved in things that are condemned in God's Word? I'm talking about such things as astrology, voodoo, palm reading and other practices associated with the occult. Hollywood is going wild with movies that encompass this theme. It's been noted that Ouija boards outsell Monopoly in some parts of the country.

It's estimated that over 20 million people carry a rabbit's foot or some other sort of good luck charm in the hopes this will help them in one way or another. Millions are afraid of the number 13 and are afraid to walk under a ladder, even if no one is on it. Who knows how many knock on wood, cross their fingers or throw salt over their shoulders?

In America today there are actually churches that worship Satan. Our government has given them tax-exempt status. A bonafide religious place of worship that will not go along with certain government standards is denied tax-exempt status while the church of Satan has a tax-exempt status! I believe false prophets today outnumber Bible-believing preachers.

Jesus said that in the end time many who claim to be prophets would be fakes. Many would have great power. Note what Matthew 24:24 says: "For false christs and false prophets will rise and show great signs and wonders to deceive, if possible, even the elect."

Time does not allow us to go into all the incredible things that people who are supposedly pastors are saying to prove themselves false prophets. I read of one minister who said, "Perhaps the task of clergy and the church is not to condemn the use of heroin, but rather to find out what's good with it so that we can understand the meaning of the text." He goes on to say "God saw everything that He had made and behold it was very good."

The president of a group of churches had this to say, "The virgin birth of Jesus Christ is unimportant. I tell everyone that has met Christ and felt His forgiving love not to worry about how He came. If He came from a harlot or was hatched from a buzzard's egg, He's still the greatest person this world has ever known."

41

It was stated from the pulpit of a mid-western church that "the prophet Isaiah did indeed go into the temple, but he didn't see God; rather, he was high on drugs when he thought that he had seen the seraphim." He tells us that a type of oil was used in the temple that caused hallucinations when the fragrance filled the poorly ventilated temple.

We're all familiar with books such as *The Passover Plot* and the rock opera *Jesus Christ Superstar* that present Jesus as immoral. A professor in a so-called Christian seminary said, "Jesus was probably married." So you see, we are living in days of unprecedented blasphemy. The blasphemy is coming not only from the unsaved. It is coming from those who claim to be leaders in Christendom. The false prophets are out there, and they are there in abundance. This is not the amazing thing. They have always been there. The amazing thing is *who* they are and *how many* there are. It's amazing how many follow them, and who those are that follow them!

Matthew 24 tells us there will be a rise in religious fanatics. Listen to verse 24 again: "For false christs and false prophets will rise and show great signs and wonders to deceive, if possible, even the elect."

From time to time every religion has produced fanatics—some more than others. The Islamic religion has produced a global terrorist network. In India, Hindu fanatics have burned missionaries and their families alive for the "crime" of preaching the gospel and feeding lepers. Those who are members of the Ku Klux Klan (KKK) misquote and twist Scripture to support their own beliefs.

Former Israeli Prime Minister Yitzhak Rabin was assassinated by a young Jewish man. This man believed he was doing God a service by taking Rabin's life. He was trying to punish the former Prime Minister for giving away parts of Israel to the Palestinians.

Perhaps more human lives have been destroyed in the name of a religion than any other ideology. Each fanatic believes he is the defender of the true faith and that others are deceived and deserve death. Fanatics believe they are operating in the will of God when they kill those who have an opposing belief.

Revelation 13 reveals a future religious leader arising shortly after the appearance of the Antichrist. He is identified as the False Prophet (Revelation 16:13, 19:20, 20:10). This man will attempt to unite two global religions under his dominion. According to Revelation 13:11-16, he will initiate the construction of a religious icon to the Antichrist, and will actually perform a supernatural miracle to make the icon speak and live. This religious fanatic will also initiate a universal system of buying and selling. This system will restrain those who do not accept his belief system from buying or selling (Revelation 13:16-18).

Today, we are seeing a rise in religious fanaticism which is threatening the very foundations of civilization. In the beginning of human civilization, Cain killed his brother Abel because he was jealous over Abel's offering to God. The first murder involved religion. The final conflict at Jerusalem will involve a religious fanatic (the False Prophet) and his military commander, the Antichrist. The rise in fanatics, especially Islamic fanatics, is another evidence of the time of the end.

The world, having rejected the true Christ, is now willing to accept anyone claiming to be Christ. They are also accepting false prophets claiming to be sent from God. It should be noted here that the signs Jesus gives in Matthew 24 are parallel to the four horsemen of the apocalypse as seen in Revelation 6.

I will conclude our study on false Christs and prophets with a warning. Do not allow yourself to be involved with things that are occult in nature even though they may seem innocent.

Allow me to give you a sampling of how Satan can influence us in ways we may never have thought of. For example, have you ever turned around to keep a black cat from walking across your path? Or have you gone out of your way to keep from walking under a ladder? Practicing these types of superstition and reading the daily horoscope may seem harmless, but they are Satan's traps and through them he influences many Christians to turn from the truth in ways never thought of.

Here are a few more superstitions. It was once thought that when a person sneezed his soul left his body temporarily. The expression *God Bless You* was used to keep an evil spirit from taking over that body while it was soulless. Knocking on wood is a way to ward off evil. Crossing the fingers has the same background. It grew from the idea that crossed fingers were symbols of the cross and acted as a good luck charm. The idea of walking under a ladder is bad luck because superstition says that Satan lurked under the ladder at the cross of Christ, and while He was foiled in that attempt he still lurks under ladders to attack others.

The ways to allow false prophets to influence you are legion and you must be on guard at all times against them.

THE FIRST HORSEMAN OF THE APOCALYPSE

The first four signs in Matthew 24 parallel the four horsemen of the apocalypse in Revelation 6. We will compare each of these as we go from sign to sign.

The first sign given, as we have seen in Matthew 24, is false Christs. The word "Christs" is plural. Of course, the culmination of this trend will be *the* Antichrist who will appear at the beginning of the Tribulation. With that in mind, note Revelation 6:2, "And I looked, and behold, a white horse. He who sat on it had a bow; and a crown was given to him, and he went out conquering and to conquer." To begin with, he has a bow but no arrow. In other words, he comes on the scene as a man of peace. This first horseman of the apocalypse is the Antichrist and parallels perfectly the first sign our Lord gave in Matthew 24 as He predicted how false Christs would arise in the end time.

First, note "a crown was *given* to him." In other words, he didn't get the crown through war or force. The national entity gave it to him. In our day, we are seeing the beginning preparations of a world that will gladly receive the coming Antichrist and give him ruler-ship. This horseman is exactly what Jesus spoke of in Matthew 24. This is one of the many things that make our time unique. Political conditions are so impossible that leaders are willing to surrender the sovereignty of their nations to anyone who can bring peace. This has never been the case in all of history, but this is *unerringly* what the Bible predicts for the end of this age.

The second thing to be learned from Revelation 6:2 is the fact that after he receives some of his power by peaceful means, he continues consolidating his power by force and becomes a man of war.

It clearly says that after he achieved power through peaceful means "he went out conquering and to conquer."

Matthew 24:5 states: "For many will come in My name, saying, 'I am the Christ,' and will deceive many." Again, the key word here is the word *many*. I refer to the first time the word many is used in the verse. True, there have always been weird people who claimed to be the Christ, but the thing that makes this sign unique to our day is the *number* of such crackpots there are. It's the significantly large number of those making this claim. So large a number has never happened since Christ ascended into heaven. That makes this sign an important one, which will consummate in the acceptance of the Antichrist.

CHAPTER 3

WARS AND RUMORS OF WAR

SIGN # 8—WARS THAT ARE MORE
FREQUENT AND INTENSE

M atthew 24:6 also reveals the next sign: "And you will hear of wars and rumors of wars. See that you are not troubled; for all these things must come to pass, but the end is not yet."

Be reminded that Jesus told us these signs would be like the birth pangs of a woman giving birth. It is *not* that there will be wars in the end time. This sign states, that while there have *always* been wars and rumors of war, the end time wars will be different in their increase in numbers and destructive intensity.

The clear implication of this is that as we come to the close of the end time, the signs will increase in number and intensity like a woman having labor pains. "The magnitude of warfare in the 20th century is another fulfillment of end time prophecy related to world politics. The 20th century was one of unparalleled war. Like birth pangs, the frequency and intensity of war increased exponentially. It is now estimated that more people died in wars during the 20th century than in all previous wars throughout recorded human history."[1]

World War I was called "The Great War." The reason it was called by this name is because until this time there was never a war that involved the entire world and was so universally destructive.

The number of troops in this war was more than in all other wars we know of in human history. But World War II was even greater in deaths and property devastation. Yes, there have always been wars and rumors of wars, but nothing of the magnitude of World War II.

May I repeat that Jesus compared the end time to a woman giving birth. He meant that as we approach the end time, the same things would be happening as have always happened, but they would increase in intensity and frequency to such a point that Jesus remarked, "For then there will be great tribulation, such as has not been since the beginning of the world until this time, no, nor ever shall be. And unless those days were shortened, no flesh would be saved; but for the elect's sake those days will be shortened" (Matthew 24:21-22).

Never before has mankind had the power to destroy all life from the earth through war in a period of seven years. That power exists today! So, the sign of wars and rumors of war as fought today are exceptionally different from the type of warfare that was fought before World War I.

Yet, while this would happen, Jesus said we should not be troubled by the devastating type wars that would characterize the end time. These end time wars are exponentially destructive because of the modern science that created weapons of incredible destructive force. Wars before World War II, in particular, could never have produced such destructiveness and loss of life because weapons of mass destruction had never existed before our day. So, Jesus declares that we should not be troubled or anxious about the end time coming immediately when these types of wars appear on the world scene. The end would not come at *that* point. As these things begin to happen, it is a sign that we are swiftly approaching the end.

SIGN # 9 RUMORS OF WAR

In Matthew 24:6 Jesus makes it plain that in the end time there would not only be a radical increase in the number of wars that would be fought, there would also be a dramatic increase in the frequency in which rumors of war would be made. It's almost a daily news story that there is the threat of war in some part of the world. Scarcely a day passes that rumors of war are not in our news media.

When we speak of 'rumors of war" we are not talking of actual war. We are talking about the fact that many nations and/or leaders are *threatening* war in one form or another.

Since Israel became a nation this rapid increase in reporting on rumors of war has been evident.

I will not take the space to give news items that verify this, as we all know it is happening as never before in the history of the world. It simply makes this sign very obvious. We are living in a day when there are unprecedented rumors of wars.

SIGN # 10 ETHNIC WARS

The real sign as it pertains to wars and rumors of wars is seen in the next verse. Matthew 24:7-8 says: "For nation will rise against nation, and kingdom against kingdom. And there will be famines, pestilences, and earthquakes in various places. All these are the beginning of sorrows."

"The beginning of sorrows" is that bridge that moves us out of the last days of the church into the beginning of the Tribulation. This is the time in which we see the deterioration of the world that will finally make the inevitable rise of the Antichrist.

In verse 7,says: "For nation shall rise against nation." This is not so much political wars, as one country fighting another country. It's *racial* wars. The primary definition in Greek lexicons for the Greek word translated "nation" is race! So racial warfare will characterize this time where there will be wars of one color against another, Islam against Christians, etc. This is what this phrase refers to. We see it in South Africa with blacks against whites, in the Middle East with Arabs against Jewish people. Hatred based on religious beliefs or skin color has never existed in such a large scale as it does today. It is undeniably the exact condition Jesus is speaking of in Matthew 24:7, that the type of things going on at the end time would be exponentially increased and much more frequent and severe.

SIGN # 11 WARS OF KINGDOM AGAINST KINGDOM

Then, verse 7 goes on to say, "kingdom will rise against kingdom." This is speaking of blocks of countries allying together against other blocks of countries. This did not happen until World War I. Why else do you suppose that they called it World War I? Simply because nothing like that had ever happened before

I believe the greatest threat to world peace today is Islamic fundamentalism. In this country we have embarked on a reckless disarmament program literally dismantling the industrial arms complex. The problem today is different from before World War II. Back then it could again be built as there would be sufficient time to do it. But not today! With the advent of weapons of mass destruction we must be totally prepared at all times to act as a deterrent to an aggressor nation.

There is an informative website, GlobalSecurity.org, that gives detailed information about actual wars. The data is listed in table form and includes things like the countries or groups involved, the number killed and the dates of the conflicts.

> There are several significant things to point out about the graph on this website: First, the number of wars increased exponentially beginning in the 1950's. Second, this exponential increase occurred only after Israel became a nation. (And, this is after two world wars that "were supposed to end all wars.") Based on these graphs, it appears the fulfillment of the prophecy Jesus made of "wars and rumors of wars" is well under way. It's no coincidence that there has been an exponential increase in wars that have occurred after Israel became a nation. Numerous scriptures tell us that the rise of Israel as a nation will be the main sign of the end time. That began in 1948.[2]

People are saying what prophecy says, "Peace and safety when there is none." The Iranian president said, "It's our goal to unite all the Islamic nations under the leadership of a coalition led by

Iran and Syria." The first efforts will be in driving the West out of the Middle East and liberating Palestine. The second goal of this unholy alliance is to replace the Judeo-Christian world order with an Islamic world order. Islamic unity and control of the Middle East oil fields is the first step. Once they have that, they believe the West is doomed.

They say that Israel would return to the pre-1967 borders, peace would result. That's propaganda. If it were true, then why did they attack Israel three times before the present borders existed? Some developments that are moving things are: Iran is building a submarine fleet in the Baltic Sea trained by the Russians. Further, Christians have increasingly become subject to attack in Islamic nations. Five former Soviet republics have formed an economic block with Iran. The vastly expanded grouping will cover 372 million square miles and include 300 million people.

> Israel's long-term survival is anathema to the Muslim Middle East. Nor have countries like Syria been reticent about their true strategic aims. In 1999, after yet another conference attempting to resolve the Arab-Israeli conflict, Syrian foreign minister Farouq al-Shara, as Stephens reports, "Delivered a speech to the Arab Writers Union in which he explained that Syria's interest in a negotiated settlement with Israel had nothing to do with actually coming to terms with Israel's right to exist, but rather that the recovery of the Golan Heights was merely a stage on the road to the destruction of Israel. Assad's government "believes that regaining the whole of Palestine is a long term goal."[3]

On top of these awesome facts, more and more Islamic nations are producing weapons of mass destruction. The emphasis in more than a half dozen Islamic nations is on buying nuclear capability. All of this, of course, reinforces the idea that we are seeing the beginning of the fulfillment of Ezekiel's prophecies about a future coalition of Russia and Islamic countries invading Israel. A total of 70 of the world's 184 countries are considered in the house of Islam. In England today, there are now more Muslims than Methodists. There are even more Muslims there than there are evangelical Christians.

Funded by the vast resources of Arab oil money, the Muslims are buying abandoned Anglican churches and turning them into mosques at such a rate that some Muslims claim that England will be the first Muslim European country. Ten years ago there were 150 mosques in England—today there are over 1,100. Even in the U.S. there are more Muslims than Episcopalians. It is said that sometime in the future Islam may well surpass Judaism as America's largest religious minority.

The goal of Islam since the days of Mohammed has been to unite all followers in a holy war against the Judeo-Christian world. The stage is now set for the kind of explosive developments students of Bible prophecy have long anticipated. The final objective is still the same, the end of the Jewish state and the beginning of a new Arab worldwide dictatorship.

In Matthew 24:7 where we are told that there would be wars of one block of nations against another block of nations. Do you see it? In this passage Jesus is not referring to usual wars as they have always existed. In part He is speaking of wars that would be on a worldwide scale involving all nations of the world at the same time.

Consider this: historians tell us that mankind to date has fought 14,531 wars that historians can identify. In all of these wars combined, over 600 million people have been killed. Half of all people ever killed as a result of war have been killed since and including World War I. The point is, that before the 20th century there is nothing with which to compare present day warfare. Note in this same chapter in Matthew 24:22, Jesus says that mankind's war-making abilities will become awesome: "And unless those days were shortened, no flesh would be saved; but for the elect's sake those days will be shortened." Neither World War I nor World War II had that potential. But today we do. This has only been so since the advent of the atomic bomb.

THE SECOND HORSEMAN OF THE APOCALYPSE

Someone has said, there will never be an atomic war as it's too risky. But tell me when mankind has not used the weapons he has stockpiled. You will then note that Revelation 6:4 speaks of the rider of the second horse of the apocalypse. We are told he has a *great* sword. I believe, as we have already pointed out in a previous sign, this great sword refers to the atomic and hydrogen bombs. What does an atomic bomb do to a city? It destroys every thing and every person. This is exactly what Jeremiah 4:6-7 predicted: "Set up the standard toward Zion. Take refuge! Do not delay! For I will bring disaster from the north, And great destruction." The lion has come up from his thicket, And the destroyer of nations is on his way. He has gone forth from his place To make your land desolate. Your cities will be laid waste, Without inhabitant."

When in world history has any thing like this ever happened? We read in our newspapers that in the event of an atomic war one third of mankind will probably be killed. Believe it or not, that's the exact figure Scripture gives for the dead of these early Tribulation wars.

We've previously mentioned that the signs Jesus gave in Matthew 24 are parallel to Revelation 6. Therefore note the second rider mentioned in Revelation 6:

> When He opened the second seal, I heard the second living creature saying, "Come and see." Another horse, fiery red, went out. And it was granted to the one who sat on it to take peace from the earth, and that people should kill one another; and there was given to him a great sword (Revelation 6:3-4).

Note again, this rider has a *great* sword, which as we have said before represents an incredible destructive weapon of war—no doubt the atomic bomb. In Revelation 18:8, in speaking of the destruction of future Babylon, note the destruction comes in one hour. "Therefore her plagues will come in one day her death and mourning and famine. And she will be utterly burned with fire, for strong is the Lord God who judges her."

Revelation 18:10 adds the following information to how speedily the destruction of a city would come: "standing at a distance for fear of her torment, saying, 'Alas, alas, that great city Babylon, that mighty city! For in one hour your judgment has come.'"

We have yet further information in Revelation 18:17 which elaborates on this destruction: "For in *one hour* such great riches came to nothing. Every shipmaster, all who travel by ship, sailors, and as many as trade on the sea, stood at a distance."

I direct your attention again to Matthew 24:3 and the words of the disciples' question: "Now as He sat on the Mount of Olives, the disciples came to Him privately, saying, "Tell us, when will these things be? And what will be the sign of Your coming, and of the end of the age?" Bing a wise teacher, Jesus gives a negative answer to remove false conceptions from their minds. He tells them the following in Matthew 24:

> Now as He sat on the Mount of Olives, the disciples came to Him privately, saying, "Tell us, when will these things be? And what will be the sign of Your coming, and of the end of the age?" And Jesus answered and said to them: "Take heed that no one deceives you. For many will come in My name, saying, 'I am the Christ,' and will deceive many. And you will hear of wars and rumors of wars. See that you are not troubled; for all these things must come to pass, but the end is not yet (Matthew 24:3-6).

In regard to this, Jesus said, these things must happen, but don't mistake them for *the* sign. After removing from their minds two points which otherwise might have been confusing, the Lord proceeds to give them a straight answer to their question. That answer is found in Matthew 24:7: "For nation will rise against nation, and kingdom against kingdom. And there will be famines, pestilences, and earthquakes in various places."

In 1914, for the first time in world history such a thing happened. The next logical question would be, "Will there be another world war? If so, how can we know which one the Lord is talking about?"

The answer is self-evident. If there is to be a succession of similar world distresses, it's only the first such event that could be called "the beginning of sorrows." Repeated occurrences of the same event will be but the continuation of increasing horrors on this earth. Luke 21:25 shares some important information with us. It declares, "and on the earth distress of nations with great perplexity."

The word "distress" is what we call a compound word in the Greek. A compound word has more than one word within the one Greek word. In this case, the first word in the Greek is "sun" which means with or together. The second word is "echo" which means to hold. The word therefore literally means a holding together of the nations—or let us say the UN.

So what we have here is a union of nations with what result? Solving the world's problems? No indeed, exactly the opposite! Rather, it produces "perplexity." The word "perplexity" means to have problems without solutions. So note now that Jesus says in Matthew 24:8: "All these are the beginning of sorrows." The Greek word used here for our English word "sorrows" is the word for travail or birth pangs. There are two reasons why this word is the best one to use here.

First, like the pains of childbirth (which is literally what the word means), the distress at the end of the age will increase in intensity and in frequency until the time of deliverance. Furthermore, the end of this age implies the birth of a new age. The first birth pains are thus spoken of as *the* sign because it's the initial or warning sign, which indicates that the deliverance is near. Later birth pains may be of greater importance in their furtherance of the conditions leading to the birth, but it's always the first birth pain that brings us to the zenith of the long expected event. Much anguish lies ahead in the future; yet, we who would stand on the watchtower of prophecy may rejoice that deliverance for a groaning creation is near.

Beginning with the prediction of end time famines in Matthew 24:7, Jesus shares a number of natural disasters that would be prevalent in the end times. These signs include such things as famines, pestilence and earthquakes. In Luke's gospel weird weather may be added to this list. In lieu of the paragraph above where we have seen that these end time signs would be like a woman giving birth, it is relevant that the way these signs exhibit themselves in these end times is unlike the way they have happened in the past. They are more frequent and much more intense. An excellent short commentary was given on this in the *Lamplighter Magazine*. It states:

> According to a report released recently by a British charity called Oxfam, the number of natural disasters around the world has increased by more than four times in the last 20 years. The data was assembled from the records of the Red Cross, the United Nations and research done at Louvain University in Belgium. The report concluded that the earth is currently experiencing 500 natural disasters per year, compared with 120 per year in the 1980s. Between 1985 and 1994, 174 million people were affected by natural disasters each year. In the following decade, this figure increased by 70 percent to 254 million people per year.[4]

CHAPTER 4

FAMINES

SIGN # 12 FAMINES

Another sign of the times is brought before us in Matthew 24:7, where Jesus said: "And there will be famines." A telling article on the subject of famine recently surfaced. It shows the direction we are heading in the matter of food supply. The article reads:

> We are facing a problem that, literally, has never been faced in human history. Surging population and food demand, food inflation, diminishing world food stocks, drought, flooding, cold, diminished credit, infestations, soil erosion, industrial farming, factory-farm pollution, aquifers/wells going dry, relocation of produce for energy production are all slamming into global financial and economic crisis. And in some places, like the United States, they don't have enough farmers. On top of that, we have desertification which is one of the world's most pressing environmental issues. New deserts are growing at a rate of 20,000 square miles (51,800 square kilometers) a year. Desertification leads to famine, mass starvation and human migration.[1]

Bernard Maquis's cattle would normally be grazing in the lush green pastures of the Limousin region in Central France at this time of the year. Instead, they are eating hay intended for the winter after months of drought that has turned the fields yellow. Third world nations are braced for riots as Europe's heat wave creates a rise in food prices and drives millions deeper into poverty.[2]

Most people who watch the news on TV or read daily news-papers are aware of the following information. The awesome part of the information on famines you will read in this section of the book is this: when so much of the information is digested at the same time, it opens our eyes as to what a disastrous situation we are seeing developing in the world. Reading an article here and there will never have the same effect on our reality as when we compile the information and take it all in at the same time.

According to the *Los Angeles Times*, the UN has declared that southern Somalia is in an official state of famine. It says, "The child malnutrition rate has soared to 55%. For months, people have been trudging out of the desert, leaving their dead children behind and carrying those who have managed to survive." [3]

In another *Los Angeles Times* article, a similar situation is reported in the African country of Sahel. The article says, "Donors waited too long on Somalia, they say. Now the Sahel region faces crisis. The new famine involves eight countries just south of the Sahara desert. A recent survey by UNICEF forecasts one million cases of severe malnutrition, with 25% to 60% of those people likely to die if emergency assistance does not reach them in time. Locust plagues in some areas further complicate the crisis.[4]

It's reported that in some parts of the world the global price of cereals has risen 71% over the past 12 months. "Europe's nuclear industry may have to shut down some riverside reactors if water levels become too low."[5] This means food production will be further reduced if water is not available.

Another Internet news source has posted a story about how the UN is painting a gloomy prediction for 2013.

The UN and the World Bank have both issued ominous warnings about the food inflation that is coming. In the developing world, a rise in the price of food can mean the difference between life and death. In 2008 food prices were so high it led to food riots in 28 countries. Today, there are approximately 2 billion people who are malnourished around the globe. Even rumors of food shortages are enough to spark mass chaos in many areas of the planet. When people fear they cannot feed their families, they tend to get desperate. That is why a recent CNN article declared that "2013 will be a year of serious global crisis."

This will be the third year that the yield of corn has declined in the United States. This has never before happened in United States history. Coming into this year, we are already in bad shape. In fact, corn reserves were sitting at a 15-year low at the end of 2011.

Farmers are using their winter hay this summer. They probably won't recover before winter. The price of hay has doubled and the availability is down 75 %. [6]

It's difficult for Americans to realize what a serious problem famine is throughout the world. A recent article shows a disturbing reality to the problem. The article states that the International Food Policy Research Institute (IFPRI) declares that one billion people have faced hunger this year. "The 2010 Global Hunger index released on Sunday, showed there was an "alarming" hunger in 25 out of 122 countries surveyed, AFP reported."[7]

In spite of the "green revolution," famine in our day is increasing. Starvation is such that over half the world's population goes to bed hungry every night! Nations of the world, who in the past were exporters of food, are now major importers unable to feed themselves. For example, because of the communist revolution in Ethiopia; that land, that once exported food, is now in a state of famine.

Russia itself was a major exporter of grain under the czar in 1917. To this day they cannot feed themselves despite massive help of technology, etc. from the West. Already some 786 million people, nearly 1 in 6 on the entire globe, are suffering from acute or chronic hunger. More than a billion more face serious malnutrition. Nations that used to feed themselves are in serious trouble. Albania relies on foreign aid for 75% of its food. In Bulgaria, 60% of the average household earnings are spent on food. Food prices in Czechoslovakia increased 70% in the last 10 years.

China, the most populous country in the world, is experiencing great famine problems. The following article is astounding in its implication:

> What underlies China's worst drought in nearly a century is a matter of great debate. Is it Mother Nature or human failure? Beyond the official explanation of "abnormal weather," Chinese environmentalists are pointing to deforestation, pollution, dams, over-building and other man-made factors. At its worst, the drought has left parched more than 16 million acres of farmland in more than four provinces, threatening the livelihood of more than 50 million farmers, according to government statistics. Up to 20 million people have been left without drinking water.[8]

The situation has become so severe that it's not newsworthy anymore. Have you noticed how the media works? When something new happens it's plastered all over the headlines, but when something becomes commonplace, they don't report it anymore. There are more people threatened by famine today than at any time in all of human history. The reason for this, in part, is because there are so many people on this planet.

It staggers me to think that half of all the people who have ever lived on this planet are alive today. Someone asks, "What's causing the hunger?" How will we feed the people? Obviously we won't be able to feed them. While you read this book over 5,000 people will have perished through starvation! That brings home the point more dramatically than by saying that this year millions will die.

> The UN warned that a major food shortage is coming, especially in third world nations. There is a spike in prices due to the global recession and inflation is impacting the Middle East, India and the Philippines. Also, a wheat fungus has reappeared in many wheat-growing areas like Iran, Africa and other places that need the grain to feed their people. In 2008, when oil prices rose to record levels, many nations held on to their grain supplies causing a shortage in numerous nations that led to food riots. We are told that "wheat stem rust" will infect major wheat production centers in Pakistan, India and Bangladesh, which produces 15% of the world's wheat and feeds more than one billion of the world's poorest people.[9]

In 2011, there was a famine occurring in Somalia and surrounding nations. The *Los Angeles Times* headline was "Somalia's Famine Is Spreading." We are told that it is one of the worst famine outbreaks in modern history.

> More than 12 million people are facing starvation, with children particularly vulnerable. About 860,000 people have trekked out of Somalia, many leaving dead children on the way hoping to find food in neighboring countries. The extreme Islamic militia Shabab, which is allied with Al Qaeda, controls much of the South. The Shabab's policies drove out Western aid agencies last year making it difficult to quickly increase food aid operations. The group imposed taxes on aid groups and banned female staff members.[10]

This Somalia famine is so bad we are now being told that the "child malnutrition rate has soared to 55% and infant deaths have reached 6 a day."[11]

Yet another newspaper report shares with us the following disturbing news about Somalia and the Horn of Africa in general:

> More than 300,000 children in the Horn of Africa are severely malnourished and in imminent risk of dying because of drought and famine, the head of the United Natioins children's agency said. The United Nations says tens of thousands of people already have died in Somalia, Kenya, Ethiopia and Djibouti, and it has warned that the famine has not peaked.[12]

Even more shocking than the famine in Somalia, is that the radical Islamic elements that control various portions of the country have declared a food ban from reaching the starving and dying because there are women aid workers and the aid is coming from countries like the Great Satan America. The headline in the *Los Angeles Times* stated, "Somalis Suffer Amid Aid Ban." The subheading lamented, "A Militia Barred Foreign Help Even As Famine and Drought Worsen."

The appalling and scandalous situation that fellow Muslims would deny food to their own because it came from non-Muslim nations is well beyond shocking and unspeakable. Judge for yourself from the following report in the *Los Angeles Times*.

> As Somalia's drought and famine worsened in recent months, the Shabab militia in the south seized families' crops and livestock and imposed taxes that made it impossible to survive, according to a report released Monday by Human Rights Watch. The militia banned international humanitarian agencies as "infidels" and told the desperate population to depend on God instead. And it stopped many hungry people from fleeing the country for survival.
>
> One man who succeeded in escaping the country said that he had fled the country when all of his 40 goats and 20 cattle died of starvation. [13]

Due to the high cost of oil and the notion that it is causing world-wide warming, the race is on to provide alternatives to oil. Thus they are using food crops to produce oil. The result is that the demand for oil is increasing faster than the new bio-fuels can be produced. The usage of food supplies to produce oil is creating rising food prices and creating a faster growth of famine. *Time Magazine* gives the following disturbing report:

> Even if all of the soybean crops produced in the United States were converted for fuel, it would only meet 20 percent of consumption needs. Is it worth it to use our food resources to produce oil and thus starvation for many around the world? This is an especially critical question when it has not been proven that fossil fuel is capable of producing "global warming." [14]

> Biofuel refineries in the U.S. have set fresh records for grain use every month since May. Almost a third of the U.S. corn harvest will be diverted into ethanol for motors this year, or 12 percent of the global crop. The world's grain stocks have dropped from 4 to 2.6 months since 2000 despite two bumper harvests in North America. China's inventories are at a 30-year low. Asian rice stocks are near a danger level. The world population is adding "another Britain" every year. This will continue until mid-century. By then we will have an extra 2.4 billion mouths to feed.

> Farmers are draining the aquifers. Environmentalist MaJun says in *China's Water Crisis* that they are drilling as deep as 1,000 meters into non-replenishable reserves. The grain region of the Hai River Basin relies on groundwater for 70 percent of irrigation.[15]

It's not because there is not enough food in the world. We can produce food to feed the world five times over, but false religion enters in here also. In India they believe the cows that roam the streets may be grandma or whoever. They have more cattle in India than we do in America yet starvation in that country is rampant. Why? Because a false religion does not allow them to eat what food there is.

What makes matters incredible is that things are happening that have never happened in human history. And we can never go back to the way it was. Take, for example, the rain forests (the lungs of our planet) are disappearing at an astonishing rate. About 80,000 square miles of rain forest vanish every year.

Industrial pollution of the air, water and soil are also responsible. Also, the food produced today has less nutritional value than it did a generation ago. After a time, chemical fertilizer becomes counter-productive. Many believe we have arrived there today. This creates soil exhaustion and corruption.

What's more, water tables are being depleted at an alarming rate around the world. Erosion of soil through poor farming techniques is also responsible. Once the topsoil is gone in marginally arable parts of the world, it's gone for good. Increasingly, there is more land, once capable of producing crops, now sitting idle.

In regard to water, underground tables are being rapidly depleted. The headline from a British news source which read "US Farmers Fear the Return of the Dust Bowl" caught my attention. The news release spoke of the Ogallala Aquifer in the United States. It reports that this aquifer, which has for decades irrigated thousands of square miles of farmland. is now running dry. It shares reports from residents from a place called Happy, TX whose population is being depleted by about 10% every year. Its population is now only 595.

This situation has placed states like Nebraska, Oklahoma, Kansas, Texas and other states at risk of losing their productive farmland. After the days of the dust bowl of the 1930's, this aquifer was tapped for its water supply. It was once the largest body of underground fresh water on the planet. The news reports give much dreadful information to absorb. Allow me to give you but a brief quote as to what is happening:

> The irrigated plains grow 20% of American grain
> and corn with America's 'industrial' agriculture

dominating international markets. A collapse of those markets would lead to starvation in Africa and anywhere else a meal depends on cheap American exports. The Ogallala supply is going to run out and the plains will become uneconomical to farm. That is beyond reasonable argument. Without the irrigation, the dust will start blowing in as few as 10 years.[16]

The fact of the matter is, the dust is already returning. In the summer of 2011, our newspapers have been full of reports of the problem with blowing dust and parched ground. Radical global warming believers blame global warming. The term, "global warming" has now been changed to "climate change" because for the past 12 years the average worldwide temperature has been cooling. The fact is, the drying up of the plains is not due to above surface conditions but a drawing out of the water from the aquifer to a point where the dust bowl is presently returning.

The farmers of the world are dependent on weather patterns. We are seeing incredible changing weather patterns along with what is known as acid rain. 60% of the world population exists on a yearly income of less than the average American makes in one day. Few realize that the average citizen of this earth will live to 30-something, and that's it.

To make matters worse, many of the fertilizers we use to grow our crops are made from Arab oil. They have raised their prices enormously making it unprofitable to make fertilizer from that source. Further, we are told that weather patterns causing drought will worsen in the foreseeable future. There are places in the Eastern areas of the world where the drought is so bad, they already walk miles to stand in line for hours just to get one bucket of water. We are told that children in certain areas of the world have never seen rain!

Bees are responsible for the fertilization of a major portion of our fruit trees and vegetable plants. It has been reported that more than 50% of the honeybees have simply disappeared in the last 50 years. More than half of that number have disappeared in the last 5 years. In an article in the *Los Angeles Times* headlined by the words,

"BUZZZZZZ Kill," they tell of billions of bees killed through lack of pesticide control. The article says, in part:

> Gaucho and other highly toxic chemicals may be responsible for the deaths of billions of honeybees worldwide. In the U.S. this year, more then 2.4 million bee colonies—36% of the total—was lost. Some colonies collapsed in just two days.[17]

In yet another article in the *Los Angeles Times* under the headline, "Flight of the Honeybees," they say that bees have been mysteriously disappearing en masse. We are given the following information:

> Something strange is happening to honeybees. They're vanishing in parts of the country. Bees are leaving their hives and not returning. The phenomenon, dubbed "Colony Collapse Disorder" has wiped out a quarter of the hives of commercial beekeepers since last summer according to the American Beekeepers Association. [18]

A follow up article in the June 10, 2007 edition of the *Los Angeles Times* had a front-page article entitled, "Suddenly, the Bees Are Simply Vanishing."

> Scientists are at a loss to pinpoint the cause. The die off in 35 states has crippled beekeepers and threatened many crops. The dead bees under Dennis VanEngeldorp's microscope were like none he had ever seen. He had expected to find mites or amoebas, perennial pests of bees. Instead, he found internal organs swollen with debris and strangely blackened. The bees' intestinal tracts were scarred, and their rectums were abnormally full of what appeared to be partly digested pollen. Dark marks on the sting glands were telltale signs of infection. "The more you looked

the more you found," said VanEngelsdrop, the acting apiarist for the state of Pennsylvania. He said, "Each thing was a surprise." Scientists have scoured the country, finding eerily abandoned hives in which the bees simply left their honey and broods of baby bees." They said, "We have never experienced bees going off and leaving their broods behind." Researchers have picked through abandoned hives, dissected thousands of bees, and tested for viruses, bacteria, pesticides and mites. So far they are stumped. [19]

A news article in the *Denver Post* warned, "If the bees go away, you'll have apples the size of quarters." [20]

In a recent British report the following disturbing information was given:

> According to a previous study, England's bees are vanishing faster than anywhere else in Europe, with more than half the hives dying out in the last 20 years. Butterflies and other insects are also in decline. Studies bear out a progressive decline in pollination over the years.[21]

The same article states that researchers have found that pollination levels of some plants have dropped up to 50% in the last two decades. The pollination deficit could see a dramatic reduction in the yield from crops.

In a recent magazine, there was an article entitled "To Be Or Not To Bee." It had this to say about the present day bee crisis around the world:

> Entomologist Stephen L. Buchmann and ecologist Gary Paul Nabhan wrote in their book, "The Forgotten Pollinators," that an infestation of parasitic mites that prey on honeybees are contributing to the depletion of the bee population. The authors also pointed out that more than 150 plants, which provide fruit and

66

vegetables are dependent on bee pollination. Without this natural process these food plants won't survive.[22]

A major source of food is found in our waterways. In a July 28 article in the *Los Angeles Times* under a headline entitled, "Alarm in the Midwest Over Fish Ebola," we were told there is a brand new problem with fish having terrible diseases which could endanger this important source of food.

> A deadly fish virus has been found for the first time in Southern Lake Michigan, and in an Ohio reservoir, causing fears of major fish kills and the virus' possible migration into the Mississippi River. The virus detection in Wisconsin, Illinois and Ohio is of particular concern, as it has never been seen in those areas before. All are routes to the Mississippi River. Officials worry that if it finds its way into the Mississippi, it will be carried by fish to other rivers and to hatcheries throughout the Midwest and the South.[23]

Another source of our food, the oceans, are being endangered through pollution. Nations of the world are allowing their fishing fleets to use smaller meshed nets, thus allowing them to catch more fish as well as smaller fish, thus depleting their numbers and futures at an alarming rate. As a matter of fact, the final result of this famine will be so great that Revelation 6 tells us that a man will have to work all day just to earn enough money to buy food enough for only himself.

Another new problem for the food industry involves a disease that is spread by the Asian Psyllid which is invading many countries of the world. Reports speak of this devastating world production of oranges:

> The pest is responsible for spreading citrus greening disease and causing catastrophic damage to orange farms in Florida and Brazil. Agricultural officials warn that the same disease could be a catastrophe to

California's $1.3 billion citrus industry. John Gless, a third generation farmer from Riverside says, "We have never been threatened with a disease like this before." He wonders whether there will be anything left of his 6,000 acres of California citrus groves to pass on to his children and grandchildren.[24]

The December 22, 2008 headline in the *Los Angeles Times* of declared: "A Global, Incurable Disease Is Wiping Out Groves In Brazil. California May Be Next." [25]

There are strange things happening that relate to our food sources -things that, as far as we know, have never happened in all of recorded history. A story from the *Los Angeles Times* is an example of the unusual things of which I speak. The story is headlined by the words, "Fishing Jobs Slip Away in the Great Lakes." Just a few comments from the large article tells it all: "Today, for the first times since the 1800's, there are no commercial fishing boats operating out of Milwaukee, Wisconsin. The boats are gone because the fish are gone. The lake is like a liquid desert."[26]

The article tells of millions of pounds of fish being taken out each year until the lake was invaded by invasive mussels. The mussels probably arrived in the Great Lakes as a stowaway in the ballast tanks of freighters that carried them across the Atlantic. The article makes an incredible, unbelievable statement. Let me quote it:

Still a rare find in Lake Michigan until just several years ago, the Mollusks mysteriously and suddenly went viral. Today they smother the bottom of the lake almost from shore to shore, and their numbers are estimated at 900 trillion. Along the way they virtually have eliminated from the lake their better-known cousins, the Zebra mussels, which also arrived as hitch hikers aboard ocean freighters. Each junior Mint-size mussel can filter up to a liter of water a day, stripping away the plankton that for thousands of years directly and indirectly sustained the lake's native fish.[27]

The U.S. Agricultural Department has said, "Enough water had been drained out of the Ogallala aqua fed in the ventral plains of the United States to half-fill Lake Erie of the Great Lakes. The problem is that in a brief half century we have drawn the Ogallala level down from 240 feet to about 80 feet. The Ogallala is going to run out and the plains will become uneconomical to farm."[28]

The *Los Angeles Times* reported that the number of Texas cows has plunged. "The state's herd shrinks 12% in a year, which will probably drive up beef prices. Since January, the number of cows in Texas is expected to have decreased by about 600,000—a 12% drop from about 5 million cows. The trend is likely the largest drop in the number of cows any state has ever seen. This is all being caused by the Texas drought and has caused an estimated 5.2 billion dollars in losses to farmers and livestock producers. Some livestock have been moved out of state, but other herds have been sold and slaughtered."[29]

Africa seems to be in the worst shape regarding food supplies because of a terrible water shortage. One magazine article put it this way, "Even now some estimates put the number of Africans without access to safe drinking water at more than 300 million and only 5 percent of the arable land is irrigated."[30]

According to the *Los Angeles Times* 20% of Californians struggled to afford food in 2010. One would never think that could be possible in America, but the *Times* declared: "The rate of people struggling to buy food in California was slightly higher than the national average of 18% . . . For them, 2010 was the third year of a terrible recession that is wildly damaging the ability to meet basic needs." The survey asked the question of those contacted, "Have there been times in the past 12 months when you did not have enough money to buy food that you and your family needed?"[31]

A few weeks later the newspaper had a similar study with the following headline: "1.7 Million Plus Face Hunger in L.A. County." Though I live in the L.A. area at this writing, I had no idea that many people were having trouble feeding themselves. The article stated that more people in Los Angeles County were at risk of hunger than people in any other county in America. On a percentage basis, nearby Imperial County has the highest rate of those at risk for hunger this year. The percentage at risk in Imperial County is 31%.[32] Would you have ever believed that hunger in the U.S. could reach such proportions?

The *Business Financial Post* tells us that the agriculture situation has worsened so much that there is increasing fear that the day may not be far off when, at least for some, "They will not be able to buy food at any price at times in the next few years." [33]

The UN and the World Bank are urging nations to pay attention to this problem before it's too late. The same article states "Monthly food prices tracked by the FAO have surged nine times in the past 11 months. The World Bank estimates that higher food prices have pushed 44 million more people into poverty."[34]

Food stockpiles in reserve are shrinking at a distressing rate. A posting on the Internet brought together a number of factors that are all happening at the same time. This could bring about the worst food crisis in earth's history. The posting does not include any information you are not familiar with. We have read about this continually in our newspapers and magazines, but reviewing it all in one short listing verifies the bleak potential for the future of food distribution. Below are the 20 danger signs listed in the post

> According to the World Bank, 44 million people around the world have been pushed into extreme poverty since last June because of rising food prices. (This is 44 million new cases of poverty not including the millions who were already in this crisis before this statistic.)

> The world is losing topsoil at an astounding rate. In fact, according to Lester Brown, "One third of the world's cropland is losing topsoil faster than new soil is forming through natural processes."

> Due to U.S. ethanol subsidies, almost all corn grown in the U.S. is now used for fuel. This is putting stress on the price of corn.

Due to a lack of water, some countries in the Middle East find themselves forced to almost totally rely on other nations for basic food staples. For example, it is being projected that there will be no more wheat production in Saudi Arabia by the year 2012.

Water tables all over the globe are being depleted at an alarming rate due to 'over pumping.' According to the World Bank, there are 130 million people in China and 175 million people in India that are being fed grain with water that is being pumped out of aquifers faster than it can be replaced. What happens once all that water is gone?

In the U.S., the systematic depletion of the Ogallala Aquifer could eventually turn "America's Breadbasket" back into the "Dust Bowl."

Diseases such as UG99 wheat rust are wiping out increasingly large segments of the world food supply.

The tsunami and subsequent nuclear crisis in Japan have rendered vast agricultural areas in that nation unusable. There are many who believe that eventually a significant portion of northern Japan will be considered to be uninhabitable. Not only that, many are now convinced the Japanese economy, the third largest in the world, is likely to totally collapse as a result of this.

The price of oil may be the biggest factor on this list. The way we produce our food is very heavily dependent on oil. The way we transport our food is very heavily dependent on oil. When you have skyrocketing oil prices, our entire food production system becomes much more expensive. If the price of oil continues to stay high, we are going to see even higher food prices. Some forms of food production will no longer make economic sense.

At some point the world could experience a very serious fertilizer shortage. According to scientists with the Global Phosphorus Research Initiative, the world is not going to have enough phosphorous to meet agricultural demand in just 30 to 40 years.

Food inflation is already devastating many economies around the globe. For example, India is dealing with an annual food inflation rate of 18%.

According to the United Nations, the global price of food reached a new all time high in February.

According to the World Bank, the global price of food has risen 36% over the past 12 months.

The commodity price of wheat has approximately doubled since last summer.

The commodity price of corn has also about doubled since last summer.

The commodity price of soybeans is up about 50% since last June.

The commodity price of orange juice has doubled since 2009.

There are about 3 billion people around the globe that live on the equivalent of 2 dollars a day or less, and the world was already on the verge of economic disaster before this year even began.

2011 has already been one of the craziest years since WW 2. Revolutions have swept across the Middle East. The U.S. has gotten involved in the civil war in Libya, Europe is on the verge of a financial melt-down and the U.S. dollar is dying. None of this is good news for global food production.

There have been persistent rumors of shortages at some of the biggest suppliers of emergency food in the U.S. The following is an excerpt from a recent "special alert" posted on *Raiders News Network*.

Look around you. Read the headlines. See the largest factories of food, potassium, iodine, and other emer-gency product manufacturers literally closing their online stores. They're putting up signs like those on Mountain House's Official Website and Thyrosafe's Factory Web page that explain, due to overwhelming demand, they are shutting down sales for the time being and hope to reopen someday.[35]

One Internet blog claims the following:

- Approximately 1 billion people throughout the world go to bed hungry every night.
- Every 3.6 seconds someone starves to death and ¾ of them are children.
- According to the UN Food and Agriculture Organization, the global price of food has gone up 240% since 2004.[36]

Along with the crisis in the shortage of food is the fact that "There are approximately two billion people that spend half of their income on food."[37] With inflation as it is, what are these people to do when the price of food doubles? An Australian source tells us cattle the world over "are eating hay intended for the winter after months of drought that has turned the fields yellow. Third world nations are braced for riots as Europe's heat wave creates a rise in food prices and drives millions into poverty. The global price of cereals has risen 71 per cent over the past 12 months.[37]

There are a number of other things that can contribute to famine conditions, which, by and large are, not thought of in this sense. One such factor is wildfires that have been increasingly exponential in the devastation they have caused in the past few decades here in America. Even Europe and Australia have reported record-breaking wild fires. The *Houston Chronicle* reported on a 2012 wildfire in New Mexico this way.

> A wildfire that has burned more than 265 square miles in the Gila National Forest has become the largest of its kind in New Mexico history. Experts warn that the mammoth fire may be just a preview of what's to come in part of the western United States after months of drought and dry conditions.[38]

This is just one of dozens of articles that report on and warn of devastation to our forests which, in turn, eliminate the life-giving oxygen so necessary to the health of our planet.

Continuing drought around the world is causing other problems in regard to farming and transporting food to delivery centers. The *Los Angeles Times* reported that the drought of 2012 has caused transportation on the Mississippi river to be limited to one lane in certain parts of its river channels. The article states "The extended drought is making passage hard or even impossible for some river vessels. In drought conditions the muddy waters recede, and squeezing barges through the narrow channels becomes an expensive and sometimes impossible chore."[39]

Whoever thought that a diminished bat population could have far-reaching effects on the lives of us all. An article in *Time Magazine* gives us stunning information on what is happening

> There's an animal apocalypse afoot in the north-eastern United States. Between 5.7 million and 6.7 million bats are estimated to have died since 2006 from white nose fungus in 16 U.S. states and Canada,

according to officials at the U.S. Fish and Wildlife Service. The new estimate finds that the death toll is far worse than wildlife biologists had believed. It could spell disaster not just for the animals but for humans as well.

As alarming as the possible extinction of these bat species is, even more worrisome is the potential loss of a critical part of the ecosystem. A female bat of reproductive age can consume her weight in insects each night and that amounts to millions of pounds of insects each year. If bats are wiped out, insect populations would explode including pests that can decimate food and agricultural yields and infest forests, not to mention the swarms that plague summer barbecues and spread disease to humans.[40]

Another frightening reality that has never before existed in all of human history exists. Terrorists in the world today claim that one of the ways they can bring down a nation is by poisoning the food supply. This could play an important role in the prophecy that there would be famines in the end time. A British news source gave the following possibility:

Manufacturers and retailers have told us that their sector is vulnerable to attacks by politically motivated groups that may seek to cause widespread casualties and disruption by poisoning food supplies.

U.S. experts have warned that the dairy industry is particularly vulnerable. Adding just a few grams of botulinum toxin or ricin to a tanker load of milk could poison or kill thousands of customers. The U.S. food "bio-terrorism" has become a major concern after documents were found in Afghanistan apparently referring to plans by terrorists to contaminate supplies.[41]

There are as many ways to poison food and water systems as there are ideas. Perhaps this is a part of what will cause famine in the end time. It seems we are heading toward an unparalleled world crisis that will end in the starvation of untold millions of people. Every year 15 million people die from hunger. It's hard for America to fathom such a thing; yet, it is true. In 2008, nearly 9 million children died before their fifth birthday with a third of those deaths related to hunger. These are staggering numbers.

In an article headlined, "What's Going On" a report is given on the mysterious and sudden weird death of millions of fish and thousands of birds. I'm sure most of the readers of this book have some acquaintance with the many news reports that shocked us with this information:

> There have been bird and fish kills that are unparalleled that no one seems to be able to explain. The sudden plummeting to the ground of thousands of red-winged blackbirds in Beebe, Arkansas grabbed the headlines around the world. However, this news report came as a horrific mass fish kill of 100,000 drum fish in the same state 160 km away on December 30, and another mass bird kill of 600 more birds on January 3 just south of Arkansas.

> In Haiti, scores of fish were found dead in Lake Azuei. In Volusia County, Florida, thousands of fish were found dead floating in Spruce Creek, Port Orange. And if that were not enough, in Chesapeake Bay lying between Virginia and Maryland, two million fish are reported dead in another kill. In California, millions of fish were found dead early one morning in the LA area. In Winnipeg, Canada, a mass kill of tens of thousands of birds occurred. To date there has been no expert agreement as to what would cause birds to fall from the sky in such massive numbers or for millions of fish to die mysteriously and suddenly.[42]

The mysterious death of all of these birds and fish show how there could be sudden catastrophes that could suddenly and unexpectedly wipe out a large part of the human food source at some future day.

What is possibly the worst news for future food supplies is that fresh, unpolluted water is getting in short supply. I recently read an Internet story that is shocking. It reads as follows:

> Every single day, we are getting closer to a horrific global water crisis. This world was blessed with an awesome amount of fresh water, but because of our foolishness it is rapidly disappearing. Rivers, lakes and major underground aquifers all over the globe are drying up, and many of the fresh water sources that we still have available are so incredibly polluted we simply cannot use them anymore.

> As sources of fresh water all over the globe dry up, we are seeing drought conditions spread. We are starting to see massive "dust storms" in areas where they've never been seen them before. Every year most of the major deserts around the world are getting bigger with the amount of usable agricultural land becoming smaller. Whether you are aware of this or not, the truth is that we are rapidly approaching a breaking point.

> According to the U.S. government, 36 U.S. states are already facing water shortages or will be facing water shortages within the next few years.

> Since 1998, the level of water in Lake Mead has plunged by more that 50%. Lake Mead supplies about 85 % of the water used in Las Vegas. At this point the Lake has 5.6 trillion gallons less water than it used to have. Lake Mead is falling so fast that some believe that the Hoover dam could actually stop producing

electricity in a few years. Needless to say, that would be a total disaster for that entire region of the country. In addition, if things continue at the current pace, it is estimated that Lake Mead will run dry some time around the year 2021.

According to the U.S. National Academy of Sciences, the U.S. Interior West is now the driest that it has been in 500 years.

Things have gotten so dry in Arizona that now giant "dust storms" have been blowing through the city of Phoenix.

Approximately 40% of all U.S. rivers and approximately 46% of all U.S. lakes have become so polluted that they are now considered to be too dangerous to fish in, swim in or get drinking water from.

According to USAID, one-third of the population of the earth will be facing severe or chronic water shortages by the year 2025.

If you can believe it, according to a UN study on sanitation, far more people in India have access to a cell phone than to a toilet.

In the developing world, 90% of all wastewater is discharged completely untreated into local rivers, streams or lakes.

Every 8 seconds, somewhere in the world a child dies from drinking dirty water.

Due to a lack of water, Saudi Arabia has given up on trying to grow wheat and will be 100% dependent on wheat imports by the year 2016.

Incredibly, a new desert the size of Rhode Island is created in China every single year because of drought and over-pumping.

In China, 80% of all major rivers have become so horribly polluted that they do not support any aquatic life at all.

Without fresh water, people cannot grow enough food. Global food prices are already starting to sky-rocket, and the coming global water crisis certainly is not going to help matters.[43]

The following are some facts about the Ogallala Aquifer and the growing water crisis that we are facing in the United States. A number of these facts were taken from one of my previous articles. I think you will agree that many of these facts are quite alarming:

1. The Ogallala Aquifer is being drained at a rate of approximately 800 gallons per minute.

2. According to the U.S. Geological Survey, "a volume equivalent to two-thirds of the water in Lake Erie " has been permanently drained from the Ogallala Aquifer since 1940."

3. Decades ago, the Ogallala Aquifer had an average depth of approximately 240 feet, but today the average depth is just 80 feet. In some areas of Texas, the water is completely gone.

4. Scientists are warning that nothing can be done to stop the depletion of the Ogallala Aquiver. The ominous words of David Bauer of the Ogallala Research Service should alarm us all. "Our goal now is to engineer a soft landing. That's all we can do."

5. According to a recent *National Geographic* article, the average rate of the Ogallala Aquifer is picking up speed. Even more worrisome, the draining of the High Plains water account has picked up speed. The average annual depletion rate between 2000 and 2007 was more that twice what it was during the previous fifty years. The depletion is most severe in the southern portion of the aquifer, especially in Texas, where the water table beneath sizeable areas has dropped 100 –150 feet; in smaller pockets, it has dropped more than 150 feet.

6. According to the U.S. National Academy of Sciences, the U.S. interior west is now the driest that it has been in 500 years.

7. Wildfires have burned millions of acres of vegetation in the central part of the United States in recent years. For example, wildfires burned an astounding 3.6 million acres in the state of Texas during 2011. This helps set the stage for huge dust storms in the future.

8. Unfortunately scientists tell us that it would be normal for extremely dry conditions to persist in parts of western North America for decades.

9. Experts tell us that U.S. water bills are likely to soar in the coming years. It is being projected that repairing and expanding our decaying drinking water infrastructure will cost more that one trillion dollars over the next 25 years. As a result our water bills will likely approximately triple over that period.

10. Right now, the United States uses approximately 148 trillion gallons of fresh water a year. There is no way that is sustainable in the long run.

11. According to a U.S. government report, 36 states are already facing water shortages, or will be within the next few years.

12. Lake Mead supplies about 85% of the water to Las Vegas, and since 1980 the level of water in Lake Mead has dropped by about 5.6 trillion gallons.

13. It has been estimated that the state of California only has a 20 year supply of fresh water left.

14. It has been estimated that the state of New Mexico only has a 10 year supply of fresh water left.

15. The 1,450 mile long Colorado River is a good example of what we have done to our precious water supplies. It is probably the most important body of water in the southwestern United States, and it is rapidly dying.

The following is an excerpt from an outstanding article by Jonathan Waterman about how the once mighty Colorado River is rapidly drying up:

> "Fifty miles from the sea, 1.5 miles south of the Mexican border, I saw a river evaporate into a scum of phosphates and discarded water bottles. This dirty water sent me home with feet so badly infected that I couldn't walk for a week. And a delta once renowned for its wildlife and wetlands is now all but part of the surrounding and parched Sonoran Desert. According to Mexican scientists whom I met with, the river has not flowed to the sea since 1998.[44]

The article further pointed out that presently approximately 40% of the entire population of the planet has little or no access to clean water. The most important lake in the West, Lake Mead and the

Colorado is rapidly having less and less water flow And capacity. Scientists are predicting that Lake Mead will be dry by 2025, which would end Las Vegas as we know it. It would be a monumental disaster for the entire Southwestern United States.

As the aquifers, rivers and lakes in the United States dry up, it will affect the entire world. This will be so as the United States will no longer be able to export food to the world as we do today.

While we have problems here in the United states with decreasing water supplies, we are in great shape as compared with the rest of the world. From the same article quoted above information is given relative to what is going on in the rest of the world.

The following are some incredible facts about the *global* water crisis that is getting even worse with each passing day.

1. Total global water use has quadrupled over the past 100 years. It is now increasing faster than it ever has been before.

2. Today, there are 1.6 billion people that live in areas of the globe that are considered to be "water stressed", and it is being projected that two-thirds of the entire population of the globe will be experiencing "water stressed" conditions by the year 2025.

3. According to USAID, one-third of the people on earth will be facing "severe" or "chronic" water shortages by the year 2025.

4. Once upon a time, the Aral Sea was the 4th largest freshwater lake in the entire world. At this point, it is less than 10% the size it used to be, and it is projected to dry up completely by the year 2020.

5. If you can believe it, the flow of water along the Jordan River is down to only 2% of its historic rate.

6. It is projected that the demand for water in China will exceed the supply by 25% by the year 2030.

7. According to the United Nations, the world will need at least 30% *more* fresh water by the year 2030.

8. Sadly, it is estimated that approximately 40% of the children living in Africa and India have had their growth stunted due to unclean water and malnutrition.

9. Of the 60 million people added to the cities of the world each year, the vast majority of them live in deeply impoverished areas that have no sanitation facilities whatsoever.

10. It has been estimated that 75% of all surface water in India has been heavily contaminated by human or agricultural waste.

11. Sadly, according to one UN study on sanitation, far more people in India have access to a cell phone than to a toilet.

12. Every 8 seconds somewhere in the world a child dies from drinking dirty water.

13. Due to a lack of water, Saudi Arabia has given up on trying to grow wheat and will be 100% dependent on what it imports by the year 2016.

14. Each year in northern China, the water table drops by an average of about one meter due to severe drought and over-pumping and the size of the desert increases by an area equivalent to the state of Rhode Island.

15. In China, 80% of the major rivers have become so horribly polluted at this point they do not support any aquatic life at all at this point.[45]

THE THIRD HORSEMAN OF THE APOCALYPSE

I have pointed out that the first four signs mentioned by Jesus in Matthew 24 parallel the 4 riders of the apocalypse. We are currently looking at the third sign of Matthew 24. Now, look at the third horse rider of Revelation 6:

> When He opened the third seal, I heard the third living creature say, "Come and see." So I looked, and behold, a black horse, and he who sat on it had a pair of scales in his hand. And I heard a voice in the midst of the four living creatures saying, A quart of wheat for a denarius, and three quarts of barley for a denarius; and do not harm the oil and the wine (Revelation 6:5-6).

The word "denarius" used in this verse stood for a day's wage. In other words, people will have to spend all of the money they make in that day on food to have just a sustainable amount of nutritious food for one day. So in Revelation 6:6, the word "denarius" should not be translated as any particular sum of money. Rather, it's simply representative of a day's work. This can be seen from Matthew 20:2 which reads: "Now when he had agreed with the laborers for a denarius a day, he sent them into his vineyard." At the present time, we in the U.S. spend about 20% of our income on food. In the Tribulation, it will be 100%. If all that a man will be able to make in a day is enough to buy food for the day, then those who are too old or too young to work will starve.

It's not only pollution that is threatening our fish supply, but fuel prices as well. In the following words, the *Los Angeles Times* carried a story about skyrocketing fuel prices hurting the Japanese fishing industry

Soaring fuel prices are killing Japan's fishing industry. The article states, "If we lose our fishing industry, we Japanese will face a food crisis," said Masahiko Ariji, a fishery specialist at the Amita Institute for Sustainable Economics in Kyoto. "About two thirds of the nation's fishing groups were in the red last year, and some are about to collapse." The price at Japan's fuel pumps has jumped to about $6.40 a gallon. About 230,000 people work in Japan's fishing industry. Lately, fewer boats have been heading out to sea. Fishing company officials say some have quit the business because they can't pay for the oil.[46]

In the Revelation passage, the color black was used in Scripture to represent famine. Let me give you one example, Lamentations 5:10: "Our skin is hot as an oven, Because of the fever of famine."

Revelation 6 tells us that at the beginning of the Tribulation, one of the first things the people will face is a terrible worldwide famine. People involved in food planning are trembling tonight because they know there is no way to avoid such a worldwide famine. Did you know that men of knowledge say that within 10 years millions will die yearly from starvation? With the population explosion there is no way to avoid it.

Then note the phrase in Revelation 6, "harm not the oil and the wine." The oil is what keeps industry humming and the wine represents our drink. That may sound strange when we seem to have so much water, but look at what has happened to certain of the Great Lakes through pollution and contamination. In the event of atomic war, think of what would happen to the lakes of the world.

It's a vicious cycle: false religions lead to war, and war leads to famine and famine leads to pestilence. Throughout the middle ages war caused food shortages and forced whole cities into periodic starvation followed by bubonic plague. What will that be like after an atomic war? As a result of the population explosion, we have four more Canada's to feed every year. Activists are also contributing to the potential coming food crisis. An example of this is the fact that environmentalists and the court system have succeeded in greatly reducing the flow of water to Southern California from the North. This will eventually result in farmers without sufficient water to grow their crops. Inasmuch as Southern California is the principle grower of fruit and vegetables in the United States, this could have very serious future implications.

Other activists have halted spraying for the apple moth. "Unknown in the U.S. until it was spotted in Berkeley last year, the light brown apple moth is a voracious eater that can threaten many fruit and vegetable crops, according to state agriculture officials."[47]

Mad cow disease is another factor that threatens our worldwide food supply. It seems to spread over vast areas rapidly. According to the *Los Angeles Times* of October 10, 2008 thousands of dairy cows are being slaughtered. This will affect milk output. Other cases of mad cow disease in other countries of the world affect meat production.

We could examine country after country where poor management or greedy profit desires are causing huge problems for food production. Take, for example, in Yemen, people are using up the already scarce water supply to grow narcotics. The *Los Angeles Times* reported this shocking story under the heading, "In Yemen, Race For Profit Is Hastening A Nightmare." The idea of the article is to point out that Yemen, which has very little water to begin with, is rapidly draining its supply of water to enable them to grow a narcotic plant. The article states:

> Water levels are falling rapidly as much of the vital resource is used to grow khat. Attempts to head off the coming crisis have failed. Wildcatters bore as much as 1,000 feet into the earth and draw out the valuable liquid. They pump it into tankers and haul it away to sell to the highest bidder. But soon the reservoirs will run dry. As Yemen's exploding population draws out more and more water from the parched land, mostly to help a voracious appetite for khat, a mildly narcotic plant. The bone-dry nation's very existence is threatened.[48]

There are numerous factors that combine to create a future food crisis, which many in the business world say is inevitable. *The Wall Street Journal* put it this way:

> When a large segment of the population is facing a drastic cut in income in the face of escalating food prices we have a catastrophic problem in the making. Today we have the simultaneous events of income deflation and food inflation; two high-speed express trains coming down the tracks at each other, a financial crisis colliding with staggering crop losses, which are cutting deeply into available planetary food reserves.[49]

We are being told that hundreds of millions of people around the world go to bed hungry each night and suffer from severe malnutrition. That's difficult for us in the United States to understand as we feel safe from that sort of thing here. Yet the *Los Angeles Times* carried an article in which it revealed an astonishing figure relative to hunger in the United States. The article had the headline, "15% of families went hungry in '09."

> The USDA says 17.4 million households lacked funds to eat at some point last year. Released Monday, the study also found that 6.8 million of these households—with as many as 1 million children—had ongoing financial problems that forced them to miss meals regularly. The number is triple the number that were having problems feeding themselves in 2006. This month, USDA officials announced that the number of Americans getting food stamps hit a record 42.4 million in August, a 17% gain over this past year.[50]

Let's hope that the *Los Angeles Times* report on a fungus disease that could wipe out 80% of the wheat crop never occurs. If it will spread as they think it might, disaster could be in the offing. How fast it would spread is probably an unknown factor in the situation.

Perhaps it could take years to get to America. The Times article is given here for you to consider:

> Working inside a bio-secure greenhouse outfitted with motion detectors and surveillance cameras, government scientists at the Cereal Disease Laboratory in St. Paul, MN suspended the fungal spores in a light mineral oil and sprayed them onto thousands of healthy wheat plants. After two weeks, the stalks were covered with deadly reddish blisters characteristic of the scourge known as Ug99. Nearly all the plants were goners.
>
> Crop scientists fear the Ug99 fungus could wipe out more than 80% of worldwide wheat crops as it spreads from Eastern Africa. It has already jumped the Red Sea and traveled as far as Iran. Experts say it is poised to enter the breadbasket of Northern India and Pakistan, and the wind will inevitably carry it to Russia, China and even North America—if it doesn't ride with people first. [51]

A recent article in the Los Angeles Times titled, "Startling State of Hunger in the U.S." declared that "one in six Americans is unsure where their next meal will come from."[52] That is an inconceivable report. It is especially hard for me to believe because I do not know of one person whom that description would fit. It is a fact, that if a thing is beyond our knowledge it is difficult to accept. We read news reports like this and are unconvinced because we have never experienced it to be so. Thus, we go our way, thinking that all is really well when it is not. Worldwide famine is a reality and getting worse each day.

I was shocked to read that a 2011 famine in Somalia claimed 260,000 lives in that one year alone.[53]

CHAPTER 5

PESTILENCE

SIGN # 13 PESTILENCE

This sign is found in Matthew 24:7 where we are told, "For nation shall rise against nation, and kingdom against kingdom: and there shall be famines, and pestilences, and earthquakes, in divers places."

Our ozone layer is being rapidly depleted. Because of this, environmentalists are telling us that weather patterns have become totally unpredictable. What's more, pestilence, such as cancer, is increasing as the ozone layer depletes. We are told that chlorofluorocarbons are the cause. However, the real problem is that there in not enough electrical charge in the upper atmosphere. Scientifically, the earth is losing half of its electromagnetic field every 1,400 years. The energy is being lost at the ozone layer. This is irreversible, and the reason why CFC's are penetrating and breaking the ozone layer down.

As the ozone is depleted and the more deadly rays of the sun flow into our atmosphere, pestilence will result—all forms of pestilence. The worst is that it will cause mutational variations on the skin of humans, which is, of course, cancer. This mutational variation is then introduced into the bloodstream, organs and deep tissues of the body.

The Environmental Protection Agency (EPA) is so pessimistic about this, they are saying it's possible that one out of three persons worldwide will die from cancer induced by the increasing rate of ultraviolet radiation. We are told that small botanical forms of life and some small creatures—insects in particular—will be drastically affected by this new alarming rate of ultraviolet radiation.

This ozone-related problems will cause these creatures to leave their ecological bounds. They are already doing that. Some examples are the killer bee and the fire ant. The migration of these creatures is dangerous for man. In addition to this, other forms of small life will spread pestilence as they move out of their normal habitations. These small creatures will make an exodus from areas where the ozone layer is the weakest. Because of this, they also become variant and behave in bizarre ways. This is in keeping with prophecies in Matthew 24 and the book of Revelation where it is predicted that pestilence caused by the small creatures of earth will run rampant.

Even with the availability of modern medicine, diseases such as malaria, smallpox and tuberculosis, are again getting out of control. Twenty years ago it was thought these diseases were eliminated from the civilized world. Now appears that the world is being readied for mind boggling end time pestilences.

Moral standards have been thrown out the window, and promiscuity is acceptable for heterosexuals and gays alike. Sodom and Gomorrah are the most notable example of cultures that went down this same road with catastrophic results. Our liberal leaders in Washington are telling us that all we have to do is practice "safe sex" and all will be OK; therefore, they pass out condoms to children encouraging them to continue on with their promiscuity.[1] Before sex education began in the public schools, teen pregnancy was declining. After the programs were established, the rates soared through the roof.

What's more, our government reacted to aids in a way that made the situation worse as they turned aids into the first politically- protected disease.

Although aids is the most horrifying of any sexually transmitted disease, *all* such diseases are on the rise. Even scarier is the long list of new sexual diseases being discovered. The center for disease control in Atlanta, GA found that a cancer thought to be a direct result of aids infections may actually be an independent sexually transmitted disease.

Within another year there could be as many as 12 million South Africans infected with the aids virus. The Central Intelligence

Agency (CIA) calculates that 75% of Africa's population south of the Sahara could be ultimately infected. If this is correct, it could be the worst pestilence in human history—worse than the black plague of medieval times. The International Aids Center at Harvard predicts that in a few years 110 million people will be infected.

Making matters worse is that sexually transmitted disease of all types has increased out of control. Over three million new cases of syphilis, gonorrhea and other genital diseases are appearing in the United State each year. Aids is growing at an alarming rate around the world. The statistics include only those individuals who have come down with full-blown aids.

We're told that 30-50 million African people will die of aids in the next few years. This is a tragedy unparalleled in human history including the black plague of the 14th century. Only 1/3 of those afflicted with the black plague died. The percentage of death of full-blown aids is 100%. Aids is the first disease in human history where there are no cases of ultimate recovery.

Is this not like what Jesus described for the last days? Are these the last days? Already, more people have been killed by aids than any single war. The problem with this disease is that the knowledge of, and protection from, it is difficult because of political control and special interest groups that squelch the truth. Already, over one million babies have been born HIV positive. Twenty million persons in the world have this disease, not counting the millions that aren't aware they have it. This figure will double in the next seven years.

According to the *Associated Press* aids in Washington D. C. is presently affecting 1 in 10 residents between the ages of 40-49.[2] The *New Tribes Mission* reports that one Christian on a Tanzania soccer team said, "Of the eleven members of my team only three are still alive, of the twenty member choir in my church only seven are still alive. I feel like an old man of 90 as all of my friends are dead or dying." In some African countries, the entire middle generation has been lost. Elderly Africans, usually cared for by their children, are now caring for their orphaned grandchildren.

We are being told that in the near future the Ivory Coast and Thailand will no longer be able to endure as nations because most of their populations will be dead due to aids. In the Ivory Coast today, aids is the leading cause of death among men and the second leading cause of death among women. There could be 30,000 deaths each year as a result of aids.

In Thailand it is estimated that nearly 50 million people will contact aids. In the next five years they expect 160,000 are expected to die. In Brazil there are already 750,000 affected. In the United States, the center of disease control in Atlanta says that one in every 250 males between the age of 20-45 is HIV positive. Every thirteen minutes in another person is infected. Every 30 minutes one dies of it. In this country there will be 40,000 deaths this year.

Because of the strong gay lobby in the United States, the treatment of aids is being downplayed. That's why former President Clinton wanted to allow people with Aids to immigrate into this country. Had it been permitted, it would have made aids the only disease immune from immigration laws.

We are officially told that the aids virus cannot live more than 3-5 seconds outside the human body; yet, in cases where aids had been contracted through dentistry we see this is not true. When a drill is used, even though it may be properly sterilized, it still could contained remnants of blood and saliva from the previous patient.

The reason the truth is not being told regarding aids, is mainly due to pressure from gay lobbyists and fear of public panic. It's difficult to protect the uninfected because of laws that disallow what's called "discrimination against aids carriers" even though all other communicable diseases are quarantined or not allowed to enter our country.

An example of this is a school teacher who contacted tuberculosis because of aids. The school board thought that this might be a threat to the students, so they transferred the teacher to an administrative job with the same pay. He hired an attorney, sued, and got his job back. So governmental policy, through pressure of special interest groups, will not protect the public.

The Moody Bible Church in Chicago had a four-year-old with aids who came to Sunday School. The student was told he couldn't attend as he might bite another student or do something else considered risky. The parents got an attorney and the court made the church accept him in Sunday School. Consequently, the thirty other children were pulled out of church by their parents. Here in America, our laws assist in the spread of aids. That's not true of any other disease.

We are told that aids and HIV positive are not the same disease, but that's not true. You can look at a baby and say it's not the same as you because it's not an adult. That child is the same as you.

Anyone who contracts HIV will die of aids. As said, this is 100% true. It may take 10-20 years or longer to die as more drugs savvy comes along to treat aids, but it will still happen. Let's say that you go to Thailand or the Ivory Coast and get in an accident or get sick and need a blood transfusion. What do you suppose will happen?

In one day in Australia an HIV positive male patient was operated on. The next four operations were all women. Each subsequently contracted the virus from the doctor that operated on the HIV man. A person who has contracted the HIV virus will not know it by a blood test for at least 3-6 months, as it will not show up until after that period of time.

Suppose you are HIV positive and don't know it, and you donate blood to a blood bank before the time it would show up on a blood test. It goes into the nation's blood supply as at the time it was tested it showed no signs of the virus; yet, it was there. Do you see how this end time pestilence can spread without hope of stopping it?

Could it be that AIDS will be this end time pestilence? The spread of aids continues: 50% of all people tested in Africa are HIV positive. Members of the Zambian army tested almost 100% Aids positive. NATO estimates that 25% of the people presently living on earth will eventually die of aids. The following is an excerpt:

Lamplighter Magazine tells us there are 40 million people currently infected with aids. It is felt within the next ten years there could be as many as 100 million infected. That's why life expectancy has gone down in many nations around the globe. In some villages in Africa an entire generation is dead—leaving the elderly and small children to fend for themselves.[3]

Dr. John Cinonci received an unsigned letter from Zimbabwe concerning aids in that country. The following communication from him is shocking to say the least. Below is an excerpt.

As you may or may not know, Zimbabwe is located in Southern Africa with a population of 10.5 million. Joshua Nkomo, the vice president accused whites of bringing aids to his country to wipe out blacks in order to take its land and wealth. The letter said, "More than 1 million people are infected with HIV. This is one in ten. Each week about 300 people die from the disease.[4]

A report from the *Associated Press* had the following scary statistical information about Washington, D.C:

A new report by D.C. health officials says that at least 3% of residents in the nation's capitol are living with HIV or aids and every mode of transmission is on the rise.

The findings in the 2008 epidemiologist report by the D.C. HIV/AIDS Administration point to a severe epidemic that's impacting every race and sex across the population and neighborhoods. Scheduled to be released Monday, the report says that the number of HIV and AIDS cases jumped 22 % from the nearly 12,500 reported in 2006.

Almost one in ten residents of the District of Columbia between ages forty and forty-nine are living with HIV. Black men had the highest infection rate at almost 7 %.

The report says the virus is most often transmitted by men having sex with men. This is followed by heterosexual transmission and injection drug use.[5]

But there is more to the plague story of the end time than just aids. Due to aids and its effect on the immune system, old diseases like tuberculosis are making a big time comeback. This means that

90 years of tuberculosis research is about to be wiped out. A disease thought to be wiped out is a coming terror for the new generation. Doctors tell us that it's perfectly clear that aids and tuberculosis walk hand in hand.

Another disease thought to be behind us is malaria. In 1955, the World Health Organization announced that this disease had been wiped out. About 2 million a year die from it. Scientists are also concerned that the world is facing a new epidemic of cholera. A strain resistant to all known vaccines has appeared in Asia and claims thousands each year. Also, we are seeing new plagues of locusts. Bubonic plague is also on the rise.

Some years ago a frightening article appeared in the *Orlando Florida Sentinel* talking about strange new diseases that could become epidemic in proportion. We've all heard about the so-called flesh- eating bug that eats the skin of a person There is nothing that can be done medically because the medical community hasn't the vaguest idea what it is. As man takes out more forests and builds in them, the contact between humans and rodents increases thus causing rare diseases to occur. Antibiotics, once thought to be the cure, have now become part of the problem. Overuse causes bacteria to become resistant to them.

A rather disturbing article was reported by the *Washington Post* as follows:

> Urinary tract infections, pneumonia and other common ailments caused by germs that carry a new gene with the power to destroy antibiotics are intensifying fears of a fresh generation of so called superbugs.

> The gene, NDM-1, which is apparently widespread in parts of India, has been identified in just three U.S. patients, all of whom had received treatment in India and recovered. The gene's ability to affect different bacteria and make them resistant to many medications marks a worrying development in the

fight against infectious diseases, which can mutate to defeat a humans' antibiotic arsenal.

"The problem thus far seems fairly small, but the potential is enormous. This is in some ways our worst nightmare," said Brad Spellberg, an infectious disease specialist at the Los Angeles Biomedical Research Institute at Harbor-UCLA Medical Center and author

The bacteria, which include previously unseen strains of E coli and other common pathogens, appear to have evolved in India where poor sanitation combines with cheap and widely available antibiotics to create a fertile environment for breeding new microorganisms

The infections were then carried to the United States, Britain and more than a half dozen countries, often through "medical tourism," which involves foreigners seeking less expensive, more easily accessible surgery overseas.

The resistance gene, NDM-1 stands for New Delhi metallo-B-lactamase 1 was first identified in 2008 in bacteria in a Swedish patient who had been hospitalized in New Delhi. The gene produces an enzyme that destroys most antibiotics.[6]

BIOLOGICAL TERRORISM

Another aspect of a coming pestilence in this world is that which may be self inflicted. I speak of the possibility of biological terrorism. While chemical attacks are frightening, a biological attack is worse because it can be contagious and reproductive. Over time, the viruses they cause may multiply and become more dangerous than when originally released.

After 9/11, a mentally disturbed person sent anthrax in the mail to various government officials. This type of biological weapon is the most dangerous because, once released, it can cause problems for decades. After testing anthrax on the island of Gruinard off the coast of Scotland some years ago, the island remained infected with anthrax spores for forty years.

One of the many problems associated with this type of warfare is that no country can protect itself against such an attack. In a tiny space, one can develop trillions of bacteria at little cost and little risk to the one producing it, and it's almost impossible to discover.

It wasn't until our lifetime that weapons of warfare could wipe out the entire human race in a short period of time. The Bible predicted that such a day would come. As I have previously quoted Mark 13, I do so again. It says: "And unless the Lord had shortened those days, no flesh would be saved; but for the elect's sake, whom He chose, He shortened the days" (Mark 13:20).

On March 20, 1995, a cult group released the nerve agent Sarin in the Tokyo subway system, killing twelve people and injuring 5,500. The only reason thousands did not die was because of an impure mixture of the agent. Just one drop of Sarin can kill within minutes after contact with the skin or inhalation of its vapor.

THE FOURTH HORESEMAN OF THE APOCALYPSE

We have pointed out earlier that the first four signs in Matthew 24 are parallel to the four horsemen of the apocalypse. The sign of pestilence is seen in the pale horse rider of Revelation 6, which says, "And I looked, and behold a pale horse: and his name that sat on him was Death, and Hell followed with him. And power was given unto them over the fourth part of the earth, to kill with sword, and with hunger, and with death, and with the beasts of the earth" (Revelation 6:8).

The Greek word translated "pale" is translated from the Greek word *choleras* from which we derive our word chlorophyll. In it's biblical usage, it's a pale green, the sickish yellow-green color of sickness or disease. This is the substance that makes plants green. But you say, "What is pestilence?" Let the Bible itself define it for you, The book of Deuteronomy tells us, "The LORD will make the plague cling to you until He has consumed you from the land which you are going to possess" (Deuteronomy 28:21). "The LORD will strike you with the boils of Egypt, with tumors, with the scab, and with the itch, from which you cannot be healed. The LORD will strike you with madness and blindness and confusion of heart" (Deuteronomy 28:27-28).

How are such diseases brought about? Note again Revelation 6:8 where it talks about this death coming as a result of "the beasts of the earth." What does the phrase *the beasts* mean? In the Greek it's literally "little beasts." It's the Greek diminutive form. In other words, these are rodents that will bring epidemics as they come into closer contact with humans due to a lack of their normal food.

They say that other small rodents that can carry the diseases will also soon leave their habitat and come into closer contact with us. It's interesting to note that the rat population is increasing at an alarming rate. It constitutes one of the greatest health hazards in the world today. The World Health Organization, for example, has pointed out that the rat population has increased from an estimated 800 million in 1919 to 4.8 billion today.

There are new strains of disease that are completely resistant to known antibiotics. But there is something more terrifying than that. There are new extremely deadly pestilences. I speak of diseases like Ebola that kills 90% of its victims in less than a week. Another new disease eats the organs and flesh of your body rapidly

But the really new development is the disclosure that biological terrorism is now a present reality. This method of terrorism can happen in any country in the world—even in our own. It comes not only in *biological* agents but in *chemical* agents as well. When the U.S. was involved in the Gulf War, we vaccinated all military personnel in the Persian Gulf. Every Israeli citizen now has a gas mask. The threat is real.

We are told that Arab terrorists already have large quantities of this material stored on American soil for use against us at the proper time. The greatest fear is that radical countries have stockpiles of anthrax. Most of these biological agents are not only fatal if inhaled, but fatal even if a mere drop gets on your exposed skin. The thing that makes this type of weapon attractive to a terrorist is the ease with which it can be made and how inexpensive it is to produce.

The spread of disease is expanded when there is famine and people are not properly nourished. Presently, out of the 171 countries in the world, only four are exporters of food. When our forefathers came to this country there was an average topsoil of 4-5 feet deep. Today, it's only a few inches. It takes a full century to produce one inch of topsoil. You figure it out. We have reduced our varieties of wheat from hundreds to fourteen. What happens if some bug or disease threatens the little variety we have left in this world?

It seems that there are all sorts of new things causing serious illness that had never before been known to mankind in its present form or its present extent. The *Los Angeles Times* reported this under the headline "Deadly 'Superbug' Infections Spread":

> The number of severe infections by a "superbug" known as methicillin-resistant staphylococcus aureus, is at least twice as high as researchers previously believed, and the bacterium now kills more Americans than AIDS. Experts attribute the emergence of the superbugs to indiscriminate use of antibiotics. The failure of patients to complete their antibiotic regimens and the use of antibiotics in animal feed are common causes of this problem. In each case, incomplete eradication of the bacteria leads to mutations that have increased resistance to the drugs.[11]

An article that appeared in the *Los Angeles Times* revealed that a San Diego Zoo outbreak of skin infections traced to staff workers tells us that something new is happening that has never happened before—a disease can be transferred from a human to an animal and vice versa. It seems like a zookeeper passed a disease to an elephant calf, which infected its caregivers. The article states:

> An outbreak of antibiotic resistant skin infections at the San Diego Zoo last year began when a zookeeper

infected an elephant calf that was being hand raised because its mother couldn't care for it, according to a zoo and county health department investigation. The calf, in turn, infected as many as 20 of its human caretakers. It is the first known transmission of a superbug from a zoo animal to a human, according to the Center for Disease Control and Prevention, which published the results of the investigation Thursday.[12]

The health department stated that the main concern is that the transmission of diseases between humans and animals, particularly pets poses a significant health problem. The article went on to say, "If the infection infects a cut or scrape and gets into the bloodstream, it can cause serious illness and even death in animals or people."[13] The point is, almost daily we hear of new health hazards that did not previously exist. It seems as though we are heading into a brand new problem that could open the door to the type of pestilences the Bible predicted.

As if all of this is not daunting enough, the *Washington Post* recently reported, "new superbugs are raising concerns worldwide." Urinary tract infections, pneumonia and other common ailments caused by germs that carry a new gene with the power to destroy antibiotics are intensifying fears of a fresh generation of so called superbugs."[14]

For years we have been hearing that bugs have learned how to defeat antibiotics, but this is something new that can cause the biblically predicted end time pestilences to attain new heights. Furthermore, we have all heard how some bugs that have become immune to antibiotics store the antibiotics in their bodies and use them to attack other bugs.

The national newspaper *USA Today* carried an article they called, "Deadly Superbugs Look Unstoppable." The story reported the following:

A family of nightmare superbugs—untreatable and often deadly—is spreading through hospitals across the USA, and doctors fear it may be too late to stop them, senior health officials said Tuesday. "These are nightmare bacteria that present a triple threat," said Thomas Frieden, director of the Centers for Disease Control and Prevention.

They're resistant to nearly all antibiotics. They have high mortality rates, killing half of the people with serious infections. And they can spread their resistance to other bacteria." These superbugs are the biggest threat that we have seen to patient safety in the hospitals. Perhaps the greatest threat from CRE is its ability to share its resistance genes with other, more common bacteria such as Ecoli. If that happened, conditions affecting millions of American—such as diarrhea, urinary tract infections, respiratory conditions and pneumonia—could become untreatable with antibiotics.[15]

The same issue of *USA Today* had a second article about superbugs. The article reads as follows:

Although many germs have become resistant to antibiotics, health leaders are most concerned about a class of superbugs called carbapenem-resistant Enterobacteriaceae or CRE. Because CRE infections can't be treated with modern antibiotics, patients are sometimes being forced to make painful choices to survive. Doctors sometimes resort to old, outdated antibiotics that can damage the kidneys because safer ones no longer work.

I've had to ask patients, "Do you want a toxic antibiotic and end up on dialysis or would you prefer to have a limb amputated?" Dr. Fishman says. Such dilemmas have led some doctors to believe the world is entering the beginning of the "post antibiotic era," says Costi Sifri, an infectious disease physician and hospital epidemiologist at the University of Virginia

Health System. Forty-two states have experienced CRE germs. [16]

These circumstances give rise to the reality of many scriptures that predict the spread of pestilence in the end time. As pointed out earlier, the signs that Jesus gave in Matthew 24 would increase in severity and frequency as the age came to its conclusion. I believe we are presently living in the very days that our Lord spoke of thousands of years ago.

A recent television program by Hal Lindsay gave the following information regarding these days of pestilence:

- Health experts tell us that the MERS-CoV Virus, which began in Saudi Arabia, could become a horrible viral threat to the entire world. It has a 50% mortality rate in those stricken by it.
- Luke 21:11 says "And there will be great earthquakes in various places, and famines and pestilences; and there will be fearful sights and great signs from heaven." The Greek word translated "pestilence" here includes not only diseases that attack humans but also livestock and crops.
- A study by Duke University concludes, "Even with the usage of pesticides over one third of our food is lost to pests." That's a pestilence of biblical proportions.
- A recently released report by the government shows that disease in the United States has risen dramatically in the past decade.
- It has been hoped germs causing disease would be eliminated by antibiotics but they often kill off weak microbes so that only the strong survive to reproduce. Over time that has produced a new generation of superbugs that are resistant to all drugs.
- Sally Davis, England's chief medical officer said, "Antimicrobial resistance poses a catastrophic threat. If we don't act now any one of us could go into a hospital 20 years from now and die of an ordinary infection that cannot bed treated by antibiotics."

- The new superbug called "MRSA" kills up to 40,000 a year in the United States alone—that is pestilence!
- Bedbug infections in the United States carry infections— a town in India was overrun with tarantulas—in Africa sleeping sickness is making a strong comeback.
- The UN health organization is predicting that cancer will surge 50% by 2020 and 75% by 2030—gonorrhea currently affects 700,000 Americans a year, Measles is making a comeback in Europe.
- In Asia they have been fighting what they called "The monkey menace." Stray dogs have become a massive deadly problem in Moscow.
- There are hundreds of variant diseases—some of them wea- ponized in laboratories around the world. This is not even to mention the many types of biological and chemical weapons terrorists could turn loose on the world.
- We are living in a time of pestilence with the "Pale Horse" of Revelation ready to charge out of the gate.[17]

In a *Los Angeles Times* report on page 1 under the heading "Campaign to prevent pandemic goes viral" it was reported that a new virus that started in Saudi Arabia (mentioned above) has killed more than half the people known to have been infected. It is called the MERS-CoV Virus. The report says "Most troubling to health experts are reports of illnesses in patients who have not been to the Middle East which would indicate a quick spreading from person to person by simple casual contact." [18]

CHAPTER 6

NATURE WILL BE UNSTABLE

SIGN # 14 EARTHQUAKES

M atthew 24:7 states: For nation will rise against nation, and kingdom against kingdom. And there will be famines, pestilences, and earthquakes in various places." Anther scripture tells us about the final earthquake. Revelation 16:18 declares, "And there were noises and thundering and lightnings; and there was a great earthquake, such a mighty and great earthquake as had not occurred since men were on the earth."

Years ago geophysicists related to us that the internal temperature of earth near the core was approximately 6,000 degrees Fahrenheit. In the last few years their measurements have been alarming, as we are now being told that this internal temperature is in excess of 12,000 degrees. They feel, if this continues, there is a possibility in the future hat some thermonuclear reactions could occur which in turn, would cause earthquakes unlike any ever known before—just as Scripture predicted.

Already earthquakes are increasing at an alarming rate. As this core warming continues something has to give. The mantle of the earth is becoming more fragile. Did not Jesus say that there would be earthquakes in various places (meaning unusual places) and more than one earthquake happening in more than one area of the world at the same time although these earthquakes would not be related to each other?

Seismology graphs show earthquakes increasing every year. Over 1 million were registered last year and more than 10,000 of those were strong enough to be felt. Scientists tell us that forces now building up under the tectonic plates will be released in various places the world over where earthquakes are not usually felt. That's exactly what the Lord said about earthquakes in Matthew 24:7 where it says, "Earthquakes in various (unusual) places." The number of earthquakes above five on the Richter scale have more than doubled every decade since 1900. This is clearly, at least, a partial fulfillment of Matthew 24:7.

Luke 21:11 tells us there will be *great* earthquakes. It is this fact that current history emphasizes. So incredible has the violence of earthquake activity increased that the Internet encyclopedia Wikipedia has informed us that there were more people killed in earthquakes in 1976 than the total number of people killed in all the earthquakes in the 19th century.

Since 1980, in California alone, there have been more earthquakes since 1980 of 5.0 or higher than in the entire century before then. The Mammoth Lakes area in California experiences thousands of quakes every year. It has been discovered it contains what they call a magma intrusion about ten miles in width, and this pre-volcanic body is rising at an alarming rate each year. They say if it erupts under these conditions it will produce 140 cubic miles of ash. This is incredibly more ash than was generated by the Mt. St. Helens volcanic explosion. If that happened, Fresno, CA and everything within seventy miles of the epicenter would be buried by ash. History tells us this has not happened before.

Jesus Himself adds great significance to the sign of earthquakes by telling us that the signs of Matthew 24 would be like birth pangs. He says, "All these are the beginning of birth pains" (Matthew 24:8).

As I have previously pointed out, by saying that the earthquakes would be like birth pangs, Jesus is saying, "Earthquakes would increase in frequency and intensity as His return drew near." Almost 2,000 years later, with so many of the other signs occurring, we are left with a question: Are earthquakes increasing? For the answer, turn to the U.S. Geological Survey's National Earthquake Information Center (USGS). The information below can be found at the USGS website. The site states: " the total number of earthquakes listed for 1990 were 16,590. Those listed for 1999 were 20,832. The year 2000 ended with 22,256 earthquakes. The year 2008 ended with 31,777.[1]

Jesus said there would be a rise in the number of earthquakes and the USGS verifies that fact, but the verse continues by telling us that not only would the number increase but so would the intensity. And so it is.

Note Matthew 24:8, which says, "All these are the *beginning* of sorrows." As stated previously, World War I could well be this beginning of sorrows. Thus in the year 1914 and the years that followed, there occurred a combination of circumstances which are identical to that which Jesus predicted would exist in the end time. We had a world war for the first time. Extreme famines began then, along with a pestilence in the form of the first worldwide epidemic. In this case it was a flu epidemic. Then as already mentioned, we have seen earthquakes occurring in different places at the same time.

Look at volcanic eruptions like the one in the Philippines. This was one of the most powerful eruptions ever experienced on this planet. Just this one volcanic eruption caused the world to lose between 1 to 3% of the sun's radiation. That doesn't sound like much, but scientists tell us that small changes create drastic consequences. That eruption lasted 24 hours with the force of an atomic bomb per second or the launching of one million space shuttles. We are seeing a dramatic increase in volcanic activity; so, look for even more bizarre situations in the future.

Related to all of this is the fact that natural disasters are happening at an ever-increasing rate. Listen to this news report:

> According to a report released recently by a British charity called Oxfam, the number of natural disasters around the world increased by more than four times in the last 20 years. The data was assembled from the records of the Red Cross, the United Nations and research done at Louvian University in Belgium. The report concluded that the earth is currently experiencing approximately 500 natural disasters per year, compared with 120 per year in the early

1980's. Between 1985 and 1994, 174 million people were affected each year by natural disasters. In the following decade, this figure increased by 70% to 254 million people per year.[2]

Scientists declared that the *entire* earth shook as a result of the 9.0 earthquake in 2004 that caused the tsunami in Indonesia. This reminds us of future earthquakes that will be even more incredible than the one we are talking about. Listen to Haggai 2:6: "For thus says the LORD of hosts: Once more (a little while) I will shake heaven and earth, the sea and dry land." In other words, there will be earthquakes that will shake the entire earth. It's most interesting that seismologists today are predicting exactly what Haggai predicted, and that such earthquake phenomena may not be that far off.

So severe was the 2011 earthquake in Japan that it "moved the entire island eight feet from its position before the earthquake."[3] Greater detail of this is included under a sign later in this book.

Seismologists tell us they are fearful that sometime soon super volcanoes will erupt causing unprecedented loss of life and property damage. The potential for a super volcanic eruption caused by earthquakes in Yellowstone National Park is becoming more and more widely known. A TV documentary on this subject was quite alarming to watch. It stated that the volcano in Yellowstone is the largest super volcano in the world. Various TV documentaries leave nothing to the imagination when they describe what the result of such an eruption would be like. Currently, sensors in the park reveal that the area is recording a lot of activity with the earth heaving and bulging. Yellowstone does not look like a volcano, but the *entire* park is a volcano. What would it be like if it exploded? One reports states:

> If it does blow, Yellowstone's volcano could kill millions of Americans—from coast to coast and border to border. It could be 2,500 times larger than the 1980 eruption on Mt. St. Helens, so say the experts. In 1993, park rangers closed the entire Norris Geyser basin because of excessive high ground temperatures. There is an area that is 28 miles long by 7 miles

bulged upward over 5 inches since
g in this area is dying: the trees, the
l shrubs. A dead zone is developing
tward. The animals are literally
'e park. An incredible bulge was
..t the bottom of Yellowstone Lake. The
..ge has risen over 100 feet. [4]

SIGN # 15 UNUSUAL WEATHER PATTERNS

Matthew 24:7 clearly lumps together several signs. When they are seen together, they tell of the overall instability of nature. Luke adds some thoughts to what Matthew said. The section there reads as follows: "And there will be great earthquakes in various places, and famines and pestilences; and there will be fearful sights and great signs from heaven" (Luke 21:11).

You can hardly pick up a newspaper without reading about some bizarre weather in some part of the world or of the increase in frequency and intensity of weather patterns. Indeed, we are living in unusual days of weather unlike anything ever experienced before.

The Los Angeles Times reported on a very unusual situation where an earthquake and a tsunami created by the earthquake were separated by only one day from a volcanic eruption not related to the other two events. All three events took place in Indonesia. That is indeed an inconceivable thing.[5]

Joel Rosenberg's newsletter of December 2010 stated, "I wanted to bring this headline to your attention, 2010 world gone wild: QUAKES, FLOODS, BLIZZARDS." The *AP* story begins, "This was the year the earth struck back. Earthquakes, heat waves, floods, volcanoes, super typhoons, blizzards, landslides and droughts killed at least a quarter million people in 2010. More people were killed worldwide by natural disasters this year than have been killed by terrorism attacks in the past 40 years combined."[6]

One news report declared that extreme weather and natural disasters are occurring simultaneously around the globe. The article states that words such as "unprecedented," "Never before in living memory" are now common, and describe many of these events. One has to wonder, "what on earth is going on?"[7]

The amazing thing is that the Bible declares all of these different natural disasters would occur simultaneously as Jesus' return draws near (Matthew 24:33-34). He said chaotic weather would be prevalent (Luke 21:25-26). He declared the seas and waves would be roaring in the last days, and He likened these signs to birth pangs in Matthew 24:8.[8]

Newsweek Magazine's issues of March 28, 2011 and April 4, 2011 sounded like a commentary from the New Testament passage on the subject. The cover of the March 28, 2011 magazine showed a tsunami-type wave with the large words, "Apocalypse Now." Thus it is, that even those who do not claim to be believers in Jesus are sitting up and taking notice of the radical changes in nature, all of which were predicted in the Bible. Also on the cover of *Newsweek* were the words, "Tsunamis, Earthquakes, Nuclear Meltdowns, Revolutions, Economies on the Brink . . . What Next?"[9]

So unusual and rare have the natural disasters of all types been that have come upon us—and with such intensity and frequency—that *Lamplighter Magazine* declared the term, "Once in a 100 years has lost its meaning."[10]

In showing the tornado history of the United States, the *Los Angeles Times* offered a graph of tornado activity over the last 61 years in which it showed exponential growth of these storms in 2011. The whole concept of exponential growth is covered in another sign in this book. The graph showed that in 2011, as of April 28, there were triple the number of tornados as compared to the year with the previous record number of tornados. The amazing thing is that the tornado season is not yet over. Who knows how many such storms will be unleashed this year?[11]

An earlier edition of the *Los Angeles Times* stated that 2011 could prove to be one of the largest convulsions of tornado history activity in U.S. history."[12]

Finally, on August 4, 2011, the *Los Angeles Times* declared that this year's tornado season was the worst and deadliest on record with 753 twisters confirmed.[13]

CHAPTER 7

PERSECUTION AND HATRED OF CHRISTIANS

SIGN # 16 PERSECUTION OF CHRISTIANS

Previously, in this book, we saw a sign of the time that declared that in the final days of earth's history Jewish people would be persecuted and murdered. This sign indicates that *both* Jews and Christians would be murdered and persecuted. We will only look at the persecution of Christians in this section as we have already shared the fact of the persecution of the Jewish people.

Speaking of what it will be like during the Tribulation after the Rapture of the Church, Matthew 24:9 and other verses quoted below give us keen insight: "Then they will deliver you up to tribulation and kill you, and you will be hated by all nations for My name's sake" (Matthew 24:9).

The irrational nature of the belief system of those who would murder Christians declares that it is God's will to kill people who are Christians. Read carefully John 16:2: "They will put you out of the synagogues; yes, the time is coming that whoever kills you will think that he offers God service."

Not only will the murder of Christians be perfectly acceptable in that age, but it will also be acceptable to persecute those who do good. 2 Timothy 3:12 states: "Yes, and all who desire to live godly in Christ Jesus will suffer persecution."

John 15 gives us the reason why the world hates true believers. "If the world hates you, you know that it hated Me before it hated you. If you were of the world, the world would love its own. Yet because you are not of the world, but I chose you out of the world, therefore the world hates you" (John 15:18-19).

The persecution and murder of Christians for no reason other than the fact that they are Christians is increasing exponentially in today's world. The reading of Revelation 13 should send chills up the spines of those living in the last days:

> And he was given a mouth speaking great things and blasphemies, and he was given authority to continue for forty-two months. Then he opened his mouth in blasphemy against God, to blaspheme His name, His tabernacle, and those who dwell in heaven. It was granted to him to make war with the saints and to overcome them. And authority was given him over every tribe, tongue, and nation (Revelation 13:5-7).

PERSECUTION OF CHRISTIANS AROUND THE WORLD

The hatred of Christians on a worldwide scale has already begun. In Matthew 24, Jesus lists things that would indicate when the end is near. He concludes His list with the fact that in the end time Jews and Christians would be persecuted. But remember, as earlier stated, the signs that Jesus gave would be like the birth pangs of a woman having a child. That means that as end time events draw closer to the birthing of the new age, each sign would intensify in its pain and increase in its frequency.

An article from the *London Times* tells of the terrifying hatred that exists in today's world toward Christian people. Here is a portion of that article:

> Paramilitary troops patrolled the streets of a town in eastern Pakistan yesterday after Muslim radicals burned to death 8 members of a Christian family,

raising fears of violence spreading to other areas. Hundreds of armed supporters of Lashkar-e-Jhangvi, an outlawed Islamic militant group, burned dozens of Christian homes in Gojra over the weekend after allegations that a copy of the Koran had been defiled. The mob opened fire indiscriminately, threw petrol bombs and looted houses as thousands of frightened Christians ran for safety. They were shouting anti-Christian slogans and attacked our houses, Rafiq Masih, a resident of the predominantly Christian colony, said. Residents said that police stood aside while the mob went on the rampage. We kept begging for protection, but police did not take action, Mr. Masih said.[1]

Today it's fashionable for terrorists to murder Christians. They do this not just by some quick way—they do it in a sadistic manner. Reports came out of Chad, Africa where we are told they took a black evangelist, bound him hand and foot and sewed him up into a huge drum. He was then left there to starve to death while natives incessantly beat on the drum with it's pulsating noise.

In Chad, thousands of Christians have been buried up to their necks in red anthills to remain until they were dead. The situation in Sudan is unspeakable as Muslim terrorists rape, massacre and murder people by the hundreds of thousands while the world stands by and watches.

It has been estimated that more Christians have been killed for their faith since 1900 than in the 1,900 years before. Does that sound like we're getting close to the end? Does this not match the words of our Lord when He predicted that as the end draws to a close, all the signs that He gave would increase in frequency and intensity?

In August 1997, an article appeared in the *Readers Digest* entitled, "The Global War On Christians. This article stated:

More Christians have died in this century for being Christians than in all other 1900 years since the birth of Christ. The atrocities against Christians just because they are Christians include torture, enslavement, rape, imprisonment, forcible separation of children from parents, and abuses that threaten the very survival of entire Christian communities. In most countries where this type of persecution exists, Christians are in a minority, but in a few places, like Cuba and Nigeria, where Christians are the majority, they are still oppressed.[2]

It is reported that in 2009 176,000 Christians were martyred. While I have not seen figures from other years, the article does not seem to indicate this was a number unusually high for a yearly total of murdered Christians. In part, the article reads as follows:

From the middle of 2008 to the middle of 2009, 176,000 Christians around the world were martyred—killed for their faith. That's 482 deaths per day—one every three minutes . . . The report cited North Korea, which reportedly used Christians as guinea pigs to test chemical and biological weapons, as the world's worst persecutor of Christians.

The report said Iran is among eight nations in the top ten of the group's ranking of the 50 worst persecutors of Christians in which Sharia, the Islamic law, is dominant. A total of the 35 nations on the list are under some form of Sharia law.[3]

On December 17, 2008 in China, the Chengnan Church, an officially registered church of the Tinghi district in Juangsu province was attacked by a mob led by government officials, according to the China Aid Association. More than 50 Christians were at the church for worship when police officers barged in and dragged several believers outside. That's where more than a thousand people were gathered, including public officials and security guards. The crowds then demolished the church's office, training center and cafeteria and confiscated church property.[4]

In England, a poll taken revealed the following stunning facts:

> The first poll of Britain's churchgoers, carried out for the *Sunday Telegraph*, found that thousands of them believe they are being turned down for promotion because of their faith. One in five said that they had faced opposition at work because of their beliefs. More than half of them revealed they had suffered some form of persecution for being a Christian. As many as 44% said they had been mocked by friends, neighbors or colleagues for being a Christian, and 19 percent said that they had been ignored or excluded for the same reason."[5]

We are told that the reason Islamic terrorists hate America is because we have helped to make Israel a military giant. We are also told that if we stop supporting Israel, the terrorists will leave us alone. but that is not the case. The goal of the Iranian president is the overthrow of the West and Christianity and to replace it with Islam, living under the Sharia law of the Muslim faith.

The belief in the twelfth Inman, discussed in other parts of this book, spells out what they believe will take place. It is claimed that when this Inman comes, he will destroy Christianity and establish the Muslim faith over all the people of the earth. He will do this in a time of chaotic war between Muslims and the West. Apparently the leader of Iran thinks he is called of Allah to prepare the way. At any rate, consider carefully the following:

Don't be fooled into thinking that if we ceased to support Israel future terrorism against us would cease. Is it possible that enough people in this country will feel we should no longer support Israel or be involved in any way with Israel in order to get the terrorists to back off? Will our *own* people put enough pressure on our government to abandon Israel? It is altogether possible that World War II and the Gulf wars were God's way to get America involved to stop the genocide of the Jewish race. Both times that America became involved, we went to war with people whose goal was the genocide of the Jewish race.

On December 7, 1941, Pearl Harbor was attacked, and God allowed it. Did God allow that to cause America to stop the German people from their attempts to annihilate the Jewish people? What about September 11, 2001? Didn't that bring us into a new war where we are again fighting against a people who are trying to destroy the Jewish people? *Both* Pearl Harbor *and* the Twin Towers of New York City were attacks from the air. Both of the attacks on America were perpetuated by people seeking to commit the genocide of the Jewish people.

Both attacks so enraged the American people they said, "We have to get these guys." Both times we were attacked to neutralize us. If they had succeeded, the door would have been opened to murder Jewish people in a wholesale slaughter.

Perhaps God allowed the attacks at Pearl Harbor and 9/11 in order for America to put a stop to the efforts to destroy the Jewish people. If that is the case, to abandon Israel will only encourage the likes of Iran and other radicals to destroy, not only the State of Israel, but Jewish people everywhere, and to turn on America and the West. God has blessed America in part, because of our support and our blessing of Israel. If we now choose to abandon Israel, will the judgment of God be our lot? Genesis 12:3 clearly states in God's own words, "I will bless those who bless you (Jews), And I will curse him who curses you (Jews); And in you all the families of the earth shall be blessed."

PERSECUTION IN ISLAMIC COUNTRIES

The continued rise of Islamic fundamentalism has made the Arab world highly volatile. There are about 1 ½ billion Muslims in the world today with a radical hatred of true Christians and Jews. They seem to have three chief goals: to conquer the world, to eradicate Israel, and to destroy America. Radical Muslims are more than willing to die if that means it's a step toward their control of the entire world. As if that were not enough, there is a new wave of anti-Semitism and anti-Christianity throughout the Muslim world.

Did you know that in countries where more than 50% of the population of the world lives, it's a crime to be a Christian? Letters with death threats are being sent to Christians in Muslim nations and sometimes are accompanied by a real bullet. The message is chilling: "Convert to Islam, leave or die."[6]

The following information is from my files, but I could not find the origin of it. The information is almost unbelievable, but nonetheless true!

In Sudan the official policy is holy war on Christians. Where the Christians are the majority in the southern part of that country, thousands of Christian children have been taken from Christian families and sold at open air slave markets for as little as $15.00 per child. Once sold, they are taken to northern Sudan, which is mainly Muslim, or to other Islamic countries. Once there, they must work as domestic slaves, field hands, soldier slaves or concubines for their Muslim masters.

In many countries Christians suffer not just torture and prison, but millions have been martyred. Southern Sudan is mainly Christian, yet believers are kidnapped and murdered. In this area of that country alone over one million have been murdered and another three million displaced. They have enslaved women and children as sex slaves. They have bombed, burned and looted villages. They have relocated entire villages into concentration camps called "peace villages." Sometimes the slave traders will bring the children back to the south to sell back to their parents so that they will get more money. Sometimes Christians have had their Achilles tendons cut so they couldn't run away from their slave owners. Another of their favorite tactics is to take busloads of Christians into the middle of a desert and leave them there without food and water.

Not only do they mass murder Christians in Sudan, they use cruel methods to accomplish their "ethnic cleansing" policies. Take this example: The *Voice of the Martyrs Newsletter* tells of "a Sudanese Christian boy who had his knees and feet nailed to a board and was left to die."[7]

What's more, they have withheld food from starving Christians who ultimately starve to death. There have been numerous accounts of Christians being crucified. Christian villages are plundered while the men are systematically murdered and their property is either confiscated or destroyed. The women are transported north and sold as slaves and concubines. Just from the Nuba mountain region alone 25,000 children have been abducted and sold into slavery.

In Pakistan, anyone who says anything against the prophet is hanged in public without a trial. Since Christians are considered apostates in this land, they can be forcibly divorced, denied any contact with their children and be disinherited. People who want to leave Islam can face death, and they may be killed by anyone with impunity.

Look at Saudi Arabia with me. In this Muslim kingdom, no public expression of Christianity is allowed. It's even illegal to wear a cross, read a Bible or utter a Christian prayer in the privacy of your own home. Christian worship is forbidden in any form, non-Muslim literature, including the Bible is forbidden. Under the law, conversion to Christianity is punishable by death. The Saudi legal system considers public flogging, amputation and beheading a right punishment just for being a Christian.

A special police force, called the muttawa, is charged with strict enforcement of religious laws. These religious police forcibly enter the homes of Christians searching for evidence of infidelity such as owning a Bible. They carry the humiliation of Christians to an extreme by delaying their execution until days like Easter or Christmas.

In Nigeria, it's common for churches to be burned to the ground while the police look on and do nothing. The story is told of one young girl in Nigeria who had a cross tattooed on her wrist and the Muslims kidnapped her and poured sulfuric acid on her wrist to remove the tattoo.

Religious minorities cannot handle food that is to be eaten by Muslims. Muslim owned shops cannot hire non Muslims. In another area Christians are often placed in metal boxes, which are very hot in the day and very cold at night. This is done as a punishment to them just because they are Christians.

> In parts of Nigeria any excuse to kill Christians will do, according to *Compass Direct News*. Muslims are murdering Christians in Nigeria because the

leaders of the radical Islamist group Tibliq died in May from injuries suffered in a 2006 auto accident. Ali Ahukade's followers now claim his death was the result of Christian prayers following an aborted evangelistic crusade.[8]

An article in *Prophecy News Watch* had this to say about the persecution of Christians throughout the world, "Christians admit to job losses, land seizures, attacks on churches, intimidation, torture, beatings, kidnappings, forced marriage and sexual harassment of Christian women. Some Christians have been killed."[9]

The plight of some of Algeria's women who refused to wear a veil had acid thrown in their faces by Muslim radicals. Things like this draw little attention in the West. The war in Bosnia has Muslim radicalism at the heart of the problem there. They want to establish a beachhead for their advancement into Europe. So, in Bosnia, Christians were mass murdering Muslims. America and the West stepped in to stop it, but they have not stepped in to stop the mass murder of Christians in Muslim countries.

This sad story was reported in the *Los Angeles times* in 2010.

The victims of Sunday's sectarian massacres were buried in mass graves in central Nigeria on Monday as survivors told horrific stories of Christian villagers being trapped in nets and hacked to death by Muslim herdsmen.[10]

The only comparison in all of world history to what is going on today is Hitler's treatment of the Jews. Terrible persecution takes place in Communist countries as well as in Muslim countries. The persecution of Christians in China is a well-documented fact.

The capital of North Korea was known as "Asia's Jerusalem" when there were 2,000 churches in the city. In 1948, when the Communists took over, they wiped out all outward signs of Christianity—all church buildings were closed, all Bibles destroyed, and religious leaders were executed or sent to concentration camps.

This sickening hatred has led to all sorts of horrific threats against the lives of believers. A recent newsletter from the *Voice of the Martyrs* reported the following situation in a Muslim country where threatening letters were sent to Christians.

> In the name of Allah, and of his final prophet, Muhammad (peace be upon him): the true religion of Islam will arise in your area. You cannot stop Allah's will. We have been watching your family: we have seen you go to church and seen you pray to your false god. We know that you are infidels, and we will deal with you as our holy Qur'an declares: In Sura 9 verse 5, it says to slay the idolaters wherever you find them; take them captive and besiege them.. It also says in Sura 9 verse 29 to fight those who have been given the Scripture and believe not in Allah or the last day or follow not the religion of truth. If you and your entire family do not leave your false religion and follow Islam, you will be killed. Your sons will be slaughtered and your daughters will become Muslim wives, bearing sons who will fight for Allah in this religion. Your only other option is to flee tonight. Leave your home and everything behind. ALLAHA AKBAR.[11]

Enclosed in the letter was a real live bullet.

THE INCREASING ANTI-CHRISTIAN BIAS IN AMERICA

SIGN # 17 THE HATRED OF CHRISTIANS

When the persecution of Jews began in Europe under the Nazi regime they did not begin by immediately sending them to gas chambers. No indeed! They began, through propaganda, inciting the population to turn against the Jewish people by a constant bombardment of propaganda that blamed Jewish people for the problems of the world. They did this through propaganda in movies, in newspapers and radio stations. The beginning of turning the populations of the world against true Bible believing Christians using the same Hitler-inspired methods is in full swing today.

One would think there would *not* be a bias against Christians in America. After all, America was founded on the Bible, Christian principles and laws; yet, today, we are seeing government, educational and media attacks on the rights and liberties of Christians as never before seen in this country. We need to look at the growing anti-Christians bias in America.

When the radical left cannot successfully debate conservative issues, they resort to vicious name calling and intolerance. They call Bible believers (and even non-religious conservatives) by the most debasing, degrading and shameful names in the English language. Let me list a few of the demeaning names given to Christians by politicians, Hollywood elite and the media.

Christians are referred to as poor, uneducated and easy to command. They are called bigots, hate mongers, fire-breathing radicals, unchristian, merchants of hate, fanatics, people who want to create a version of Ayatollah Khomeini, mean-spirited, Nazis, extremists, radicals, terrorists, arrogant, narrow-minded, ignorant, old-fashioned, crazy, the radical right, the far right, the extreme right, the Christian right and people who have a message of hate and fear. Can you imagine anyone referring to other groups like liberals, black people, Jewish people, gays or whoever by these terms? It would surely be called a hate crime. It seems that the only group that it is acceptable to commit hate crimes against are Christian people.

I am certain that most of you reading this have heard or read of Christians being called by at least some of these names. The most incredible part of it all is that those doing the name-calling refer to themselves as tolerant and rational while Christians are said to be just the opposite. Have you ever heard the liberal news media refer to left wingers as extreme, radical, narrow-minded or Nazis? Yet the liberals declare they are tolerant while conservatives are non-tolerant. Imagine that!

Everything Christian is under attack as well as Christians themselves. The entire scope of moral behavior accepted in this country since its founding is being ridiculed as bigoted and narrow-minded.

Many of our TV programs make fun of anyone who is a Christian. Anything a Christian believes is belittled.

This hostility to Christians and Christian beliefs is an apparent attempt to wipe out every moral and cultural principle that is represented by Christianity and the Bible. I have heard this referred to as "religious cleansing." This can be seen in the following examples:

- It has, for some time now, been illegal to express religious beliefs in public schools.

- Although Christmas is a celebration of the birth of Christ, the singing of Christmas carols in public places is deemed "unconstitutional." Even in privately owned business establishments what for generations has been traditional to greet people with the words "Merry Christmas" has been changed to "Happy Holidays." For years, many have referred to Christmas as "Xmas."

- Prayers offered in legislatures, schools, etc. can no longer be said "in Jesus name."

- Government has legislated laws and rules that undermine the Bible's concept of a family.

- Government denies the sacredness of human life by abortion and euthanasia.

- Government has outlawed the teaching of creation, and they now declare that evolution is a fact, when in reality it is a theory—not a fact.

- Divorce is now allowed for any reason. The purity of the marriage relationship is denied by pre-marital sex.

- God's chain of command in the home and church is ridiculed by modern feminism.

- While Christian morals and principles are ridiculed and slandered, obscenity, pornography, nudity, filth and violence are treated with tolerance.

- New hate crime and human right laws are a means to prosecute believers in Christ. The radical left can use the new laws to keep people quiet who disagree with their extreme agenda.

- The American Family Association is barred access if you use Cyber Patrol to block pornography. The reason? The

American Family Association is considered intolerant to fanatic left wing promotion of immoral issues.

A book documenting radical cases of bias and hate being aimed at Christians had this to say:

> It's now possible in America to be arrested and charged with a misdemeanor for praying in the name of Jesus. Such was the case in Fredericksburg, Virginia, where the city adopted a penalty of disorderly conduct for anyone violating a city council ban on praying in Jesus' name in public meetings.
>
> Unquestionably, the city council's policy aimed directly at Councilor Turner and his practice of closing prayer in the name of Jesus Christ. After the policy was adopted, other city council members were permitted to pray in the name of other deities and to utter prayers reflecting denominational influence, whereas Councilor Turner was precluded from praying.[12]

The same book has also documented the following cases where bigoted prejudice was exhibited.

> In San Diego, Pastor David Jones and his wife, Mary, were issued a citation barring them from holding Tuesday night Bible studies in their home. Otherwise, they would have to spend hundreds of dollars and apply for a major use permit from the county or pay big fines. The incident might be chalked up to a misunderstanding on the part of an overzealous code enforcer, but no such actions were brought against people holding poker nights or Tupperware parties in their homes. Only after a deluge of bad publicity and a demand letter from the Western Center for Law & Policy did the county see the error of its ways. The

citation was withdrawn, and the Joneses were given an official apology for the "unfortunate events."[13]

Christmas parades are open to everybody—except Christ and Christians. That was the case in Denver in 2004, when Faith Bible Chapel was banned from having its float in the annual Parade of Lights because of its overtly religious theme. Instead, the parade featured homosexual American Indians, Kung Fu artisans, belly dancers, and Santa Claus. In a masterpiece of understatement, Pastor George Morrison responded, "I think there's an agenda that is anti-Christian."[14]

In Texas, students were told they could not wear red and green because those are Christmas colors.[15\]

A recent release by the *Associated Press* tells of a federal judge in Georgia who ordered a suburban Atlanta school district to remove stickers from high school biology textbooks that call evolution "a theory and not a fact," saying the disclaimers are an unconstitutional endorsement of religion.

Writing in the *Washington Post*, Michael Lind made a connection between the Oklahoma City bombers and pro-lifers. He wrote, "The story of Oklahoma City and the militias should not make us forget that the main form of political terrorism in the United States is perpetuated by rightwing opponents of abortion." [16]

As a result of dehumanizing Christians and making them appear to be enemies of the state, they move on to the next step, which is silencing Christians. They embarrass, insult, shout them down and mischaracterize Christians as fools—as the ones who are responsible for the ills of the world. Is this not exactly what Adolph Hitler did in Germany in the 1930s?

You do not have to look far to see these tactics in play. It may be the case when a conservative speaker who addresses a college assembly is shouted down so that his speech cannot continue. The root of this type of intimidation is not difficult to discover. It only takes picking up a history book on the subject of the rise of the Nazi party in the 1930s in Germany.

In his best selling book, "Persecution: How Liberals Are Waging War Against Christianity," David Limbaugh makes this general statement, "This anti-Christian bias manifests itself in unflattering portrayals of Christians in Hollywood films and entertainment television, and also in the demonizing of Christian conservatives in the media." [17]

In his book, Limbaugh cites numerous examples of media bias and hate mongering by liberals, but it is absolutely radical when Christians are called Nazis and the "American Taliban." As quoted in the *Newsmax* article, Limbaugh states, "Christians have been called "the American Taliban," with one reporter for a Florida newspaper, Bob Norman, referring to "evangelical loonies" and "way out there Christian wackos." In the *St Petersburg Times* columnist Robert E. Blummer wrote that the "religious right" is trying in "Taliban-like" ways to inject religion into public schools and the operations of government."

Speaking of how Hollywood and the TV media depict Christians, *One News Now* shares this viewpoint:

> Christians are far too often the bad guys in mainstream entertainment. Frankly, though, I think it goes beyond that. We are in a strange place where so-called mainstream entertainment doesn't represent mainstream at all and in no area is that more true than in the area of religion. When you consider the huge majority of Americans self-identity as Christians and yet how unusual it is to see the hero of a movie make that identification, it really is an almost bizarre disconnect, isn't it?[18]

There is a deluge of anti-Christian books sold all over the world today. These books blame Christians for everything wrong and evil just AS Hitler unjustly blamed the Jewish people in his day. Books such as the following titles are on sale everywhere. Allow me to list a few, which Rabbi Daniel Lapin shared in an Internet message:

- *American Fascists: The Christian Right and the War on America*
- *The Baptizing of America: The Religious Right's Plans for the Rest of Us*
- *The End of Faith: Religion, Terror, and the Future of Reason*
- *Piety and Politics: The Right Wing Assault on Religious Freedom*
- Atheist Universe: The Thinking Person's Answer to Christian Fundamentalism
- *Thy Kingdom Come: How the Religious Right Distorts the Faith and Threatens America*
- *Religion Gone Bad: The Hidden Dangers of the Christian Right*

Rabbi Lapin goes on to say, "The alarming thing is that there are more of these books available than those warning against the perils of fervent Islam."[19]

The American Family Association reported that the Feds ordered Christian signs and symbols and "Merry Christmas" buttons removed from a bank in Oklahoma City. Some of the items that had to be removed were paintings by Thomas Kinkade.[20]

Throughout the nation even the word Christmas is banned and public schools no longer call Christmas "Christmas," but they refer to it by pagan names such as "Winter Festival."

We see an anti-Christian bias in government when they allow colleges to make special accommodations for Muslim footbaths and Muslim only prayer rooms. While a Muslim group (meeting on college facilities) can suspend membership or revoke it for fifty-seven Christian groups are denied the privilege of meeting on campus because it requires officers and voting members to agree with its Christian beliefs. Such is the hypocrisy of our government.[21]

The article from *The Christian Post* reveals that a San Diego elementary school created an extra recess period to allow 100 Muslim students to pray, while a Federal judge upheld a Knoxville, KY., jury's decision that a public school could prohibit its 5th grade students from studying and discussing their Bibles during recess.[22]

Outrage spread across America and around the world when a small fanatic group burned the Koran as an expression of protest. Certainly here in America, we should respect all ideas that differ from our own. Yet when Palestinians tore up Bibles and used the pages for toilet paper, there was no outrage in America or anywhere else.[23]

I believe these things show an anti-bias toward Bible believing Christianity, but there's a lot more to it than just that. The Christian Law Association (CLA) publishes a monthly newsletter called The *Legal Alert* that shares events going on in America that are increasingly, and even exponentially, showing the chilling direction as to how American new laws single out Christians to limit their rights. We are talking about rights that have always existed since the founding of our country.

These former rights are now being taken away by liberal judges who write laws from the bench based on their own narrow opinions, which are contrary to the Constitution. After all, if the laws listed below are what is meant by the Constitution of the United States, then how is it that those who wrote the Constitution had the opposite interpretation of these things?

Wouldn't you think that those who wrote the Constitution would understand what they wrote better than liberal judges could understand it over 200 years later? The following examples are all out of various issues of the CLA monthly magazine:

- A church in Tennessee was told to cover a cross in its sanctuary for a public event held in their church. If they did not do this, the event would be cancelled.
- A co-worker heard a conversation of other employees talking together about religion during their lunch hour. The co-worker complained to management that these discussions should cease because overhearing them offended her.
- A church-run medical clinic in Georgia is being told that its medical personnel must discontinue praying with patients. This faith-based clinic takes no government money.
- The California Supreme Court ruled that a doctor could not refuse to perform medical procedures that violated his religious beliefs.

- A church in Missouri was threatened by the IRS unless its pastor removed a political sign from the front yard of the home that he, as a private citizen, owns.

- Pastors are being banned from praying at city council meetings across America because they pray in the name of Jesus. Praying in such meetings has been practiced in America in civil meetings ever since the founding of America.

- The chief justice of the Supreme Court in Alabama had a display of the Ten Commandments in the lobby of the courthouse and the Federal government made him remove it, and then they removed the judge from the bench.

- A fast-food worker in North Carolina has been told that she may not listen to a Christian radio station or read her Bible on her break time. She could listen to any other radio station.

- A man who works for a Fortune 500 Company was told that he could not meet with fellow Christians in his workplace. Meanwhile, other groups, like homosexuals, are allowed to use company resources and promote their group's agenda.

- A Christian business owner who owns a printing company, was sued by a witch for refusing to print advocacy materials about witchcraft.

- A Christian employee was ordered not to wear a Christian T-shirt, while other employees were allowed to wear T-shirts with secular themes.

- Countless Christian soul-winners face hostility on American streets every day for simply handing our gospel tracts.

- A pastor was cited by government officials for holding a Bible study group in his own home.

- Certain states do not allow Christianity to be taught in public schools even though Islam and other non-Christian religions are often taught as "cultural" subjects.

- A workplace supervisor in Florida was terminated after he shared comforting scriptures with an employee who was contemplating suicide.

- A student in Ohio was forced to read a book about witchcraft in English class.

- A school in Indiana is considering using pagan charts and worship symbols during its football halftime show this fall.
- Workers in a hospice facility in Florida were told that they could no longer get together in the hospice building to pray for their patients during their break.
- A judge in North Carolina has ordered that witnesses testifying in his courtroom would no longer have to say the part of the usual oath, which says "So help me God," and that their testimony would not include the words "so help me God." He also ordered that witnesses would no longer have to place their hands on a Bible when they take the witness oath, He also ordered that God's name should be removed from traditional court announcements. These orders brought an end to the traditional language used in North Carolina courts for the last 200 years.
- A man in Texas has been told that he cannot witness to others at a recreation center. Further, he cannot invite anyone to attend his church while he is there.
- A teacher in California was told he could not present historical material to students, such as the Declaration of Independence and the diaries of George Washington and John Adams because they contain references to God.
- The Air Force Academy in Colorado has banned Bible verses on e-mails of its staff.
- When a student in Michigan was overheard talking about religion with another student during free time, his teacher made him spend the rest of the school day in the hallway as punishment.
- Evangelists in Virginia were told they could no longer hold religious services at a private nursing home and that they may no longer visit residents there. The residents who have relied on this ministry for their spiritual food for many years have been greatly upset by this ban.
- Many college professors across America discuss inappropriate sexual topics in class and demean Christian and conservative students.

- Recently, in the California Miss USA pageant, a contestant was leading in the contest until the time of the final spontaneous question she was asked. The moderator (who was a gay man) knowing she was a Christian, asked her about her views of homosexuality. After she answered, the moderator of the pageant said he was giving her a score of zero. Thus, she lost the contest.

- A recent widow in Florida has been threatened with a lawsuit because she has been honoring her deceased husband with religious memorials in her front yard and in the local newspaper.

- A church in Virginia is being told it may not erect a cross on church property.

- A school district in Maine is considering banning the Pledge of Allegiance because the phrase "under God" might offend some students.

- A Ph. D scientist in Massachusetts was dismissed from a research position because he mentioned to his supervisor that he believes in creation.[24]

The cases brought out above are not even the tip of the iceberg as to what has been happening in our country regarding religious freedom since World War II. I have given the cases above to show how government intervention in what has *always* been the rights and liberties of Christians is ever expanding its attempts to silence Christianity and place it in an appalling light with the citizens of this country.

Perhaps anti-Christianity is nowhere more manifested than in the stifling of America's celebration of Christmas by governmental, educational and business attacks on the meaning of Christmas. These traditional ways of celebrating Christmas have been observed ever since the founding of the country. Allow me to share some examples as to how this is being carried out:

- An Illinois 4th grader enjoyed hearing her public school teacher read a book to her class about the origins of the Jewish holiday of Hanukkah, but when the little girl brought a book about the origins of Christmas the teacher refused to read it.

- A principle in a public high school in Pennsylvania told a teacher that he could not include Christmas carols in the annual Christmas concert. He almost lost his job when he protested.
- An employee in Florida was fired from her job after she sang a religious song during karaoke entertainment presentations at an office Christmas party.
- A teacher in Texas discontinued all Christmas celebrations in her classroom and substituted a celebration of Kwanzaa instead, during which her first graders were taught to worship their ancestors.
- In a Florida city, a citizen complained to the city council because stars and angels were included as part of lamppost decorations in the downtown area.
- Students in South Carolina were told to write an essay on a topic of their choice during the month of December. When one student decided to write about Christmas, the teacher refused to grade his essay.
- Bible club students in Pennsylvania and New Jersey were told they could not distribute candy canes to their classmates during the Christmas season because the candy package included an explanation of the religious origins of the candy cane.
- Kindergarteners in Missouri were told they could not sing Christmas carols during the holidays.
- Stores, restaurants and other places of business have told their greeters and workers that they are not allowed to say "Merry Christmas" as shoppers enter their stores, but are told to say "Happy Holidays."
- A high school student "D.J." in Florida was told it would be unconstitutional to play religious music, including instrumental versions of carols, over the school's loudspeaker system during the Christmas season.
- City officials in Georgia told the private owners of an amusement park they could not present holiday entertainment shows that mentioned the religious meaning of Christmas.

- Private citizens were banned from setting up religious displays in a public park area that had been set aside for private expressions of the holiday spirit.
- A drugstore in North Carolina removed a manger scene from an advertising display when a customer complained that viewing this religious item offended her.
- When a school multicultural committee in Pennsylvania set up a holiday display that included a crèche (a manger scene), a menorah, and a Kwanzaa scene, the principal demanded that the crèche be removed, although the other items could stay.
- In a Pennsylvania community, police ordered the local firehouse to take down its Christmas tree after neighbors called law enforcement officials claiming to be offended by the display.[25]

The article concluded with a quotation by President Franklin D. Roosevelt, which he made on December 24, 1944 during a national wartime address:

> Here at home, we will celebrate this Christmas day in our traditional way—because of its deep spiritual meaning to us, because the teachings of Christ are fundamental in our lives, and because we want our youngest generation to grow up knowing the significance of this tradition and the story of the coming of the immortal Prince of Peace and Good Will.[26]

I suppose there are those today who would feel that any president that would make a public statement like this statement of President Roosevelt would be violating the Constitution.

> In December 2009, the D.C. City Council passed an ordinance that legalized gay marriage in the District. But that's not all. Private charities that provide social services within the District would be required to hire gay men and women, provide employee benefits to

same-sex married couples, and allow them to adopt. The Catholic Church, which is one of the largest social service providers in D.C., rightly noted that such a mandate would violate its right to operate freely, under the First Amendment, in a manner that reflects the Church's values and principles.

When the Church told the Council that it may have to cease providing its services in D.C., Democratic council member Tommy Wells fumed: "It's a dangerous thing when the Catholic Church starts writing and determining the legislation and the laws of the District of Columbia." This is the precise flawed logic that pushes so many voters into the anti-gay marriage camp. The Church isn't writing the law. The Church is saying that the law violates its beliefs, and as such, it can't operate within the law's structure. And given the choice, it would rather stay true to its belief system than scrap a care tenet of its faith because a few D.C. council members said so.[27]

The violation of the rights of Christians are being crushed by our own government whose ancestors left their homelands over the last two centuries to get away from socialism, bigotry and hatred of Christians and what they believe. Our forefathers who founded America to escape this form of antagonism would turn over in their graves if they knew that the country they founded is turning into exactly what they came here to escape.

Other violations of the civil rights of Christians can be seen in the following examples.

At the University of Virginia, even abject blasphemers apparently are welcome. You want to publish a cartoon depicting God talking dirty and smoking in bed after having sexual relations with Mary? No problem. In fact, just such a cartoon was deemed worthy of publishing in the student newspaper, *The Cavalier Daily*, in March 2008. Only after a national protest spearheaded by the American Family Association did the newspaper remove the cartoon from its web site.[28]

The Foundation for Individual Rights in Education (FIRE) reports that hundreds of major public and private universities routinely trash the First Amendment and violate their students' rights to free speech.

In a 2006 assessment of U.S. institutions of higher learning, FIRE found that more than 73% of public universities maintained unconstitutional speech codes despite court rulings striking down similar policies.[29]

The long arm of this particular kind of totalitarianism is reaching down even into secondary schools and home schooling. How? Higher education exerts substantial leverage over "lower" education through the curricular and textbooks it recognizes in college entrance requirements—and those it shuns. See where this is going? Yes, those shunned materials just happen to be Christian curricula and textbooks.

Consequently, students taught using textbooks from Bob Jones University Press and Beka Books may have trouble getting admitted to any school of the University of California, which adopted a policy in 2007 that science, literature and history textbooks from such publishers would not qualify for core admissions requirements because of their Christian perspectives.[30]

An article in The *Los Angeles Times* said, "Prayer Day is ruled illegal."[31]

Yet another incredible violation of Christian rights had the headline, "Florida Principal, Athletic Director Faces Six Months in Jail Over mealtime Prayer."[32] The court refers to the case as one of "criminal charges." We are indeed living in inconceivable times that are so very different from the America in which I grew up.

Still another headline appeared in The *Pacific Justice Institute Press* release, which read, "Atheists Ask Federal Court to Ban Highway Memorial Crosses." [33]

Another report carried the announcement that private schools can't pray before athletic games even when both are private schools playing each other.[34]

> ACLU's war on religion was illustrated when the organization set out to sue Carolyn Rusher, mayor of Inglis, FL for denouncing Satan. Every Halloween night for nine years Rusher had issued a proclamation banning Satan from city limits. Taking up a complaint from a resident, ACLU eagerly planned to file suit, that, if successful, would ostensibly make Satan welcome in Inglis.[35]

Another shocking event from Ohio is that, while I lived there, an effort was being made to remove B.C. and A.D. from the history books that our children and grandchildren use. This method of telling time has been used by all Western nations to identify our calendars for hundreds and hundreds of years. This is to be replaced by the words, "Common Era" and "Before the Common Era." It's incredible how far the radical left will go to obliterate our history and culture and reduce America to something unlike anything it has ever been.

In Butte, Montana, the valedictorian of Butte High School was not allowed to speak because she made mention of God in the speech that she submitted, Following is this sad story:

> A judge in Montana ruled against a high school vale-
> dictorian who wasn't allowed to speak at her gradu-
> ation ceremony because she wanted to give God the
> credit for her success in high school. She was asked,
> as were the other valedictorians, about what helped
> them to get through school—the others spoke about
> all kinds of things, but the only thing they would not

permit, by their own admission, was, to attribute any achievements to belief in God.[36]

In Philadelphia, the cradle of American liberty, four evangelists were arrested for conducting traditional open-air services to those passing by on the sidewalk. In San Diego, a Christian attorney was arrested for standing in front of a doorway to an abortion clinic and he was sentenced to nine months in jail. In Adams county Colorado the 10th circuit court of appeals upheld a lower court ruling prohibiting a fifth grader from keeping a Bible on his desk. In Houston, Texas the head of an anti-abortion group served a four-month sentence for a criminal trespass conviction for handing out pro-life literature in front of a high school.

Just look at the way that Hollywood demeans, vilifies and ridicules Christian characters in movies and TV shows. While Hollywood promotes ideas of social deviates and ensures that they are not usually presented in a negative light, Christians are ridiculed and made to look stupid. Municipalities and state governments are under siege from the American Civil Liberties Union and other radical secularists who are determined to rid the American culture of all publicly displayed Christmas scenes and others like the Ten Commandments, Bibles and crosses.

The groups that claim to be promoting free speech are in fact successfully promoting censorship of Christian beliefs while participating in blatant Christian bigotry. In short, it seems like anything goes in our society except that which reflects a positive attitude about Christian thinking or American tradition.

We are told it's censorship to restrict public tax money from being spent on obscene art works and the like, but yet the same people seek to keep public spending from being used to promote anything that would place traditional religious beliefs in a positive light. A leading movie producer recently said publicly, "Christianity is a religion for losers." Can you imagine him publicly saying that about abortionists or gays or blacks—and getting away with it? A rock star said, "When you see the Christian fish symbol on the car in front of you, know that that's the enemy."

It's not just that Christians are under attack — it's Christian values that are under attack as well. Just think of the way the government is crusading for condoms in the public schools and public funding for abortion on demand. When Christians protest about such things, the liberal news media describes Christians as poor, uneducated and easy to command. Can you think of another group of citizens so insulted by a major newspaper?

Racial Islamists who are American citizens have taken to the streets again and again to oppose the Jewish people. They have such slogans as "God hates Jews," "Death to Israel," "Use the Jews as fossil fuel."[37] It's hard to believe that such things are going on here in America, but it's even harder to believe that American politicians and police, etc. don't put a stop to this.

According to the *Pacific Justice Institute*, in California there was a policy in place in some areas that the word "God" was prohibited from being used at county-sanctioned wedding ceremonies. A couple was denied a marriage license after adding the terms "bride and groom." In San Leandro a pro-transvestite film was to be shown in an elementary school. In one city there was a city ordinance that censored churches from their religious content on their signs.[38]

In California, various cities are trying to shut down home Bible studies. It's home churches that are persecuted in China and other repressive governments. The problem is not that a traffic problem is created as most home Bible study groups have fewer than a dozen attendees. Proof of the fact that traffic is not the problem is seen because these same cities do not place similar restrictions for Monday night football parties or various other events.[39]

Muslim students who attended and graduated from Trinity University in Texas, a Christian college, are demanding that the university remove the phrase, "In the Year of Our Lord" from their diplomas. One wonders how far it is going to go![40]

Many Christians are home-schoolers, and liberals have long been opposed to this since they feel that the state and the state alone should have the education of America's children as their singular duty. A shocking article has shared the following outrageous information about a proposed regulation:

Parents who teach their own children at home must undergo criminal record checks, say government education inspectors. The estimated 40,000 parents who choose not to send their children to public schools should be vetted, says Ofsted. It said that parents whose records throw up suspicions should be barred from teaching their own children. If it's unsafe for children to be with parents during normal school hours, it is equally unsafe for them to be with their parents in the evenings, on weekends and during school holidays.[41]

In another similar case in another country we have this report, "Home schooling in Sweden will be banned altogether, with a few minor exceptions. They are following the German statute, following the German model. In Germany, parents face stiff penalties if they are caught illegally home schooling their children, they face severe penalties and the potential loss of custody rights for their children."[42]

In other words, the idea of not allowing parents to teach their own children because of suspicious records has nothing to do with education, but rather, it has to do with the denial of parental rights.

Rev. Franklin Graham was invited to offer a prayer at the annual Pentagon National Day of Prayer in 2010. Because Rev. Graham had criticized Islam for the murder of Christians, particularly in the Sudan, he was "disinvited." This is just another of the overwhelming number of incidents showing a direction that seems to be leading to the downfall of America's past greatness.

Further news reports regarding the National Day of Prayer tradition in America grew even more shocking than the situation with Franklin Graham. It's amazing to note that in 2010, President Obama canceled the annual National Day of Prayer ceremony at the White House under the guise of "Not wanting to offend anyone." Yet our President, that same year, hosted a day to honor the Muslim religious holiday of Ramadan in the White House.

Also, on September 25, 2009 from 4 AM until 7 PM, a National Day of Prayer for the Muslim Religion was held on Capitol Hill, beside the White House. There were over 50,000 Muslims that day in Washington, D.C.

Apparently having a National Day of Prayer might offend someone, but it would not matter if a Muslim National Day of Prayer would offend the majority of Americans. This is especially so in that the Muslim religion (The Koran) teaches that if Christians cannot be converted they should be annihilated.

Even in regard to the honoring of our servicemen who were killed in wars defending America, efforts are made to eliminate religious memorials from our society.

> In 1934, the Veterans of Foreign Wars decided to pay tribute to the memory of the fallen. They erected a simple white cross atop a large outcropping of rock in the California desert. For more than seventy-five years that cross kept a silent vigil as a reminder of those who laid down their lives for freedom. The U.S Congress supported the project and officially designated the site a "war memorial." For years thereafter the area was a gathering site for Easter sunrise services. Recently, by court order, the top of the cross has been covered by a large plywood box, courtesy of a lawsuit filed by the American Civil Liberties Union (ACLU) on behalf of a lone, retired park employee who feels the cross violates the separation of church and state. The ACLU located a judge who agreed with the plaintiff, who, in turn, ordered the "offending" symbol removed.[43]

This is not an American problem only, as it's showing up all over the world. The Romanian parliament is considering a law that would restrict non-orthodox minority religions such as Baptists. Greece is adopting a law that would forbid proselytizing. Indonesian authorities have announced new regulations that would allow missionary activity there only among those who are not already members of a major world religion. Such people represent only 0.3% of it's 187 million people. In Islamic African nations, like Ethiopia and Sudan, Christians are routinely attacked and killed by government forces. In

Vietnam, police routinely arrest Christians for holding unregistered meetings and worship services. Church property is often confiscated.

Newsmax Magazine recently reported the following astonishing statement by a U.S. senator that further documents anti-Christian bias and hatred:

> Anti-Christian hostility became blatantly obvious when Sen. Charles Schumer (D-N.Y.) and his leftist comrades began attacking some of President Bush's nominees to the federal bench for the crime of having religious principles he feared might influence their judicial decisions.[44]

Another scary development is that many of the New-Age people who direct the environmentalist movement suggest that Christianity is responsible for the environmental crisis the world is in. They thus declare that these beliefs must be eliminated before our problems can be resolved.

The American liberal policies of the past twenty years are contributing to a one-world government. The plan would require schoolchildren to be indoctrinated as citizens of the world. Thus, they are being educated that the American way of doing things and the Judeo-Christian heritage of the nation are simply anachronistic, oppressive, racist, sexist and imperialistic.

Some of the breakdowns in our society that the liberal establishment promotes are forced busing of children to school, mandates that businesses hire by quota rather than merit, making sure that banks lend money to people who won't repay and requiring landlords to rent to undesirables.

The Equal Employment Opportunity Commission (EEOC) has created some guidelines for the workplace, which, in essence, makes it a violation of the law to share one's faith, or to even show evidence of it. This means not only a spoken word but even a symbol of religious faith such as a woman wearing a necklace with a cross on it would be illegal.

When the EEOC'S changes come into existence here is a partial list of what that would prohibit:

1. Wearing a cross around the neck or wrist.
2. Displaying a picture of Christ on an office desk or wall.
3. Wearing a T-shirt, hat or other clothing that has a religious emblem on it.
4. Having a Bible or any other religious book on a desk.
5. Hosting Christmas, Hanukkah, Thanksgiving or Easter celebrations.
6. Opening or closing a company program with prayer.
7. Witnessing verbally while on the job.
8. No business would be allowed to a display a nativity scene at Christmas.
9. Inviting a fellow employee to a synagogue, church or temple.
10. Conversations about religion or religious groups.
11. Sponsoring prayer breakfasts.
12. Singing or humming a religious tune while at a copy machine.
13. Giving a fellow employee a holiday card or birthday card that includes any religious reference.
14. Praying while in the work place.

The Jeremiah Project has identified three methods that those who want Christian standards and morals removed from our society can do to accomplish that goal. Let the Jeremiah project speak for itself:

> Secularists appear to have agreed upon three specific mechanisms to complete the task of immobilizing and silencing Christians. You can find evidence of these strategies in your own communities and schools. These strategies are:

> 1. Deny our Judeo-Christian roots and rewrite our historical record.
> 2. Convince the American people that Christians are in violation of the Constitution.
> 3. Embarrass, insult, shout down and mischaracterize Christians hoping to intimidate them into being silent.

The article went on to quote a page of the *New York Times* where Robert H. Meneilly writes, "The religious right confronts us with a greater threat than the old threat of Communism."[45]

As a result of the clash between the government and the cult group in Waco, Texas in 1993, the establishment press has begun to define for us how to recognize a dangerous religious cult. They said, "It's a group who has a preoccupation with Jesus Christ and with Bible prophecy, with Jerusalem, and with Bible studies in homes." We are told those who are a part of a dangerous religious cult can be identified. They are often home schoolers, and radical extremists who believe in spanking their children, which they say is child abuse. They also state that radicals are those who support the right to bear arms.

In short, this definition includes millions of Bible believing Christians; thus, a cult today is increasingly being defined as Christianity or a religion that the government and establishment do not approve of. This will have a tendency to turn the public thinking against Bible believing Christians. It should be known that in the Roman Empire Christians were looked upon as a dangerous cult and were everywhere spoken against.

I picked up on a shocking post on the web that carried an unbelievable attack on a college student who posted an advertisement on her church bulletin board in Grand Rapids, MI seeking a Christian roommate. Apparently someone saw the ad and felt that it discriminated against non-Christians; so, that person filed a complaint with the fair housing center of West Michigan. The following words of the report are hard to believe, but it was reported on TV news, in local newspapers, and many other types of news outlets:

> It's a violation to make, print or publish a discriminatory statement, Executive Director Nancy Haynes told Fox News. She said, there are no exemptions to that. Haynes said the unnamed 31-year-old woman's alleged violation was turned over to the Michigan Department of Civil Rights. Depending on the outcome of her case, the Christian woman could face

several hundreds of dollars in fines and fair housing training so it doesn't happen again.[46]

We are living in a day when we are being told that tolerance is the "politically correct" approach to all things. By this, it is meant that there is no absolute truth. When Jesus said in John 14:6: "I am the way, the truth, and the life: no man cometh unto the Father, but by me," according to their logic—He was wrong. The idea is that all religious beliefs are bonafide ways to get to heaven and are acceptable to God; therefore, when someone says the way of Mormonism or Islam is wrong, you are considered intolerant. This incorrect definition of tolerance, along with hate crime laws being passed, is undermining the very fabric of our society. It was Aristotle who said, "Tolerance is the last virtue of a dying society." James Newton said:

> The culture of our day has redefined tolerance to mean the acceptance of the idea that all beliefs are equally true. If you say 2+2=4, and I say 2+2=31, both of us are equally right! Your "truth" has no superiority over my "truth." According to today's mindset, the only belief that matters is the belief that *nothing* matters. And the only thing that is *not* tolerated is the belief that some things are intolerable. The newly defined "tolerance" has become the ultimate virtue. The only unpardonable sin to a society that does not admit the existence of sin is the belief that indeed that "Jesus Christ is the way the truth and the life and that no man comes to the Father except though Him."[47]

The whole thing smacks of Hitlerism just before World War II when the persecution of the Jews got underway. As public opinion follows like sheep with these declarations, there will be stronger and stronger pressure brought to bear against gun owners, pro-lifers and other resistors to their vision of a new socialist America. The hate bill passed by a liberal Congress and House in 1994 was voted in and approved before the actual bill was even in print for the congressmen to read. It is, among other things, an anti-political-action bill or political dissident bill, which calls for property forfeiture and prison sentences for a variety of things like speeches, writings and assemblies which are not "politically correct."

It is exactly the kind of legislation that Adolph Hitler used to put the people of Germany in chains in the 1930s. Should the Lord tarry, you will discover that it may cost you your freedom—or even your life to stand fast by your faith.

Much of what Christianity stands for and what America was built on is being eroded as this anti-Christian sentiment spreads. The problems facing this country and the world seem overwhelming. We're threatened with over-population, pollution, deforestation, nuclear proliferation, ozone depletion, new and deadlier strains of disease, famine, war, lawlessness and disorder.

No matter where we turn, we are confronted with the sad state of the human race. We see pre-teenage pregnancies, free condom distribution in public schools, drive-by shootings, kiddy porn, abortion on demand, rampant child abuse and suicide machines. Euthanasia is now on the law books in Oregon.

What is good is being called bad, and what's bad is being called good—just as God's Word predicted it would be in the end time. For example, can someone explain how the Boy Scouts of America are now considered a subversive organization by the establishment?

Many cities have eliminated the Boy Scouts from receiving funds through the United Fund. For generations the Boy Scouts have received funding through this organization. Boy Scouts, in some communities, are also being denied the use of public parks for their activities.

In a *Lamplighter Magazine* article, the harassment of the Boy Scouts is reported in the following way:

> In November of last year, the Pentagon suddenly announced that it had decided to ban all U.S. military bases around the world from sponsoring Boy Scout troops! This action was taken at the urging of the ACLU because the Boy Scouts insist that their members hold a belief in God. Here is the horrible

oath required of Boy Scouts that so troubles the ACLU and the Pentagon: "On my honor I will do my best to honor God and my country and to obey the Scout law, to help other people at all times, to keep myself physically strong, mentally awake, and morally straight." Is there any hope for a country that objects to such an oath?[48]

Since 1960, there has been a 560% increase in violent crime. Illegitimate birth rates have increased 419% while there has been the murder of 50 million unborn human beings. In the same period, divorce rates have tripled and the number of children in single parent homes has also tripled. The teen suicide rate has increased by 200% while student achievement scores have plummeted 80 points.

Abortion, now officially pushed by the federal government, recently went overseas to push it on to the rest of the world. In one generation, abortion has become the most common surgical procedure in America. Why has abortion become so accepted, so popular? This is due, in part, because in the 1970's we were told that if we eliminated unwanted children child abuse would plummet. Has it worked? As the value of life has been cheapened by abortion, child abuse has reached epidemic proportions. The push that is now on to accept euthanasia cheapens life at the later years of life as abortion cheapens life when it begins.

When children are more neglected and abused, they become abusers themselves; thus, the fastest growing segment of the criminal population of America is children. Let me ask you, if you were born before the Viet Nam War, do you think our day is different from when you were growing up? Do you believe that the pre 1960's era was more moral or law abiding than today?

Inasmuch as more Christians have been murdered in the 20th century than there have been collectively since the Church was founded, this speaks eloquently of the day in which we live.

"Soul-winners in New Hampshire and in Tennessee have been criminally cited for public preaching and handing out tracts. In Georgia, a soul-winner has been told that he may not pass out tracts in a city public park without paying for and obtaining a permit."[49]

Various news sources are reporting incredible stories about the wave of Christians being brought to trial because they have simply been doing what they have done all their lives. One such article reads as follows: "The Christian owners of a hotel are being prosecuted for a crime because they defended their faith and criticized Islam in a debate with a Muslim guest."[50]

A United Methodist church in New Jersey owns a campground retreat that they founded in the 19th century as a place for spiritual revival. The denomination has come under attack for refusing to abandon its religious beliefs. The story goes like this: "The New Jersey Division of Civil Rights has ruled in favor of a couple that filed a civil rights complaint against Ocean Grove Camp-Ground Association for declining to host a same-sex marriage. The United Methodist Church has an official disapproval of same-sex marriage.[51]

A headline in *One News Now* newspaper stated that a student by the name of Ryan Dozler was witnessing at the Yuba Community College when a campus police officer said that if he continued to do so without a permit, he could be arrested and face possible expulsion from the school. Several weeks later he received a letter from the college president which told him that if he shared his faith on campus again, he would face expulsion from the school.

The *Columbus Ohio Dispatch* headlined an article that reads, "Christian Candy Now Forbidden." The article states: "They arrived every December: gaily wrapped gifts designated for children at a kindergarten in rural northern France. But this year, teachers unwrapped a few, took a look and sent all 1,300 packages back to city hall. The presents were innocent, but strictly speaking, illegal: seasonable chocolates shaped like Christian crosses and St. Nicolas."[52]

In Hitler's Germany, once the hatred of Jews had become widespread, the persecution began, but not before this important first step. "Christian missionaries are as dangerous as terrorist activists and of the illegal drug trade," Islamic theologians in Uzbekistan declared.[53]

So today we see the flames of hatred being stirred up against Christians and Jews in our own country. What's going on here is very subtle. We are not led before firing squads. We don't see our churches burnt down, but we are seeing seeds being sown that are causing non- Christians or lukewarm Christians to be stirred against true Bible believing Christians. Because of our liberal government and court system we see that what Christians believe in is losing on every front while the anti-Christian agenda moves forward.

For example, in the 1980s when a family association tried to get X- rated movies removed from motel TV sets, liberals cried, "Censorship." Their defense was, "If you don't like those movies, just don't turn them on." They won. Later, a 3,000 member atheistic organization began a campaign to make hotel chains remove Gideon Bibles from their dresser drawers. No liberal came forward and said, "If you don't want to read the Bible just don't open it." No liberal stepped forward and screamed "Censorship."

In Solvay High School in New York, the liberal English teacher was having the students read writings entitled "The Pope's penis" and "Outside the Operating Room of the Sex Change Doctor." When attacked by the local PTA, the Liberal Aid Society said that attempts to eliminate that literature from the school was an attack on the freedom to learn. Is it any wonder that God said this in Isaiah 5:20: *"Woe unto them that call evil good, and good evil; that put darkness for light, and light for darkness; that put bitter for sweet, and sweet for bitter."*

The liberals tell us that Rush Limbaugh fans are a threat to democracy. Who are his fans? Essentially, they are Christians. Thus liberals sow seeds of doubt about good people and the same people make evil look good.

Let me give you a few examples.: The Transit Authority in New York City has announced that they will no longer arrest women riding in the subways topless. Why? Because New York judges declared that arresting topless women would be discrimination against women since men are not arrested for going topless.

There are secular humanist groups who publish books on how to get schools, TV and other places *not* to say "Merry Christmas." They declare saying "Merry Christmas" is an infringement on the rights of atheists. They say it's wrong to say grace in your own home in front of guests who might not want to do that. A syndicated columnist wrote an article in which she said, "If your religious beliefs lead you to fight sex and violence on TV, you're mentally ill." And

146

what's that all about? It is an effort just like you find in Islamic countries to eradicate Christian principles and morals from society.

The *Legal Alert Newsletter* asked their readers to "pray for state trooper chaplains in Virginia who are being told they can no longer pray in Jesus' name. Several troopers have resigned their chaplaincy in protest and the issue is being addressed at various levels of state government. The Fourth Circuit Federal Court, which includes the states of Virginia and North Carolina, have been especially hostile toward the use of Jesus' name in public prayers."[54]

The clearest indication of liberal intolerance is to resort to name calling whenever they cannot win an honest debate. Their favorite is to call conservative Christians "Nazis!" The news media constantly refers to Hitler as an extreme rightwing leader. I don't understand that. Look at what Hitler believed politically:

- He didn't want citizens to own guns.
- He believed in, and practiced euthanasia.
- He believed in abortion.
- He wanted to control the lives of Germany's citizens.
- He took over the news media.
- Before he took over the news media he restricted freedom of the press and spied on and intimidated journalists.
- He was a radical environmentalist.
- When Hitler came to power, he overturned the old traditions that had long existed in Germany.
- He appointed judges, etc. that would make up laws from the bench rather than make rulings based on Germany's long standing constitution.
- He based his ideas on the elimination of inferior races, such as Jews, and on the evolutionary ideas of Darwin.
- Hitler dabbled in the occult.
- In regard to the family, he felt that the children belong to the state, not to the parents.
- He hated Jewish people.
- He used political power to punish those who didn't fall in line with him.

There are other things Hitler believed that could be mentioned, but this gives you an idea of what he believed and practiced. When politicians, educators and others call Christians Nazis, they don't know what they're talking about. Christians do not believe in *any* of the above beliefs of Hitler. Determine in your own mind who are today's Nazis based on the beliefs of Hitler himself.

As a matter of fact, one of the greatest problems in America today, from the standpoint of the conservative, is that the federal government wants to control your child's choices; therefore, they advocate abortions without the parents' knowledge, the passing out of condoms to school children without parental consent and the authority to take a child away from his parents on virtually any allegation.

Another group that frequently speaks out against Christians is the gay group. Gays blame Bible believers for all of their persecution, but the fact is they have been jailed in every atheistic nation in the world. Another way to turn people against Bible believing people is to rewrite history.

How did the Nazis deal with the Jewish people before World War II? They began by making the Jews look evil, as though they caused all the problems in Germany. We are seeing this trend even here in America today regarding Bible believing and conservative people.

Education is one of the main methods that liberals use to turn the nation's children against their Christian parents' beliefs. Children are enrolled in anti-Christian programs without the knowledge of their parents. When the children are asked why they didn't tell them, they say, "because the teacher told us not to."

> In April, the Obama Administration published an assessment of "Rightwing Extremism" in the United States. The nine page document was produced by the Department of Homeland Security. It stated that the possibility of right wing acts of terrorism was increasing due to "the economic downturn" and "the election of the first African American president."

The document warned local police departments to monitor those who are "antagonistic toward the new presidential administration," as well as those opposed to immigration and restrictions on firearms. It also warned of those who were opposed to a "New World Order." Incredibly, the report warned that two groups in particular are terrorist threats: returning war veterans and believers who deem end time Bible prophecy as important.[55]

The *Christian Law Magazine*, already quoted, puts out monthly newsletters. Below are several articles from magazines I have read:

In a junior high school in San Marcos, CA, for example, the students were being taught that anything goes. These students were told there *is* such a thing as safe sex by receiving condoms and the whole nine yards. That year forty-seven girls who attended that school got pregnant.

For more than 40 years the University of New Hampshire car-illon has played religious tunes twice a day. It's silent now because liberals say they don't want it influencing students. The same liberals tell us that the filthy, obscene lyrics of rock music won't influence anyone.

In Vienna, VA when Christmas carolers showed up for the decades long tradition of singing carols in the town square, they were met by armed guards and forced to leave.

The city council of Oak Park, IL prohibited a Catholic hospital from putting a cross on its own smokestack because some residents might be offended.

Dr. Dean Kenyon has taught biology 101 at San Francisco State University since 1977. He was told he is no longer qualified to teach biology there! The reason? He believes God had a part in creation.

A seven-year old boy wanted to join the Boy Scouts but he refused to take the Boy Scout oath, which professes faith in God. He was an atheist. The boy and his parents sued the Boy Scouts. In other words, the court was asked to declare that this private organization cannot have only members that believe in God.

A San Jose, CA school recently erected a twenty-five foot tall statue of an Aztec god at public expense, but they will not allow a temporary nativity scene at Christmas at no public expense.

There was a junior high school boy in Maryland who wanted to make a wooden cross in his wood workshop class to put on his mother's grave, but the teacher told him that he couldn't do that at school.

Students at Oyster River High School in Durham, NH are allowed to write senior memories in their yearbook, but four boys who made mention of Jesus had to delete what they had to say. In Missouri an elementary girl was reprimanded for praying over her lunch.

In Norman, OK an eleven-year old boy was told he could not read from the Bible on the playground. A public school teacher in Georgia told a girl that she could write a biography on anyone except Jesus. In Frederick County, VA the principal issued orders that no one could refer to December 25th as Christmas but must speak of it as winter holiday. In Decatur, IL, a teacher told her 4th grade class to strike the word God from their phonetic workbooks, telling them that it's against the law to mention God in the classroom.

Years ago, the assistant police chief of Los Angeles, a born-again believer was under investigation to see if his beliefs disqualified him from holding public office. All across America good men are being disqualified from office because they are Christian. Imagine the cries of protest we would hear if people were disqualified because they have New Age beliefs, or are Muslims, gays or whatever.

There was a day when Christians were presented as bigots. Now we are being presented as *dangerous* bigots. Bible believers are presented by Hollywood as sleazy people, liars, narrow-minded, bigots and mean-spirited and other hate-filled terms.

The preceding are but a few examples from the *Legal Alert* which is a monthly publication of the Christian Law Association as to how today's Christians are being singled out and ridiculed and made to look like evil people. This is the same as the Nazi propaganda made Jewish people look before World War II.[56]

Where is all of this leading and what is the agenda behind it? The *Jeremiah Project* in an article on their website titled "Religious Cleansing" had this to say:

The result is that Christians are being depersonalized. Depersonalization makes it easy for people to accept negative stereotypes and tolerate abuse and persecution of the people who have been depersonalized. Historical precedent for this can be found in Nero's treatment of Christians, racism in all forms, and Hitler's treatment of the Jews. Dictators, tyrants, and other opponents of the truth don't want churches and Christians to interfere.[57]

This hatred and bigotry directed toward Christians and the moral standards that the Bible teaches is accelerating throughout the country. Almost daily, businesses, government leaders and others are declaring that the Constitution of the United States forbids anything Christian. To show you how radical blasphemy and hatred are spreading across our land, note the news article below that is not even the tip of the iceberg.

Students from the Pioneer Valley Performing Arts Charter Public School, which serves 400 students, grades 7-12, in South Hadley, Massachusetts—on March 15 performed the controversial play, *The Most Fabulous Story Ever Told*. The play alters the biblical book of Genesis to include homosexual couples Adam and Steve and Jane and Mabel in the Garden, as well as a "horny" rhinoceros that tries to seduce men on the ark, and Mary the mother of Christ, arguing she can't be pregnant because she's a lesbian "bull-dyke."

A Christian church in America's heartland redefined the birth of Jesus in its living Nativity scene in December 2010. It featured two women, instead of a man and a woman, starring as Joseph and Mary.[58]

Our liberal government is finding all kinds of new ways to intimidate and force Christians to go against what they believe and deprive them freedoms they possessed even since Columbus came to America. An example of this has been reported about a Christian husband and wife who own a photography business in Albuquerque, New Mexico. They were approached by Vanessa Willock—a lesbian—who wanted them to photograph her "commitment ceremony" to her lesbian partner.

They refused based on their Christian faith. Rather than seek another photographer, the lesbian filed a complaint with the New Mexico Human Rights Commission. The Human Rights Commission ruled the photographers engaged in sexual orientation discrimination and ordered them to pay Willock $6,639.94 in legal fees.

Jordan Lance, senior vice-president of the Office of Strategic Initiatives for the Alliance Defense Fund commented about the ruling saying, "Americans in the marketplace should not be subjected to legal attacks for simply abiding by their beliefs. Should the government force a video photographer who is an animal rights activist to create a video promoting hunting and taxidermy? Of course not, and neither should the government force this photographer to promote a message that violates his conscience."

This effort by liberal politicians and judges who write laws from the bench to make Christians violate their moral conscience is completely contrary to the Constitution of the United States. The matter is clearly seen by the demand that hospitals owned and operated by the Catholic Church perform abortions. This is obviously a form of persecution against a religious entity.

Another recent development in the United States and around the world has been to create laws called "hate crimes." What constitutes a hate crime is in the eye of the beholder. Actually, it's in the eye of liberals who *only* see criminal activity when it's at one of their protected classes. An example of this is when a man in New York placed bacon around a park for wild animals to eat. Later in the day a group of Muslims went to the park for a time of prayer. This act of putting bacon out for the animals was determined to be a bias event. He was charged with a hate crime. On the other hand an artist unveiled a photograph of a plastic crucifix in a glass of the artists urine. The piece was the winner of the Southeastern Center for Contemporary Arts. This event was sponsored by the National Endowment of the

Arts. The art show was put on with tax dollars. Yet, this disgusting put-down of a Christian symbol was not a hate crime.

The end time persecution is not only against Christians but also against Jewish people. To address this problem, I cite that a Scottish municipality has banned books from its libraries by Israeli authors that were printed or published in Israel. A government that boycotts books is not far from a place that burns books like Hitler did before World War II.

We are living in the end time the Bible speaks of and prophesied about. Changes are being made so fast that no one could possibly keep up with them. They all seem to have one and the same goal — "political correctness" which has made bad things good and good things bad. They create hate crimes that protect those who practice liberal beliefs and punish those who practice beliefs that were always acceptable in the United States.

As a result of the persecution that Jesus spoke of, there will be negative results that Matthew shares with us. These results are unfolded for you in the next several signs.

SIGN # 18 APOSTASY WILL DEVELOP AS A RESULT OF THE PERSECUTION

As a result of the persecution in Matthew 24:9, horrific problems arise in the Christian community pitting one Christian against another Christian.

Note how clearly this is stated in the book of Matthew: "Then they will deliver you up to tribulation and kill you, and you will be hated by all nations for My name's sake. And then many will be offended, will betray one another, and will hate one another" (Matthew 24:9-10).

The words, *and then*, in Matthew 24:10 are chronological in nature. In other words, after verse 9 — and only after the persecution spoken of in that verse — do the events of verse 10 take place. Therefore, we are given to understand that the apostasy is the result of the persecution.

The English word translated by the Greek word "offended," according to Augustus Strong means *to entice to apostasy.*[59]

153

SIGN # 19 BELIEVERS WILL BETRAY ONE ANOTHER

This sign follows right on the heels of the previous sign. As a result of the apostasy, many will betray others who were at one time bonded friends. Now they are separated as a result of some leaving the faith and turning on those who did not leave the faith.

A skillful analogy of what this verse teaches is as follows:

> The rulers of Communist states had chosen the following course of action in their strategy for the destruction of Christianity: Their secret services would work with the population. Members of the Communist society were to betray and hand over one another underhandedly. Over the years and decades this course of action destroyed normal interpersonal trust. No one could be sure, for example, whether the friendly neighbor who always greeted you so nicely in the morning was not an informer and co-operating with the KGB, the Securitate (Romanian secret police), the Stasi (East German secret police) or whatever secret intelligence agency it might be. Teachers at school, colleagues in the workplace, or friends and acquaintances were also potential informers. All this was prophetically foretold in Matthew 24:10.

> Even within a family, no one could be certain as to whether someone was working as an informer and a betrayer of the family members. The Communists did not even hold back from breaking into the family with its methods and destroying the closest family relationships. The Lord prophesied this in Mark 13: "Now brother will betray brother to death, and a father his child; and children will rise up against parents and cause them to be put to death" (Mark 13:12). [60]

This is exactly what is going on today in virtually every society on earth. This is what the last days will be like, and as the end approaches it will increase in intensity and make life more and more unbearable.

SIGN # 20 PEOPLE WILL HATE ONE ANOTHER

We are living in radical times when division is the order of the day. We see believer against nonbeliever, black against white, poor against rich, liberal against conservative, union members against non-union members, etc. The list goes on. This should not be. It seems like our politicians are leading the way in creating these divisions. It is noticeably tearing our country apart. Certainly nothing like this has ever happened in our history.

This sign seems to continue in the chronological order of Matthew 24:9-10 in which one thing comes out of the previous thing. Thus, Christian hating Christian is the main emphasis here. We see this on every hand today. Truly, this sign is getting more and more prominent and observable as the years pass by. As you read this, I'm certain you are well aware of it, and you can remember multiple situations where it is true from your own experience.

CHAPTER 8

MISCELLANEOUS SIGNS
FROM THE GOSPELS

SIGN # 21 A DAY OF TRAITORS

Matthew. 24:10 says, "And then many will be offended, will betray one another, and will hate one another." We will not dwell on this sign long as it's so obvious it hardly needs comment. We have high government officials, servicemen, the FBI and the CIA who all seem willing to sell our top priority secrets to our enemies. That's how Russia came to possess the A-bomb and many other secrets. It's a day when everyone is only interested in his own well being, so everyone is betraying everyone. There was a day when Benedict Arnold and Judas stood out by themselves. Now there are many traitors in all nations. It's so commonplace, we can't even think of their names

SIGN # 22 AN EXPLOSION OF CULTS

Matthew 24:11 (quoted above) means there will be a proliferation of false cults. You need to catch the word *many* in that verse which says, "Then *many* false prophets will rise up and deceive many."

This verse is talking about a unique time in human history when there will be *many* cults. It's not just that there are cults—the point Matthew makes is there are a multitude of cults—enticing away even true born again people. There have always been cults in our world. What is unique about the cult situation today is that they are so profuse with so many influential people being a part of them.

SIGN # 23 INIQUITY WILL ABOUND

True to the end time days in which we live, well did Matthew 24:12 announce, "And because lawlessness will abound, the love of many will grow cold." When society reaches a breakdown of morality, that society cannot long survive. This is the condition predicted in Matthew 24, but note also 2 Timothy 3:1-2: "But know this, that in the last days perilous times will come: For men will be lovers of themselves, lovers of money, boasters, proud, blasphemers, disobedient to parents, unthankful, unholy."

As a result of what we have just said, we have 2 Timothy 3:13: "But evil men and seducers shall wax worse and worse, deceiving, and being deceived." The moral base has all but virtually disappeared in western civilization. This moral breakdown could bring on exactly the conditions of the Tribulation. Evil is growing since nothing remains static, and it's becoming worse and worse. Everything has a breaking point—a point where it can no longer support the degree of corruption that has come upon us.

A recent news item said: "For the first time ever, the percentage of married households fell below 50% according to the Census Bureau with figures derived from the 2010 Census." [1]

A great deal of the problem is the immoral conduct promoted by teachers in public schools. Just a couple of examples will suffice. A report from the Santa Fe, New Mexico newspaper, *The New Mexican* says this: "The New Mexico Health department is standing behind a sex-education teacher in New Mexico who encouraged ninth-graders to taste flavored condoms she passed out to the students." [2]

Think of the legalized mass murder worldwide of countless millions of unborn babies. Think of how many highly intelligent blessed personalities there are who have been slaughtered before birth. This is illustrated in the following account I read which states, "A professor asked his medical students what they would do in the following case: 'The father has syphilis, the mother has TB. They already have four children. The first one is blind, the second one is dead, the third is deaf, and the fourth one has TB. The mother is expecting her fifth child. The parents are willing to have the pregnancy terminated.'" The professor says, "If you had to decide, what would you do?" Most of the students were in favor of an abortion. "Congratulations," said the professor, "you have just murdered Beethoven."[3]

An American eagle was found wounded in Maryland and was rushed in for emergency treatment, but it died anyway. A $5,000 reward was offered for the arrest of the killer. The Massachusetts Supreme Court has ruled that goldfish cannot be awarded as prizes in games of chance. This violates the state's anti-cruelty law. This same court upheld mandatory state funding for abortions.

The *AFA Journal* reports that, "One in five of all American moms have children with multiple birth fathers. When the researchers look only at moms with three or more children; 28% have children with at least two different men."[4]

An article in the *Los Angeles Times* reports that "a Massachusetts judge has ordered the state to pay for sex-change surgery for an imprisoned murderer."[5] The article goes on to explain that the "new woman" was moved to a women's prison after the surgery.

Years ago, an appointed leader had this to say, "We taught our children what to do in the front seat of a car through driver's training, now we need to teach them what to do in the back seat." She insists that sexual promiscuity isn't a problem. It's OK for the youngest of kids to do it. "The problem," she says, "is being protected by a condom when you do it." There are those who want the nation to institute explicit, no holds barred sex education in our public schools to everyone from kindergarten and up.

In a featured article in the *Whistleblower Magazine* there was a report on various classes being taught in major universities in America. These were courses for credit that have very explicit topics that would turn your stomach inside out just at their mention.[6]

There was an article in the *Los Angeles Times* that was giving a report on the Sundance Film Festival under the title, *"Role of Sex is Being Recast."* It went on to describe the various film offerings for the festival. It was so filthy and low-life, I would be embarrassed to quote any of it.[7]

When asked, what if the condom doesn't work and the girl gets pregnant? Then they will get into their second most important agenda. We are told in such a situation that the young girl should have an abortion "without parental knowledge" as she doesn't feel that parents should have a say in the matter. Those wanting this say that parents are old-fashioned and dumb, and the rights of parents are non-existent anyway. Note again Matthew 24:12: "And because iniquity shall abound, the love of many shall wax cold."

The media liberals are even shoving their sick ideas on children's TV shows. One report tells of a cartoon on a children's show at Christmastime. The report goes like this:

> A man wearing a Santa hat sits on a roof. He's talking to his ex-girlfriend on a cell phone trying with feigned cheer to wish her a Merry Christmas. He asks if she's with her new boyfriend. "Yes," she replies and says, "I'm with my whole family opening presents." He says, "That's great, because I have a present for you," and he saws off his own head so it falls down the chimney into the fireplace.
>
> This isn't a horror movie. It's a cartoon, filmed in animation like *"Rudolph the Red-Nosed Reindeer."* It runs on the cartoon network, and it's aimed at children."[8]

The article shares how offensive much of children's programming is. The following sums up just how offensive it is:

> In a new survey of the top 20 animated shows, the Parents Television Council gave an A grade to Disney and Nickelodeon for its top cartoons. But the Cartoon Network and its "Adult Swim" blog earned an F for excessive sex, violence, profanity and drug use. In watching 123 programs in a four-week study period, the PTC documented 1,487 examples of offensive material in cartoons. On average, young

viewers were exposed to this junk once every two minutes and 19 seconds.[9]

While it's true that iniquity has always been present in our world, there never has been anything quite like it is now. We see one of two marriages ending in divorce. The teacher of eleven-year-olds found that one day several of her students came to class drunk. The national crime bill amounts to $120 for every man, woman and child in the country. In a recent year 20% of all marriages in this country were based on pre-marital pregnancy.

Teens involved in doing something wrong used to scatter when a police officer walked down the street, but now they hold their ground and yell curses at him.

I read where a bus went over an icy embankment killing one and injuring the rest, and motorists who stopped went through the wreckage and stole the people's jewelry and wallets. We have underworld crime at an all-time high with government officials and everyone getting in on the act of lawlessness. Things that were condemned by Christians fifteen years ago as wrong are now accepted by them.

The Ashley Madison Agency of Toronto, Canada has launched a dating service designed to help married people commit adultery! The motto on the website proclaims: "Life is short. Have an affair." They claim to have more than 3.5 million subscribers. They are advertising their "Infidelity Service" through television and magazine ads and through their website. One of their commercials was rejected by NBC for national broadcast during the Super Bowl, but was aired by some local stations during the game. One of the ads shows a stone tablet that looks like the Ten Commandments. The commandment that is highlighted reads: "Thou shall make money from adultery."

SIGN # 24 LAWLESSNESS WILL INCREASE

Another aspect of Matthew 24:12 is that the word "iniquity" is the Greek word for *lawlessness*. This is seen from Augustus Strong's concordance # NT: 59.

We have already seen that lawlessness is an end time sign, but here we add something new. You will recall it has been pointed out that Jesus told his disciples in Matthew 24:8 that the word *sorrows* is the Greek word for a woman in childbirth. As the day of the birth draws nearer there is an increase in both the intensity and frequency of her pain. Our Lord has declared that this is a picture of the end time signs. As the end nears the signs will increase in intensity and frequency. Unquestionably, this is the case with the sign of lawlessness. It will increase in intensity and frequency exponentially. There can be no doubt that any observant person has noticed the exponential increase in lawlessness in our day.

It seems that every year we say that lawlessness cannot get worse, but every year you look back on the previous year as the "good old days" when lawlessness wasn't so bad. Is there anyone out there who thinks that things are getting better? It seems like there are increasing numbers who are doing what they think is right in their own eyes.

SIGN # 25 LOVE WILL DIMINISH

Matthew 24 has a great variety of end time signs and Matthew 24:12 declares one of them: "And because lawlessness will abound, the love of many will grow cold" (Matthew 24:12).

I believe this to be a reference to true believers in particular, as those who are not saved cannot possess the type of love God's Word speaks of. Romans 5:5 states, "The love of God is spread abroad in our hearts by the Holy Ghost." An unsaved person does not possess the Holy Spirit and therefore cannot have the love of God in him. That the love of Christians is "waxing cold" is seen in the words of Jesus when He said, "If you love me you will keep my commandments." In other words, when we violate God's Word, it's a sign that we don't love Him as we ought to love Him.

Only 2% of the American population is in church on Sunday night. In a recent year we spent 50 million for Christmas trees and 90 million for ornaments. This is more than all of our giving to missions. In some Christian schools there are now signs asking students and professors not to smoke. Most Christian families do not have a family altar, personal devotions or a concern for the lost. We are so involved in worldly things that our Christian life has grown cold.

The main emphasis of Matthew 24:12 is that the loss of love for Christ on the part of Christians will be because of iniquity. The Greek word translated by the English word "iniquity" does not adequately describe the intent of the verse. *Strong's Concordance* shares the following meanings of this word. It says the word means lawlessness or the breaking of the law — meaning God's law.

Christians today are breaking every rule and law that God has ever laid down. We see it in their sex lives, in the breaking of their marriage vows, in drug usage and in a list of violations of God's Word as long as your arm. We see a departure from the faith and the basic doctrines considered foundational.

Even our educational system will not allow prayers in school. You cannot have public Bible readings or even carry a Bible into many school buildings. You cannot publically pray "In Jesus name." Our schools are allowing every other religion into the curriculum of our children in the form of the Eastern religions like Yoga, Hinduism, Muslim beliefs, etc.

SIGN # 26 THE GOSPEL WILL BE PREACHED AROUND THE WORLD

Matthew. 24:14 is very clear relative to this sign: "And this gospel of the kingdom will be preached in all the world as a witness to all the nations, and then the end will come."

We need to continuously remind ourselves that Jesus said all of the signs He gave in Matthew 24 would increase in frequency and intensity. In the last few decades, the Bible is being preached around the world as never before, particularly on the radio. Matthew 24:12 is now possible for the first time in human history since Jesus spoke these words. This is so because mass media communications, communication satellites, radio, the Internet, short wave and TV are all adding to the impact of this prophecy.

The latest statistics say there are 78,000 new Christians every day around the world. There are about 66,000 missionaries around the world, and they say 1,000 new churches are formed in Asia and Africa each week. The largest churches in the world are in South Korea where the largest one there has about 500,000 people. In

Santiago, Chile, one church now has 250,000 people. This has never been seen before in history. The Bible has now been translated into 1,673 languages. Ethnic groups, not yet reached with the gospel of Christ have decreased to only hundreds. We are on the verge of seeing this prophecy fulfilled.

SIGN # 27 CHRISTIANS WILL NOT THINK THE RETURN OF CHRIST IS IMMANENT

In Matthew 24:42-51 our Lord talks about a servant who in his thinking, delays the possibility of the Lord's return in the near future. Remember, Matthew 24 is a chapter dealing with signs of the times. Note that this unfaithful servant did not deny that the master would return, he simply delayed it in his thinking.

Listen to 1 John 2:28: "And now, little children, abide in Him, that when He appears, we may have confidence and not be ashamed before Him at His coming." Apparently there are those who will have an abundant entrance into heaven while others will be saved by the skin of their teeth. 2 John 1:8 declares: "Look to yourselves, that we do not lose those things we worked for, but that we may receive a full reward." Here again, some receive a full reward and, obviously, others do not. Our Lord is going to reckon with His servants when He comes again.

Note carefully that in the Matthew 24 passage, Jesus is not talking here about two different servants; rather, He's talking about two *possibilities* for the same servant. This is clearly observable by the word "that" in Mathew 24:48. It is therefore the same servant. He belongs to the Lord. In verse forty-eight, the servant calls Him "Lord." What's more, Jesus calls Himself "the Lord of that servant" in verse 50.

Notice please the mistake that the servant made. It lists certain things he did which were wrong. Indeed they *were* wrong, but according to verse forty-eight, the reason he made these fatal mistakes is because he said in his heart, "My Lord delays His coming." He *believed* that his Lord would come, but not right now—perhaps at some far off distant date. Furthermore, note that he didn't say it aloud. Rather in verse 48 he said this in "his heart." Now what's involved in delaying the Lord's return? It's denying that He *could* come even right now!

If we believed and lived as though Christ could come back this very day, I dare say it would affect how we live. There is no greater influence to holy living than the constant expectation of the Lord's return. What do you suppose God means when He says this in 1 John 3:3?: "And everyone who has this hope in Him purifies himself, just as He is pure." The apostle Paul says the same thing in the book of Titus.

> Teaching us that denying ungodliness and worldly lusts, we should live soberly, righteously, and godly in the present age, looking for the blessed hope and glorious appearing of our great God and Savior Jesus Christ, who gave Himself for us, that He might redeem us from every lawless deed and purify for Himself His own special people, zealous for good works (Titus 2:12-14).

Therefore, the thought of the imminent return of Christ is associated with holiness and right living. That's the way you will want to meet the Lord when He comes. Is that not the force of Matthew 24:48-49?: "But if that evil servant says in his heart, My master is delaying his coming, and begins to beat his fellow servants, and to eat and drink with the drunkards."

There is a strange silence in the majority of pulpits today regarding the soon return of Christ. In spite of the many signs of His soon return, we hear people scoffing at the possibility of it. This is no doubt why Peter wrote these words in 2 Peter:

> Knowing this first, that there shall come in the last days scoffers, walking after their own lusts, And saying, Where is the promise of his coming? for since the fathers fell asleep, all things continue as they were from the beginning of the creation (2 Peter 3:3-4).

This is a prophecy inspired by the Holy Spirit and written by Peter just before he went home to be with the Lord. He says there shall come in the *last days* scoffers. These are certainly the last days for we believe that the return of the Lord is near.

There are three possible avenues of attack on the imminent return of Christ. Satan will use these avenues to convince people that the Lord will *not* return soon. They are to deny, delay or debauch the subject.

Satan's first attempt is to try to get you to deny its literalness. There is only one interpretation, for example, to a verse like Acts 1:11 which affirms the literalness of Christ's return. "Ye men of Galilee, why stand ye gazing up into heaven? This same Jesus, which is taken up from you into heaven, shall so come in like manner as ye have seen him go into heaven" (Acts 1:11, KJV). This verse teaches that His coming will be bodily, visible and personal.

Failing to deceive the believer by causing him to deny this crystal clear truth, he will try his second ruse. He will allow men to believe that Christ is coming—but not for a long time. This is called delaying His coming and is our subject at this point.

If the believer cannot be deceived into doing this, Satan will try to get us to debauch it! He then seeks to push us to a fanatical extreme, and deceives preachers as to the exact timing of the return of Christ. Thus, down through the years, many preachers have set dates as to the exact day of His return. Of course they are all wrong, as no one can know the day or the time of Christ's return. This is the dogmatic teaching of Jesus Himself. Matthew 24:44 is one of several verses that teach this. "Therefore you also be ready, for the Son of Man is coming at an hour you do not expect."

Satan gets people to make fantastic interpretations about prophetic events. I have seen such hair splitters where they claim they are actually able to measure to the fraction of a millimeter the horns on Daniel's beast. They claim to be able to give the dimensions of the bells of the seven trumpets in the book of Revelation. As a result of this, Bible prophecy has been brought into disrepute. Most people who are involved in the error of delaying the immanency of Christ's return do not recognize it as an error.

While the Bible lists wrong activities of this servant, the emphasis is on the reason he was doing these things. It was because he did not believe the Lord would come soon, He delayed the Lord's coming in his *thinking*. As a result of this, he became careless and bad habits developed.

Apparently this man was orthodox. He didn't deny the fact of the Lord's return. He believed all that! But he did deny the immanency of that return. He believed the Lord was coming—at some time— *but not now*! Remember, he didn't say it aloud. He said it only in his heart. But his outward conduct revealed what was in his heart!

If we lived as though Christ would come back today, we wouldn't be carnal or sinful. If enough Christians really believed this, we would see the greatest revival in the history of the world.

Our trouble is, that just like the unfaithful steward, we confess Jesus with our lips but in our minds we don't think He'll come today. There is no greater influence to holy living than to live with the constant expectation of the Lord's return. What do you suppose 1 John 3:3 means when it states: "And every man that hath this hope in him purifieth himself, even as he is pure."

Paul had this to say in the book of Titus: "For the grace of God that brings salvation has appeared to all men, teaching us that, denying ungodliness and worldly lusts, we should live soberly, righteously, and godly in the present age, looking for the blessed hope and glorious appearing of our great God and Savior Jesus Christ" (Titus 2:11-13).

The Bible teaching of the coming of the Lord is always associated with holiness and right living. You would not want to meet the Lord at a point in time when you were walking in sin.

If the church, for example, must pass through the Tribulation or even a part of it—even a week of it—then, of course, Jesus cannot come *today*. If there were no possibility that Jesus could come back today, the admonitions of Scripture to look for—to watch for—and to prepare for the Lord's coming lose all meaning and force. How can we look for something *today* that will not happen until next year, or perhaps even later? This is delaying our Lord's return, and this is what this servant is guilty of. Inasmuch as Jesus is talking about the signs of the times in Matthew 24 where this servant is used as an illustration, then the thinking of this man is one of those signs that Jesus gives as an indicator of the end time.

SIGN #28 PEOPLE WILL MAKE FANTASTIC CLAIMS AS THEY PERFORM SIGNS AND WONDERS

We have already seen the fact that in the end time many false prophets will arise, but this sign is a bit different in that we are told here that these false prophets would be able to perform signs and wonders. This sign is given in Matthew 24 also: "For false christs and false prophets will rise and show great signs and wonders to deceive, if possible, even the elect" (Matthew 24:24).

While this sign will be completely fulfilled in the person of the Antichrist and False Prophet, we can't help but observe that we are living in a day of incredible feats by those claiming to perform them in God's power. It is not necessary to cite examples of such things as everyone is conscious of what is going on today in this realm.

The Bible declares that the end time will be like the days of Noah and also like the days of Lot.

SIGN # 29 THE POPULATION EXPLOSION

The Bible is clear about this sign. We will start our study of it beginning in the book of Matthew. There we are told the following:

> As the days of Noah were, so also will the coming of the Son of Man be. For as in the days before the flood, they were eating and drinking, marrying and giving in marriage, until the day that Noah entered the ark, and did not know until the flood came and took them all away, so also will the coming of the Son of Man be (Matthew 24:37-39).

To understand this verse, we must know what it was like in the days of Noah. This will not be an exhaustive commentary just a few of the more obvious things.

Note Genesis 6:1 proclaims: "And it came to pass, when men began to multiply on the face of the earth, and daughters were born unto them." Here we are told about a population explosion. Henry Morris, in his book on Genesis, states there is proof that in the day of

Noah, the population on earth was over one billion. That population size was not reached again until 1840. In other words it took from the days of Noah until 1840 to again get one billion people living on earth at the same time. Less than a century later the population was two billion—thirty years later it was 3 billion.

We are now over seven billion. From this point forward, approximately one billion will be added every five years. To make matters worse, not all humans live evenly distributed across the earth. Most live in urban areas. India adds more people to its population in one year than there are presently living in all of Australia. The Bible says: "As it was in the days of Noah so shall it be in the day of the coming of the Son of Man." One of the things that characterized that day was a population explosion. A second characteristic of Noah's day brings before us another sign of the time.

SIGN # 30 THE EARTH WILL BE FILLED WITH VIOLENCE

Genesis 6:11 tells us: "The earth also was corrupt before God, and the earth was filled with violence." The days of Noah were days of violence. Do you think this typifies our day? We have terrorists everywhere. We have people meeting violent deaths in cars and on planes, etc. What's so disturbing about the violence of our day, however, is that so much of it is just violence for the sake of violence. We see it on our TV sets, in our movies, in our novels. It's everywhere! Years ago a foreign movie produced somewhere in South America had a scene where the actress, after all sorts of unimaginable sex acts were portrayed, was literally murdered in the movie. She didn't know it was to happen, but it did—deliberately. The people of New York City loved it. They packed out the movie houses until this movie was banned.

We don't need to document how violence is present in our day as it never has been before. Our daily newspapers and news broadcasts report on almost nothing else. It's seen in the incredible number of wars going on all over the world. We see it in terrorism, gang violence, random violence and in ways that are too numerous to name. These are indeed days just like Noah's day.

An interesting sideline to the Hebrew word translated by the English word *violence* is the Hebrew word for *Hamas*. Is it just a co-incidence that a radical group—a part of the Muslim Brotherhood—goes by that very name today? The headquarters of Hamas is located in the Gaza Strip and their main attribute is violence against the Jewish people.

Perry Stone had a noteworthy observation of this word in a video program called "The Noah Code." The amazing comment by Stone is as follows:

> When Abraham had relations with Hagar, a child was born to them by the name of Ishmael. Later Sarah had Hagar and her son expelled from the family. After that, we see Genesis 16:5, which says: "Then Sarah said to Abram, My wrong be upon you! I gave my maid into your embrace; and when she saw that she had conceived, I became despised in her eyes. The LORD judge between you and me." Believe it or not, the Hebrew word translated by the English word *wrong* in this verse is the identical Hebrew word translated *violence* in Genesis 6:11. Sarah is saying, ":*violence* is going to come upon me because I gave Hagar to you." The children of Ishmael, in particular, are the ones, who show extreme violence to the Jewish people

You may obtain a copy of this message by Perry Stone by calling The *Voice of Evangelism* at (423) 478-3456. Ask for the DVD "The Noah Code."

Another amazing thing about Noah's day is that though the truth was preached to them, they failed to hear God. Listen to Genesis 6 where we are told: "And the LORD said, My Spirit shall not strive with man forever, for he is indeed flesh; yet his days shall be one hundred and twenty years" (Genesis 6:3). As a matter of fact, Peter declares this to be one of the primary signs of the last days. 2 Peter 3:3-4 says: "Knowing this first, that there shall come in the last days scoffers, walking after their own lusts, And saying, Where is the promise of his coming? For since the fathers fell asleep, all things continue as they were from the beginning of the creation." The days of Noah are further understood by the next sign—the imagination of men was only wicked continuously.

SIGN # 31 THE IMAGINATIONS OF MEN WILL BE EVIL CONTINUOUSLY

In Genesis 6:5 God tells us: "And God saw that the wickedness of man was great in the earth, and that every imagination of the thoughts of his heart was only evil continually." Today we see impurity in our music, our movies, our jokes and in all imaginable areas of life. I hardly need to go into any detail here. We are so numb to it that we are insensitive and unconscious as to what's going on. With the evil in our books, magazines, TV, music, movies and through the use of narcotics, men *think* evil thoughts continually. The desire to think impurely has even gone over to music. In rock and roll, and other types of music, song writers have written immoral lyrics in their songs. In other words, in this regard, we are getting just like the days of Noah.

SIGN # 32 MEN WILL NOT FEAR GOD

Even though Noah had preached to them and warned them about how God would punish their sins, they laughed and failed to respond. That's why God said in Genesis 6: "And the LORD said, My Spirit shall not strive with man forever, for he is indeed flesh; yet his days shall be one hundred and twenty years" (Genesis 6:3). The people of today have heard the Word of God until their hearts have literally been hardened. As a matter of fact, the people of our day are fulfilling the word of 2 Peter 3: "Knowing this first: that scoffers will come in the last days, walking according to their own lusts, and saying, "Where is the promise of His coming? For since the fathers fell asleep, all things continue as they were from the beginning of creation" (2 Peter 3:3-4).

SIGN # 33 GLUTTONY

The conditions in the time of another Old Testament character named Lot typified the end days spoken of by Jesus. Luke 17 says: "Likewise as it was also in the days of Lot: They ate, they drank, they bought, they sold, they planted, they built; but on the day that Lot went out of Sodom it rained fire and brimstone from heaven and destroyed them all. Even so will it be in the day when the Son of Man is revealed" (Luke 17:28-30).

As we did with the days of Noah, we must look back to the book of Genesis to see what the days of Lot were like. Note the idea of gluttony is expressed in the words, eating and drinking. The idea is eating and drinking to excess. This is also brought out in Ezekiel 16 where it says:

> As I live, says the Lord GOD, neither your sister Sodom nor her daughters have done as you and your daughters have done. Look, this was the iniquity of your sister Sodom: She and her daughter had pride, fullness of food, and abundance of idleness; neither did she strengthen the hand of the poor and needy (Ezekiel 16:48-49).

Only three times in the Bible is food so plentiful that it's mentioned as being a sin. The occasions are the days of Noah, the days of Lot and at the end of this age. It's almost a paradox that *both* gluttony and people starving is a sign of the time. But isn't that exactly the way it is today. We have half the world engulfed in famine and the other half in overeating. In this country hundreds of books have been written on how to curb your diet, and thousands of books are written on diets.

America's 50 million housewives would have to labor fifty-seven years to can all the corn canned for them by companies in one year. There is enough coffee drunk in this country alone in one year to float 453 battleships the size of the USS Missouri. The frozen food packaged in one day weighs more than thirty Empire State Buildings. Last year America manufactured enough hot dogs to wrap 26.5 times around the earth, and we emptied enough food cans to stretch to the moon and back three times.

SIGN # 34 GOVERNMENT CORRUPTION

Ten righteous people could not be found in the entire cities of both Sodom and Gomorrah. Lot was a judge there, and the suggestion is found in Genesis that the court system was corrupt. We find the same thing today where the rich can commit murder and get away with it while the poor commit a much lesser crime and are severely punished. No comment is needed at all on how corrupt things have become in Washington and virtually all the governments of the world.

SIGN # 35 HOMOSEXUALITY

According to God's Word, *the* sign of Lot's day was homosexuality. *Webster's Dictionary* definition of the word "sodomy" explains that it is homosexuality. This is a sign of the time in that a significant portion of the population practice homosexuality as was true in the days of Lot. In our day, homosexuals in this country are the third largest minority next to Hispanic and black peoples. Our churches are now accepting into the clergy gay people, and that is gaining acceptance in churches all over the world. Inasmuch as God said that in the last days things would be as they were in the days of Lot, we are not at all surprised at the widespread activities of mankind along these lines.

If, a few years ago, someone told you that people of the same sex would legally be getting married in America, would you have believed it? The Massachusetts Supreme Court was the first court that ruled that homosexuals had the right to marry. Since that ruling thousands of gay couples have been legally married in that state.

SIGN # 36 AN AGE OF PRIDE

Again referring to the days of Lot, I would have you note with me one more time Ezekiel 16: "As I live, says the Lord GOD, neither your sister Sodom nor her daughters have done as you and your daughters have done. Look, this was the iniquity of your sister Sodom: She and her daughter had pride, fullness of food, and abundance of idleness; neither did she strengthen the hand of the poor and needy" (Ezekiel 16:48-49). Note that pride was one of their great sins. Everyone everywhere is full of this noxious sin. With our scientific achievements we have deified man, and pride is at an all time high.

SIGN # 37 IDLENESS

Note that the other sin of Lot's day mentioned in Ezekiel 16 is the sin of idleness. Today, what with welfare programs and all, people are idle in unprecedented numbers and being paid for that idleness. In the presidential election of 2008, it was suggested that if you were opposed to paying higher taxes so that people not working could get a government check you were "unpatriotic" or "selfish." Men are seeking four-day work weeks, longer lunch hours, more coffee breaks and other benefits. It seems like everyone wants to work less and get paid more. We are a lazy people. Workers were on strike at an industrial giant a few years back. One of the demands was that a conveyer belt be installed throughout the plant so that the men would not have to walk from one place to another.

SIGN # 38 TSUNAMIS

Luke 21 tells us that in the end time we will see tsunamis unlike any other time in history. I had not known of tsunamis in my lifetime until the one in Indonesia in December 2004 when 230,000 people lost their lives. There have been others since then. The most notable one was in Japan in March, 2011. Listen carefully to the words of Luke 21: "And there will be signs in the sun, in the moon, and in the stars; and on the earth distress of nations, with perplexity, the sea and the waves roaring" (Luke 21:25).

The idea of the sea and waves roaring from the Greek seems to be horrific wave action caused by an earthquake at sea. A loud noise is associated with this word.[10]

In Matthew 8:24, when it speaks of a storm like this on the Sea of Galilee, it uses the Greek word "seismos." You will recognize the closeness of this Greek word to our English word seismograph, which is the word for earthquake activity. It's amazing how common tsunamis have become whereas in the past they were extremely rare. This is just another of the multitude of signs of the times that are increasing in frequency and intensity.

SIGN # 39 REVOLUTION AND INSURRECTION IN MANY COUNTRIES

The original Greek language in which the Bible was written makes this sign very clear. The prophecy is found in Luke 21 where we are told: "But when you hear of wars and commotions, do not be terrified; for these things must come to pass first, but the end will not come immediately" (Luke 21:9).

Perhaps the most trusted authority on the original biblical languages is Augustus Strong. He has this to say about the word "commotions" in Luke 21:9. He said, "The word can be translated *tumult, instability, disorder or confusion.*"[11]

Obviously, the intention of the word is to explain what constitutes a revolution or insurrection against constituted authority. The so-called Arab Spring is the most obvious example of what this verse is talking about.

SIGN # 40 TERRORISM

Strong's Concordance claims that one of the definitions of the Greek word translated "fearful sights" in Luke 21:11 is, in fact, *terrible events* or *terror*. [12] If that is in fact the case, then we have a biblical statement that in the end time there would be acts of terror that will spread fear to people the world over. Inasmuch as this is such a well-known fact of our day, it seems unnecessary to even comment or try to explain what is going on. The news media tells us about it daily.

Robert Liebi gives keen insight into this Greek word when he shares the following:

The meaning of Luke 21:11 cannot be restricted to terrorism. The sense of the (Greek) word *phobethra* is broader. If we take the meaning "terrible events (as shared above)", the long list of floods, heat waves, forest fires, flooding, oil spills, volcanic eruptions, nuclear reactor accidents, etc. falls under the signs of the last days. Tsunamis, famines and earthquakes are mentioned separately in the Olivet Discourse. But all other types of disasters are summarized under the concept of *terrible events*. The signs of the Olivet Discourse are "birth pains" which are cyclinal and tend to become more painful. Natural disasters have increased dramatically and steadily from 1900 to the present. This increase over the last decade has been incredible and most frightening.[13]

SIGN # 41 SIGNS IN THE HEAVENS

We are living in strange days when there are sights in the heavens that are causing men to fear things they believe are going to bring terror on the earth. Because of a more accurate understanding of scientific truth, we are now able to understand certain Bible prophecies about the end time that would never have been understood before our day.

There are two passages of Scripture that prophesy there would be signs in the heavens. The first passage is Luke 21: "And there will be great earthquakes in various places, and famines and pestilences; and there will be fearful sights and great signs from heaven" (Luke 21:11).

The second passage is also found in Luke 21 where we are told: "And there will be signs in the sun, in the moon, and in the stars; and on the earth distress of nations, with perplexity, the sea and the waves roaring; men's hearts failing them from fear and the expectation of those things which are coming on the earth, for the powers of heaven will be shaken" (Luke 21:25-26). With these scriptures as a foundation, we can examine parallel passages to get the complete understanding of what this sign encompasses.

The heavens have always intrigued men. They have interested men religiously as well as otherwise. With the invention of the telescope, man learned many exciting and new things about the heavens. With the advent of satellites and space travel, our knowledge has increased beyond all imagination.

In Genesis we read: "In the beginning God created the heaven and the earth" (Genesis 1:1). We must first ask, "Why did God create the heavens? The answer is two-fold. First He created them to reveal His eternal power. We read in the book of Psalms, "The Heavens declare the power of God" (Psalm 19:1).

Then, secondly, God tells us that He created them for *signs*: "And God said, let there be lights in the firmament of the heaven to divide the day from the night; and let them be for *signs*, and for seasons, and for days, and years" (Genesis 1:14). King Darius exalted God in Daniel's day in Daniel 6:27 because he said Daniel's God "Works signs and wonders in heaven and on earth" (Daniel 6:27).

Since God has announced that He created heavenly bodies as signs for mankind, it's important to know how and when He will do this. When the disciples asked Jesus what would be the sign of the last days Jesus said this in Luke 21: "And there shall be signs in the sun, and in the moon, and in the stars; and upon the earth distress of nations, with perplexity; the sea and the waves roaring" (Luke 21:25).

Joel had previously pointed this out in Joel 2: "And I will show wonders in the heavens and in the earth, blood, and fire, and pillars of smoke. The sun shall be turned into darkness, and the moon into blood, before the great and the terrible day of the LORD come" (Joel 2:30-31).

Astronomers believed that the beginning of a star's violent death throes should become fairly obvious to any inhabitants within its life zone. One such sign is increased activity, such as violent solar flares, magnetic storms and a sudden surge of x-ray and radio wave emissions. I am constantly reading about worried scientists who have been observing our sun going through just such a strange hyperactive stage at this very moment.

This is nothing new to God's Word. God's Word, as we have shown, states that the sun will experience a cosmic catastrophe. The

Bible declares that this great solar disturbance will occur at the time of our Lord's return to earth. Therefore, it would behoove men to take note as all life on the earth is possible only because of the sun, which, in reality, is simply a small star.

That the sun is created for extinction some day is clear from the book of Revelation which teaches us the reality of this: "Now I saw a new heaven and a new earth, for the first heaven and the first earth had passed away. Also there was no more sea. Then I, John, saw the holy city, New Jerusalem, coming down out of heaven from God, prepared as a bride adorned for her husband" (Revelation 21:1-2). The same chapter goes on to give further information. It says: "The city had no need of the sun or of the moon to shine in it, for the glory of God illuminated it. The Lamb is its light" (Revelation 21:23).

According to certain scientists, this day may be much nearer than anyone imagined. The point here is not when their predictions will come to pass, rather, it's that scientists are now predicting what the Bible has always said.

Our sun is about an average size star. Some stars are smaller— some infinitely larger. There are stars so huge they could not pass between our sun and the earth—a distance of 93 million miles.

The sun is composed of mostly gaseous substances, yet it's remarkably compact. Temperatures on the sun range from 10 million degrees to 70 million degrees centigrade. Near the sun's surface, hydrogen is much in evidence. As the temperature becomes hotter nearer the core, helium is found, then silicon and finally iron. Astronomers have concluded that once the iron nucleus of a star begins to break down into helium, thus overturning the balance between hydrogen and helium, the end is rapidly approaching. When that occurs, the star either explodes, which is a supernova, or there is a total collapse of gravity, which is a nova. Either cosmic event would mean the end of all life on this planet unless God intervened.

Heat moves outward from the core of the sun to the surface, throwing out clouds of burning gas thousands of miles into space. While the atmosphere of our earth is only twelve miles, the flaming atmosphere of the sun extends outward more than 1 million miles

The life of all stars is dependent upon their supply of hydrogen. According to current scientific belief, the sun has used up about 50%

of its original hydrogen supply. By and large, they are predicting that the sun has about 4 billion years of life left in it. That is based on the idea that the sun will continue as it is until 90% of its hydrogen is used up. But due to the powerful telescopes and computerized abilities we have today, astronomers are now telling us that stars throughout the universe have reached nova or supernova once 51%—not 90%—of its hydrogen content has been used up.

Thus, current findings indicate that when 50% of a star's hydrogen is gone, drastic changes begin to occur. Helium and other gases and matter begin to build up inside the sun, thus trapping more and more heat inside. A star *must radiate* approximately the same amount of heat that is produced internally or it explodes or collapses. Thus we are told that when a stars hydrogen supply is 49% as compared to 51%, helium, it will *expand* and heat up to more than 100 times it's normal temperature. At that point the remaining hydrogen will be eaten up at a very fast pace until the sun goes into either nova or supernova. We are now being told that the future life expectancy of our sun is between ten years to several thousand years.

What is a supernova? Astronomers used to think that a supernova resulted when a star explodes. This false theory is understandable since 90% of all that science knows about the heavens has been discovered since 1955. Most of that knowledge has come in just the last few years.

Proof that the heavens are not being built up was always known to true believers for Psalm 102 teaches us: "Of old You laid the foundation of the earth, And the heavens are the work of Your hands. They will perish, but You will endure; Yes, they will all grow old like a garment; Like a cloak You will change them, And they will be changed" (Psalm 102:25-26).

The first documented supernova was by Chinese astronomers in 1054 AD. Since that time, many supernovas have been seen and recorded. This could never happen to our sun as atomic scientists have proven beyond any shadow of a doubt. Our sun is too small to experience such a thing

Then we ask the next question, "What is a nova?" The nova of a star is far more common than a supernova. This happens, on the average, to twenty stars per year in the Milky Way alone. The nova of a star begins in the same way that a supernova begins. But in smaller stars, the pressure is built up by the imbalance of more helium than hydrogen and it is not great enough to cause an explosion.

What happens is that the increasing gravitational pull in the center of the star begins to crush the atoms shells, sucking millions of tons of gas and matter into a tiny ball. Once the process begins, it cannot be reversed! Once the cycle is complete, no light or heat will be able to escape. Thus, the sun will become totally dark unless there were an outer glowing ring which some nova appear to leave when the star collapses. These dark and midget stars may have been what Jude referred to in Jude 1 when he said: "Raging waves of the sea, foaming up their own shame; wandering stars for whom is reserved the blackness of darkness forever" (Jude 1:13).

As pointed out previously, when the breakdown begins, the remaining hydrogen would be burned up at an accelerated rate. Our sun would become exceedingly bright and hot. The temperature would shoot upward drying up the rivers and scorching the trees and the grass on the earth. This condition would continue for from seven to fourteen days and then the collapse of the sun would begin.

What about the idea of the nova of our earth's sun? Does the Bible teach such a thing? In considering this, we could quote many scriptures, but I will quote only four. The first verse is found in Isaiah 30:26 where we read: "Moreover the light of the moon will be as the light of the sun, And the light of the sun will be sevenfold, As the light of seven days, In the day that the LORD binds up the bruise of His people And heals the stroke of their wound."

This is obviously referring to when Christ comes back to set up the millennium. Isaiah 30:26 is a description of the scientific process called nova. The sun becomes exceedingly bright and hot. When it does, what appearance will the moon take on as it reflects all this? It will turn red. Further, the heat of the nova fits in perfectly with numerous Tribulation prophecies where we learn of intense heat, which burns up grass, etc.

The second passage I would refer to is found in Revelation 16:8-9 where John teaches the following truth: "Then the fourth angel poured out his bowl on the sun, and power was given to him to scorch men with fire. And men were scorched with great heat, and they blasphemed the name of God who has power over these plagues; and they did not repent and give Him glory."

The third passage I want to share is found in Joel 2:30-31 where it states: "And I will show wonders in the heavens and in the earth: Blood and fire and pillars of smoke. The sun shall be turned into darkness, And the moon into blood, Before the coming of the great and awesome day of the LORD."

The fourth and final scripture we'll look at is found in Matthew 24:29 "Immediately after the tribulation of those days shall the sun be darkened, and the moon shall not give her light, and the stars shall fall from heaven, and the powers of the heavens shall be shaken."

Is there a contradiction here? Isaiah and John say that the sun will become exceedingly bright and hot. Jesus and Joel say the sun and the moon will not give light. There is certainly *no* contradiction here because what all four are describing is the nova of our sun. There is not an astronomer in the U.S. who would not understand that to be the case. During a nova, the sun gets super bright. It then collapses and no longer gives light! This is exactly what the verses above have predicted would happen.

Jesus said that *before* the catastrophe of the sun's nova takes place, the people of the earth would be warned. This is what the following passage we have previously referred to, is all about. "And there will be signs in the sun, in the moon, and in the stars; and on the earth distress of nations, with perplexity, the sea and the waves roaring; men's hearts failing them from fear and the expectation of those things which are coming on the earth, for the powers of heaven will be shaken. Then they will see the Son of Man coming in a cloud with power and great glory" (Luke 21:25-27).

Before it happens, men will know it will happen, and their hearts will be filled with fear! This is not an uncommon view. The current increase in the number of sunspots, floods, tornadoes and hailstorms are signs that pre-nova forces are at work in our sun. I would further share a thought from Matthew 24:21-22 here: "For then there will be great tribulation, such as has not been since the beginning of the world until this time, no, nor ever shall be. And unless those days were shortened, no flesh would be saved; but for the elect's sake those days will be shortened."

As previously said, the sun is having strange things happen to it even at this present time. Solar storms increasing in intensity and number are having a strange effect on lower forms of life here on earth. For example, many homing pigeons are unable to find their way home. With all that has been noted throughout sign 41, it is obvious that all major predicted signs of the Tribulation are in a state where the stage is set for their complete fulfillment.

SIGN # 42 PEOPLE WILL HAVE HEART FAILURE FOR FEAR OF WHAT THEY BELIEVE IS COMING TO EARTH

This sign is found in Luke 21:26 where we read: "men's hearts failing them from fear and the expectation of those things which are coming on the earth, for the powers of heaven will be shaken."

Almost daily we read in our newspapers how men are fearful because they believe a cosmic catastrophe is coming sometime in the near future. They fear a comet may strike the earth or that an EMP attack would wipe life off the planet. They fear the extreme sun spot activity presently going on because we are told that the activity of the sun could damage or destroy the power grid. On and on it goes. The fear regarding the predictions are sincerely believed by those who worry about them. This sign in not just that they fear what will *certainly* happen—they fear what they *think* will happen.

CHAPTER 9

THE WEAK WILL SAY THEY ARE STRONG

SIGN # 43 THE WEAK WILL SAY THEY ARE STRONG

God's Word declares that in the end time weak nations will boast that they are strong. Joel 3:10 says: "Beat your plowshares into swords And your pruning hooks into spears; Let the weak say, I am strong." How can the weak say they are strong? They can do that because we live at a unique time in history. Anyone who can develop an atomic bomb or some sort of chemical or biological weapon can bring a powerful nation to its knees. We are living in the era of terrorists in the midst of a world that seems to make every effort possible to protect the terrorists.

When the terrorists in Gaza shot deadly rockets at random into Israeli cities with the intent of killing non-military citizens, Israel responded by sending a shell to the location where the rocket was fired. Of course, innocent Palestinians were killed because the terrorists used their own non-military citizens as shields. The world, and the UN then proceeded to call the Israeli's "terrorists" that should be punished. As long as the world holds attitudes like that, terrorists can bring a more powerful nation down. If the world of the 1940's had said we could not attack the enemy *wherever* he might be, we would still be fighting World War II today.

That's not the only way that terrorists could gain the upper hand.

A terrorists' letter arrived at the mayor of Los Angeles office on Nov. 30, 1989. A group calling itself "the Breeders" claimed to have released the Mediterranean fruit fly in Los Angeles and Orange counties, and threatened to expand their attack to the San Joaquin Valley, which is an important center of California agriculture.

With perverse logic, they said that unless the government stopped using pesticides they would assure a cataclysmic infestation that would lead to quarantining California produce costing 132,000 jobs and $13.4 billion in lost trade.

Insects are one of the cheapest and most destructive weapons available to terrorists today—one of the most widely ignored. They are easy to sneak across borders, reproduce quickly and can spread disease and destroy crops with devastating speed.[1]

Now, suppose a strong country experienced terrorists unleashing attacks like that, or suppose it attacked a strong nation with all sorts of biological and chemical weapons that could kill millions of its citizens. In all probability that country would give in to the weak foe. It would have no way of stopping it so, it's ominous as far as Bible prophecy is concerned. Thus, we live in a day when the weak are saying they are strong.

Today, many weak countries with no military industry or any other kind of industry for that matter, are saying they are strong when *really* they are *weak*. Thus we have what Joel spoke of where weak nations like Iran, and others are saying, "We are strong." Simply stated, the problem is that weak nations of the world, in seeing the affluence of the industrial nations want that for themselves. Countries with mineral wealth are saying, "You industrial nations are going to have to give us your wealth to continue to get our minerals that keep your economy going." With shortages and rising costs of what is available, industrialized nations will be provoked to trade-wars, which economists say could bring on a worldwide depression. What's the solution to it all? There is only one logical solution that the one-world crowd gives, and that is a worldwide dictatorship. As you can see, all of these signs are inter-related.

A number of years ago, when Spain had troops in Afghanistan as a part of the NATO war against the Taliban, Spain had a president who believed this was the right thing to do. Just before their national elections, this president led in the polls by a wide margin. The Sunday before the election, terrorists blew up several trains loaded with passengers. When the election came, the opponent of the president won hands down. The terrorists won—they got their man elected and the troops of Spain were brought back from Afghanistan.

The thing I want to focus on in this study is the worst and most logical scenario of all. That scenario is when nations like Iran or North Korea can use an EMP bomb on a strong nation like the United States. Few people are aware of the devastation that an EMP bomb could cause on a country virtually sending it back to the eighteenth century. We need to look at the facts in great detail to see exactly where we are in the history of the world and Bible prophecy.

In presenting the above possible scenarios as to how a weak nation can claim it is strong is not the real heart of the problem and prophecy. The fact is, weak nations like Iran or North Korea could completely destroy the United States in a matter of seconds with the advent of a weapon called the Electro Magnetic Pulse Bomb known as the EMP bomb. I feel that this is such an important potential end-time weapon that I want to spend adequate time on this subject. I do not believe that most people have even a scant idea of the horrific reality that such a weapon could pose. I have spoken to people and read articles on this subject that show an incredible ignorance of the subject. Most people seem to feel that the damage done by an EMP would be no greater than what a regular atomic weapon could do to an individual city.

You may ask, "What do you know about the subject of an EMP bomb?" I must confess, I know nothing about such things. I am not an expert on any military matter, but because of the sign under present consideration, I have done extensive research on the subject in order to show you how a weak nation can utterly destroy a great nation like the United States. It would do us well to be aware of the extreme dangers posed by weapons like this in the hands of our enemies. The following is the result of my research:

Mahmoud Ahmadinejad, the president of Iran, has said, "Israel is the little Satan and the United States is the great Satan. Both must be destroyed in order for the world to live at peace with the worldwide rulership of the Muslim religion." He goes on to say that the world will soon see the total annihilation of these two nations (Israel and the U.S.). How is it possible, that a man who is the head of a weak nation like Iran, can declare that he will have the ability to completely destroy the United States of America, the most powerful nation that has ever existed in human history? Believe it or not, one of the ways his vision could be realized would be if he ever got his hands on just *one* EMP bomb.

Allow me to share my research with you on this matter by answering a number of important questions that will give us needed insight into this subject.

WHAT IS AN EMP BOMB?

An EMP bomb is a nuclear bomb that is detonated about 200-300 miles above the earth's atmosphere. As the bomb explodes, it emits a powerful wave of gamma rays. When these rays are unleashed outside the earth's atmosphere, they react with the air molecules of the upper atmosphere that will result in an enormous pulse current that will interact, in turn, with the earth's magnetic field. When this energy release hits the upper atmosphere it creates an electrical disturbance known as the Compton Effect.

> The intensity is magnified. View it as a small pebble rolling down a slope, hitting a larger one, setting that in motion, until finally you have an avalanche. In an instant, an invisible radio frequency wave is produced—a wave of almost unimaginably immense intensity, approximately a million times as strong as the most powerful radio signals on the earth. At the speed of light this disturbance races toward the

185

earth's surface. It is not something you can see or hear. As the pulse strikes the earth's surface, with a power that could range up to hundreds of amps per square yard, it will not affect *you* directly.

The higher the altitude of the weapon's detonation, the larger the affected area would be. For example, at a height of 300 miles, the entire continental United States could be exposed, along with parts of Canada and Mexico.

Dr. Lowell Wood of Lawrence Livermore Laboratory, a member of the *EMP Threat Commission*, has warned in testimony before Congress that an EMP attack could reduce the United States to a pre-Industrial Age capacity, in terms of its ability to provide vital food and water for its population. [3]

Dr. Wood explains how the EMP bomb has such a widespread destructive potential as follows:

Electromagnetic pulses propagate from the burst point of the nuclear weapon to the line of sight on the earth's horizon, potentially covering a vast geographic region . . . simultaneously, at the speed of light.[4]

In simple terms this means that upon the explosion of an EMP, the destructive electromagnetic pulse traveling at the speed of light can create destruction of all electronic devices in the path of its movement. The geographic territory covered by this destructive pulse will be horizon to horizon within the view of an area from the altitude at which the EMP was exploded. That means that the higher the altitude of the explosion, the larger will be the area covered by the destruction of the attack.

Scientists tell us that what is meant by the terminology *horizon to horizon* is as follows: if you were personally in a spaceship at that altitude, all that you could see out the spaceship window would be affected. That's why the higher up the explosion, the greater the territory that would be affected. Another factor is this, if the explosion took place at an elevation too high, it would not effect the electric devices on earth. At a certain level, there is enough space the pulse would travel through before reaching the earth, and the pulse would be filtered out and would cause no damage. The pulse occurs so quickly that the damage is done before automated emergency shutdown systems can react.

> The pulse effect would cause a power surge similar to lightning, which would burn circuits and immobilize electronic components and systems. The surge will flow through electricity transmission lines, damaging distribution centers and fusing power lines and possibly creating fires. This will cause irreversible damage to our electronic systems. Then the United States would effectively be set back to the 19th century, to a world without cars, cell phones, computers and any other electronics.

> If history is any guide, an EMP attack would be catastrophic. In 1859, British astronomer Richard Carrington observed an unusually large solar flare. Later, the flare reached earth. Telegraph operators were knocked unconscious. Their machines caught on fire as the EMP effect from the flare surged through the lines. When this event occurred, only a small fraction of the world was electrified (used electricity). [5]

Another source declares that such an attack on a country could "Send that country into a new Dark Age." In it's October 27, 2010 edition, the mainstream poster child, *USA Today,* ran an article warning of the dangers of an EMP attack. Titled, *One EMP Burst and the World Goes Dark,* Dan Vergano leads with, "The sky erupts. cities darken, food spoils and homes fall silent. Civilization collapses."

The bad news is, whenever it strikes wires, metal surfaces, antennas or power lines, it will now travel along those metal surfaces in the same way a lightning bolt will always follow the metal of a lightning rod or the power line into your house. The longer the wire, the more energy it will absorb. A high-tension wire, miles long will absorb tens of thousands of amps. The destruction begins as it slams into any electrical delicate electronic circuit. This means computer chips, relays, etc. will be destroyed. In that moment, they are over-loaded by the massive energy surge, and they will short circuit and fry.

Your house, via electric, phone and cable wires is connected, like everything else, into the power and communication grids. This energy surge will destroy *all* delicate electronics in your home, even as it destroys all the major components all the way back to the power company's generators and phone companies' main relays. In far less than a mille-second the entire power grid of the United States will be destroyed. The pulse can melt important components in whatever equipment is affected by it.

Put simply, an EMP produces radiation that rapidly changes electric and magnetic fields and produces a destructive current and voltage surge. An EMP is generated when gamma rays from a high altitude nuclear explosion interact with the atmosphere to produce a radio frequency wave pulse that would hit everything in line of sight of the explosion. An EMP attack on America could cause such widespread damage that it could take months, years or even decades to fix. With all generating stations knocked out, where would new sophisticated generators come from? How could we produce them when there is no electronic power, which is needed to build such things? The fact is, the United States is more vulnerable to this type of attack than any other country on the earth. The reason this is so is because we are more totally dependent on electricity and electronics than any other nation.

I understand that twenty-eight countries have explored the ability to have the type of ballistic missile capabilities to carry out such an attack.[7]

The United States, Russia, China, North Korea and Iran are developing it. Terrorists could obtain this technology from any of these countries or other countries presently doing research on it.

Former CIA double agent Reza Kahlili spent time as a member of Iran's Revolutionary Guards Corps. He said the Iranians have conducted missile tests off ships in the Caspian Sea, which are consistent with an EMP-style attack. They plan going to the Gulf of Mexico with ballistic missiles on board cargo ships, and they're going to launch one at a moment's notice.[8]

So the Iranian government has been practicing launching missiles from container ships for some years now. The ship would pretend to be a normal container ship carrying cargo to America under the flag of any one of several countries. When they position their ship a few miles from the Texas coast, they would open special doors on the ship and fire their missile to launch it about 300 miles high over a state in the Midwest (like Kansas). They would then detonate the missile while at that height thus producing an EMP explosion. Seconds later, the EMP would travel at the speed of light and the entire power grid of America would be doomed. Ten minutes after the ship launches the missile, the war is over. America would have lost and would now be incapable of any communications or military actions emanating from within the U.S. borders. This is how a weak nation like Iran could destroy the U.S. whom they declare is the "Great Satan."

The potential of an EMP bomb was discovered accidentally when the United States conducted an atmospheric test over the mid-Pacific ocean in 1962 in a program code named *Starfish Prime*. The test was conducted 250 miles high with a small atomic bomb. The scientists were surprised at what a high altitude explosion did. Hawaii, 898 miles away experienced all sorts of power blackouts and damage to electronic systems. The effects were felt even in Australia. It was through this test and others like it that scientists discovered the destructive potential of what they termed an Electromagnetic Pulse Bomb.[9]

Some time after this, Russia did her own experiments named The K Project. These tests were conducted in space over Kazakhstan. Their tests did extensive damage to an underground power line that caused a fire in the power plant in the city of Karaganda.

The EMP travels so fast that there can be no power surge protection device that will work to prevent the catastrophic damage that results from such a pulse. This fact makes it impossible for power surge protection devices to do any good.

THE EFFECTS OF AN EMP ATTACK

Various news sources tell us that all major transportation systems would cease to work, all financial systems and banks would collapse. There would be no TV, phones, cell phones, electricity, heat or air conditioning. Water could not be delivered, trucks and cars would not run; so, food could not be delivered. What little food would be left after panic buying would have to be rationed. There would be no access to money, and the stock market would be closed. Our money would become worthless and a worldwide depression would result. Because there would be little production of anything, the United States would default on its debt.

Time Magazine of March 30, 2010 reported under an article "EMP: The Next Weapon of Mass Destruction" the following:

> If America needs a new threat around which to organize its defenses, try this one: Bad guys explode nuclear weapons miles above U.S. soil, sending out electromagnetic pulse (EMP) that fries the electronic guts of everything in America. The nation's financial and transportation systems collapse, hospitals and the Internet go dark, water and electrical grids freeze and runaway Toyotas with electronic throttles are finally brought to a stop. The EMP resulting from the blast would cause widespread damage devastating the economy and resulting in the deaths of millions of Americans.[10]

When Bill Clinton was president, he established a blue ribbon panel commission to determine how severe the threat of an EMP attack on the United States is:

The commission's chairman testified that within one year of such an attack, 70-90% of Americans would be dead from causes such as disease and starvation due to the interruption of the national food supply, which is entirely automated and needs a functioning power grid to operate.[11]

Senator Jonb Kyl, who chaired the Senate Subcommittee on Terrorism, Technology, and Homeland Security, wrote the following about the EMP threat in the April 15, 2005 edition of the *Washington Post*:

An electromagnetic pulse attack on the American homeland is one of only a few ways the United States could be defeated by its enemies—terrorist or otherwise. A single scud missile, carrying a single nuclear weapon, detonated at the appropriate altitude, would interact with the earth's atmosphere, producing an electromagnetic pulse radiating down at the surface at the speed of light. Depending on the size and location of the blast, the effect would be to knock out our already stressed power grids and other electrical systems across much or even all of the continental United States, for months if not years.

Few, if any people would die right away. But the loss of power would have a cascading effect on all aspects of U.S. society. Communication would be largely impossible. Lack of refrigeration would leave food rotting in warehouses, exacerbated by a lack of transportation as those vehicles still working simply ran out of gas (which is pumped with electricity). The inability to sanitize and distribute water would quickly threaten public health, not to mention the safety of anyone in the path of the inevitable fires which would rage unchecked. And as we have seen in areas of natural and other disasters, such

circumstances often result in a fairly rapid breakdown of social order.[12]

The *Hawaii Free Press* carried a story about the potential effect
of an EMP attack on the United States, which gives several of the
resulting damages to our entire society and how our individual lives
would be affected. In part, the report reads as follows:

> Medical services would not be available because they
> need electric power. Telephones wouldn't operate.
> The traffic lights would stop working. Big traffic
> jams. Transportation would be shut down. Electronic
> fund transfers won't work so you wouldn't get your
> paycheck. You won't be able to use your credit card.
> Food stocks would run out very quickly. Everything
> we know about life today that makes it convenient
> and efficient would be shut down.
>
> The result of a massive EMP event would be devas-
> tating. Communications would collapse, transporta-
> tion would halt, and electrical power would simply
> be nonexistent. Not even a global humanitarian
> effort would be enough to keep hundreds of millions
> of Americans from death by starvation, exposure,
> disease, social collapse or lack of medicine.
>
> Nor would the catastrophe stop at U.S. borders. Most
> of Canada would be devastated too, as its infrastruc-
> ture is integrated with the U.S. power grid. Without
> the American economic engine, the world economy
> would quickly collapse. Much of the world's intel-
> lectual brainpower (half of it is in the United States)
> would be lost as well. Earth would most likely recede
> into the "new" dark age.
>
> Yet, despite the threat—and the fact that six
> national commissions and major independent

U.S. government studies have concurred with the significance of the danger—Congress has merely deliberated it but has not taken substantive action. Meanwhile the administration and federal agencies remain mostly ambivalent.[13]

It is estimated by experts that the bottom line result of such an attack would be the death of 70-90% of the entire population of the United States of America. One report tells that Iran is developing missiles on which to launch their nuclear weapons once they develop them. We are told that intelligence officials have noted that Iran is testing detonating its nuclear-capable missiles by remote control while still in high-altitude flight. This development makes a potential attack on the U.S. more probable. Let me quote a part of the report:

> We believe this is the only reason why Iran would be testing SLV's within-flight detonations. With this kind of weapon, Iran would simply need to strike first. Once the weapon goes off, it would be difficult to determine where it came from, and to respond appropriately, as all form of traditional communication would be wiped out.

> The effects would be nothing short of disastrous— literally the end of the world as we know it. All unprotected and unhardened electrical devices would be left useless. The recovery period from a collapse of this magnitude would be counted in decades, not years.[14]

Newt Gingrich gave a very insightful analysis on the threat of an EMP attack on America in the following words:

> Former House Speaker, Newt Gingrich is one who spoke at the American Israel Public Affairs Committee annual conference in May 2009, saying,

"Three small nuclear weapons at the right altitude would eliminate all electricity production in the United States." A few months later, Gingrich spoke at a conference hosted by EMPACT a leading EMP advocacy group. He ramped up the urgency of his message: "An EMP attack may be the greatest strategic threat we face, because without adequate preparation, its impact would be so horrifying that we would basically lose our civilization in a matter of seconds."[15]

Try to imagine a world where:

- Nobody had electricity; therefore, none of your electronic gadgets work.
- You had no heat or air conditioning in your home—there was no light in your home.
- You could not talk to anyone who wasn't near enough to hear your voice.
- You could not use your credit cards or get any money.
- If you got government checks, they could not deliver them.
- Most vehicles would not start and all cell phones would be dead.
- You could not cook warm meals.
- You couldn't flush a toilet or take a bath or shower.
- How would you brush your teeth when your toothpaste ran out and there was no water?
- There would be no trucks to deliver food.
- There will be no electricity to pump water where it was needed. You would turn on the faucet in your sink and nothing would come out.
- No planes could fly—no trains could move.
- You would not be able to get medicines and medical supplies as they could not produce them. Even if they could, there would be no way to transport the medicines to your local pharmacy.

- Unemployment would be almost 100%. No one could work if there was no electricity, no communications and no transportation.

- You were unable to go from place to place except by walking, biking or riding a horse.

- You could not use your computer or any type of electronic device.

- Your car would not run. Even if it could run, you could not get gas as there was no electricity to pump it.

- You could not get any clean water to drink. Grocery stores would have no food.

- What if all of these things happened and could not be fixed for weeks? For months? For years or decades?

- Social unrest, break-ins, muggings and rioting would be the usual results of society breaking down. What would you do if that happened? How could you go anywhere when transportation would not be available? You could not call 911 or anyone for help.

- People who were ill and dependent on electronic devises to stay alive would die quickly. There would be no more dialysis treatments or surgeries. No manufacturer could make medicine. Even if they could, how could they ship it to your town?

- An EMP would destroy the computer that was a part of your car, anything that was solid state in the car and the ignition system. Some police departments are even now experimenting with using a specially designed bumper on their cars for high-speed chases. If they can brush up against the car they are pursuing, the officer just hits a button, and through his bumper a high energy surge will be released flooding into the car being pursued and shorting out its computer system. Result? The energy surge, which is the same principle as an EMP blast, when fired into your car essentially makes it a useless hunk of metal that will slowly roll to a stop. In that instant, most of America will be on foot again.

- An airplane would be the worse case scenario for this reason: Commercial airlines are all computer driven. It's estimated that at a given minute during regular business hours, somewhere between three to four thousand commercial airliners are above America in the skies. If an EMP hit while a plane was flying, that plane would be doomed. The pilots would be sitting there impotent, staring at blank computer screens, pulling on controls that no longer responded as the plane finally nosed over and crashed. Somewhere between 250,000-500,000 people would die on these planes in the first few minutes after the attack.

- Law enforcement would be powerless without radios, cell phones and squad cars, unable to know where there was a crisis and how to react.
- Nursing homes and hospitals are required by law to have back up generators, but those generators are "hot wired" into the building so that power can instantly kick back on if the main system shuts down. That "hot wiring" means the EPM pulse would take out the generators and their circuitry as well.
- The American financial system would break down as it's completely dependent on the electric power grid.

A detailed analysis of what would happen in our hospitals was given by F. Michael Maloof. He was a former senior security policy analyst for the office of the Secretary of Defense. He has almost thirty years of service in that capacity. He gave the following warning:

The hospitals in every affected city will be scenes of chaos and carnage as backup generators and battery-powered systems that were not fatally damaged begin to falter and run down. Respirators, cardiac monitors, intravenous drip pumps, and dialysis machines all stop. Patients die, first by the scores, then by the hundreds, then by the thousands. How can anyone who has a problem get help when there is nothing to call with, or nothing to transmit the call on the other end? The big farms, dependent on power for everything from milking machines to harvesting combines, are shut down. Powerless and darkened slaughterhouses and chicken processing plants are scenes of confusion, for people and animals alike.[16]

Mr. Maloof continues his comments on some of the specific problems an EMP attack would cause as follows:

> In widespread power outages of the past, people reacted with behavior ranging from rioting and looting (as many did during the 1977 New York outage) to patiently waiting for the crisis to be over (as with the 2003 outage). But if the recovery period were to be longer, and if electronic communications were down for a period of weeks or even months, civilization in the United States could reach a tipping point where people's worst impulses would be on display and recovery would be very difficult.

> Damage to large numbers of insulators and pole-mounted transformers would also result in a shortage of replacement parts, since they are considered sturdy and reliable items under normal conditions. Consequently, spares are not kept to cover wide-spread losses, resulting in delays in finding replacement parts.

> Delivery of a new large transformer ordered today is nearly three years, including both manufacturing and transportation. An event damaging several of these transformers at once means it may extend the delivery times well beyond current time frames.[17]

Is it any wonder that the Bible speaks of a coming day when weak nations could declare themselves strong and take down strong nations? Friend, we are living in the last days. You'd better be ready to meet God.

WHY WOULD ANYONE DROP AN
EMP BOMB OVER AMERICA?

America has many enemies that would like to see us destroyed. Countries like Russia, China, North Korea and Iran are certainly on the list of our enemies.

Yet the fact remains that Russia would probably not carry out such an attack. They know that if they did, the same thing would happen to them. The cold war proved that the ability of both countries to retaliate deterred either one from doing such things.

Probably China would not drop such a bomb on us as they have become rich due to the transfer of jobs from the United States to China and the subsequent bundle of money they make by America buying their goods. What's more, the United States owes them trillions of dollars; so, it would make no sense for China to kill the goose that laid the golden egg. This job transfer came about because of environmental restrictions in the U.S and also enormous red tape our government imposes on companies in America. These restrictions do not exist in China.

North Korea would do it at the drop of a hat, but they do not have the technological ability to do so. and will not have such capability in the foreseeable future.

That leaves Iran, which, we are being told, will do that very thing in the near future. They have stated that when they "Destroy Israel," even if Israel wiped out ¾ of Iran's population, it would be worth it. In other words, they have no fear of death. They love death because of the promise that all Muslims that murder Israelis or Westerners will have a special place in heaven.

Recently, for the first time ever, the main Ayatollah in Iran has spoken out about his intentions. His plan is shocking, but in complete line with the pronouncements of the president of Iran. The following information came from Reza Kahili, who was formerly an officer in the Iranian Revolutionary Guards Corps. Then he became a double agent for the CIA. He has published articles on what is going on in Iran. You'll want to hear this as it reveals the true intentions of the country of Iran. The article that published what Kashili said was sent out by Joel Rosenberg in July, 2012. Following is, in part, what Reza Kahili had to say:

- Iran's supreme leader, for the first time, is telling his nation that it must prepare for war and "the end of times" as it continues to develop nuclear weapons. State-owned media outlets, in a coordinated effort, all ran a similar story Friday highlighting Ayatollah Zali Khamenei's message on the coming of the last Islamic messiah.

- Until now, the Iranian media would mostly quote clerics from seminaries on the issue of the last Islamic messiah to avoid the regime being labeled "Messianic." However, the wide publication of Khamenei's statements on a need to prepare for the end time as it confronts the West over its nuclear program, is alarming to Western leaders.

- "The issue of Imam Mahdi is of utmost importance, and his reappearance has been clearly stated in our holy religion of Islam," Khamenei said. "We must study and remind ourselves of the end of times and Imam Mahdi's appearance — we must prepare the environment for the coming so that the great leader will come."

- Shiite theology holds that great wars must engulf the earth, during which one-third of the world's population will die in the fighting and another third will die from hunger, lawlessness and havoc. Israel is to be destroyed, and only then will the 12th imam, Mahdi, reappear and kill all the infidels, raising the flag of Islam in all corners of the world.[18]

As far back as July 2008 it was discovered by U.S. intelligence services that Iran is planning a nuclear attack on the United States as soon as it gets the bomb. Meanwhile, they are testing ballistic missiles being fired from cargo freighters and then exploded by remote control at high altitudes. The only possible logic for these kinds of tests is so they will be prepared to launch a weapon that will be capable of acting as an EMP bomb over Israel and the United States.

Let me highlight information reported by *Newsmax Magazine* on July 29, 2008.

Iran has carried out missile tests for what could be a plan for a nuclear strike on the United States, the head of the national security panel has warned.

In testimony before the House Armed Services Committee and in remarks to a private conference on missile defense over the weekend, hosted by the Claremont Institute, Dr. William Graham warned that the U.S. intelligence community "doesn't have a story" to explain the recent Iranian tests.

One group of tests that troubled Graham, the former White House science advisor under President Ronald Reagan, were successful efforts to launch a Scud missile from a platform in the Caspian Sea. Another troubling group of tests involved Shahab-3 launches where the Iranians "detonated the warhead near Apogee, not over the target area where the thing would eventually land, but at altitude," Graham, said. "Why would they do that?

The only plausible explanation we can find is that the Iranians are figuring out how to launch a missile from a ship and get it up to the altitude and then detonate it," he said. "And that's exactly what you would do if you had a nuclear weapon on a Scud or a Shahab-3 or other missile, and you wanted to explode it over the United States.

The first indication of such an attack would be that the power would go out. We would not physically feel anything in our bodies," Graham said. The food distribution system would grind to a halt. Even warehouses with backup diesel generators would do no good, because "we wouldn't be able to pump the fuel into the trucks and get the trucks to the warehouses."

"The United States would quickly revert to an early 19th century type of country, except that we would have ten times as many people with ten times fewer resources," he said.

Within a week or two of the attack people would start dying. "People in hospitals would be dying faster than that, because they depend on power to stay alive. But then it would go to water, food, civil authority, emergency services. And we will end up with many people not surviving the event."

Asked how many Americans would die if Iran were to launch the EMP attack it appears to be preparing, Graham gave a chilling report. "You have to go back to the 1800s to look at the size of the population that could survive in a nation deprived of mechanized agriculture, transportation, power, water and communication. I'd have to say that 70—

-90% of the population would not be sustainable after this kind of attack," he said. America would be reduced to a core of around 30 million people—about the number that existed in the decades after America's independence from Great Britain."

In his recent Congressional testimony, Graham revealed that Iranian military journals, translated by the CIA at the Commission's request, discuss a nuclear EMP attack that would gravely harm the United States. Furthermore, if Iran launched its attack from a cargo ship plying the commercial sea lanes off the East coast—a scenario that appears to have been tested during the Caspian Sea tests—America would never be able to be certain who was to blame for the attack.

Graham said, "An EMP attack on America would send us back to the horse and buggy era—without the horse and buggy. Today America has no missile defense against such an attack."

Arizona Republican Jon Kyl, a long-standing champion of missile defense, told the Claremont conference on Friday that Obama has opposed missile defense tooth and nail and as president would cut funding for these programs dramatically.[19]

Dr. Graham was the chairman of the Commission on EMP Readiness appointed by President Bill Clinton. We will discuss their full report below.

WHAT CAN BE DONE ABOUT IT?

Barak Obama, our current president, as quoted earlier, is tooth and nail against a defense system. Congress hears lots of testimony about the problem, but does nothing. We are even told that if the news got out in the mainstream media, it would so overwhelm the average citizen psychologically, he would be overcome by hopelessness and helplessness. The fear is, that should word of this get out people would have the attitude, why bother, if it happens, we're all finished.

During the cold war something happened in the mid 1960's. The threat was no longer fifty to a hundred small atomic bombs dropped from airplanes it was a rain of thousands of hydrogen bombs delivered within minutes by ballistic missiles. In the atmosphere of overkill, attempting to prepare seemed ridiculous, futile. The standard phrase became, "The living will envy the dead, so why bother?" Civil defense became an object of derision, the realm of a few survivalist nut cases. An EMP attack is different since it requires but one nuclear weapon 300 miles above the middle of the United States. One bomb. The launch could be done from a container tanker somewhere in the Gulf of Mexico. In that instant, the war is already over and won.[20]

In 2009, NERC went under new management. The new chief executive officer, Gerry Cauley, recently testified to the Senate Energy and Natural Resources Committee, and according to reporting from Dr. Pry, he insisted that "Geomagnetic storms cannot threaten transformers, the operation of the electric grid or the survival of the American people."

NERC's official position has clearly evolved. Now they are maintaining that a geomagnetic super-storm, like the 1859 event, would not cause widespread damage to big transformers or a catastrophic collapse of the national electric grid for a protracted period. So the NERC is now at odds with reports by the 2008 EMP Commission, the Department of Energy, the Federal Energy Regulatory Commission and national laboratories at Los Alamos, Lawrence Livermore, Sandia and Oak Ridge. Reports from all these government groups concluded that a great geomagnetic storm or EMP event could damage and destroy hundreds of electrical transformers and take down the national electronic grid for three to ten years. That, in turn, as Dr. Pry has told us, could cause "millions of Americans to perish from starvation and societal collapse." [21]

Once the entire system collapses, how and where does one build it back? Where does he get the generators and millions of miles of wire, connectors and numerous fried parts to put it all back together. Perhaps some parts could be gotten from some place in Europe or Asia, but how could we get in touch with someone to order it and what nation would have as many parts as would be needed. Even if the parts were available overseas and they were able to ship them all to America, how could they be transported to where they are needed all over the country?

The task would take decades and perhaps, no matter what happened, could never again be like it was. The bottom line is simply this: each one of us would be on his own. Not only that, but what would happen if some progress were made on restoration and the enemy simply sent another EMP bomb to destroy all the rehabilitation work done?

Without plenty of clean water and waste removal, disease will spread rapidly. Millions will die from those problems. Couple that with the problem of lawlessness and people breaking into homes to get "things" to barter with others so that their own needs can be met. How could the National Guard be sent in to quell the lawlessness when there would be no way to transport them to the place of need, which would be just about everywhere?

One writer asked, "What about the multi-million dollar condo on the 40th floor that would then become a nightmare hike straight up, lugging whatever food and water you might get? Where do we get safe water? The nearby stream is a known dump for raw sewage since purification plants are offline. Once stricken by the results of drinking this water, where does one get basic help, basic medication, more water to keep you hydrated? By 60 days starvation will be killing millions and by 120 days mass starvation will be the norm."[22]

We, in America, have a greater vulnerability to an EMP attack because we are more advanced in the usage of electronics than any nation in the world.

> The U.S. has developed more than most other nations as a modern society heavily dependent on electronics, telecommunications, energy, information networks and financial and transportation systems. This asymmetry is a source of substantial economic, industrial and societal advantages, but it creates vulnerabilities and critical interdependencies that are potentially disastrous to the United States.[23]

Gaffney pointed out further that our antimissile systems might not always be able to defend against missiles launched from the sea close to our shores: "The determining factor would primarily be the location and readiness of the Navy's missile-defense equipped Aegis ships. Our West coast deployed ground-based interceptors will be unable to do the job against short-range missiles fired off our East or Gulf coasts.

The cargo vessel could be out on the waters, going around our coasts through the normal channels used by other commercial cargo vessels. It could go back and forth for weeks or months and appear to be routine as it goes in and out of various ports along the U.S. East Coast, ports in the Gulf of Mexico, or even visit ports on the West Coast. The ship would be registered with any number of countries to provide legitimacy and show a flag of a very neutral country, with no prior reference to any other vessel that may have been used by countries of concern. The ship however, actually could have a crew of highly trained missile experts who know how to launch SCUDS especially from a ship.[24]

Unfortunately, most Americans who see reports that describe the problem will write it off, They think it is written by a nut case and totally ignore it. However, to do so, they will have to write off the Blue Ribbon Panel of experts that Bill Clinton appointed to study this potential problem. The Commission was established in 2004 and reported its conclusions to Congress. I have a complete copy of the report they issued to the president and Congress. It is called, "The report of the Commission to Assess the Threat to the United States from Electromagnetic Pulse (EMP) Attack." It is 180 pages long, not counting the appendix pages. The men chosen by President Clinton are the foremost experts in their areas of expertise. To refer to this distinguished panel as "nut cases" would prove the person making such a statement to be the real "nut case." The people that President Clinton placed on the panel to discover what, if anything, is the threat to America from an EMP attack are as follows:

- Dr, John S. Foster Jr.
- Mr. Earl Gjelde
- Dr. William R. Graham (chairman)
- Dr. Robert Hermann
- Mr Henry (Hank) Kluepfel
- Gen. Richard L. Lawson, USAF (Ret.)
- Dr. Gordon Soper
- Dr. Lowell L. Wood, Jr.
- Dr. Joan B. Woodward

See appendix B-2 for the biographies of each panel member.

It's not even remotely possible that there is any individual who could have more knowledge and understanding on the subject of an EMP Pulse bomb that would be greater than the collective research of the elite members of the Commission listed above.

THE REPORT OF THE COMMISSION TO STUDY THE IMPACT OF AN EMP ATTACK ON THE UNITED STATES OF AMERICA

There is no way I can quote the 180 pages of material that are contained in the Commission's report, but I can share the highlights of its conclusions in each of the specific areas of their investigation. All the material under this heading is based upon or quoted from the report of the Commission appointed by President Bill Clinton.

When a nuclear explosion occurs at high altitude, the EMP signal it produces will cover the wide geographic region within the line of sight of the detonation. This broad band, high amplitude EMP, when coupled with sensitive electronics has the capability to produce widespread and long lasting disruption and damage to the critical infrastructures that underpin the fabric of U.S. society. A single EMP attack may seriously degrade or shut down a large part of the electric power grid in the geographic area of EMP exposure effectively and instantaneously. There is also a possibility of functional collapse of grids beyond the exposed area as electrical effects propagate from one region to another.

Some critical electrical power infrastructure components are no longer manufactured in the United States,. Their acquisition ordinarily requires up to a year of lead time in routine circumstances. Damage to, or loss of, these components could leave significant parts of the electrical infrastructure out of service for periods measured in months, to a year, or more. There is a point in time at which the shortage or exhaustion of sustaining backup systems occurs.

Electrical power is necessary to support other critical infrastructures, including supply and distribution of water, food, fuel, communications, transport, financial transactions, emergency services, government services, and all other infrastructures supporting the national economy and welfare. Should significant parts of the electrical power infrastructure be lost for any substantial period of time, the Commission believes that the consequences are likely to be catastrophic. Many people may ultimately die for lack of the basic elements necessary to sustain life in dense urban and suburban communities.

The recovery plans for the individual infrastructures currently in place essentially assume, at worst, limited upsets to the other infrastructures that are important to their operation. Such plans may be of little or no value in the wake of an EMP attack because of its long duration effects on all infrastructures that rely on electricity or electronics. The number of people knowledgeable enough to support manual operations is limited.

The physical and social fabric of the United States is sustained by a system of systems, a complex and dynamic network of interlocking and interdependent infrastructures. It is important to realize that the vulnerability of the whole of all the highly interlocked critical infrastructures may be greater than the sum of the vulnerability of its parts. Coordinated activity is enabled by the growth of technology, and failure within one individual infrastructure may not remain isolated, but, instead it may induce failures into other infrastructures. The bottom line in testing observations at the end of the testing was that every system tested failed when exposed to the simulated EMP environment.

The Commission considered the implications of these multiple simultaneous control system failures to be highly significant as potential contributors to a widespread system collapse. Based on the testing and analysis outlined in the previous section, we estimate that a significant fraction of all remote control systems within the EMP affected area will experience some type of impact.

Planning for multiple failures, particularly when they are closely correlated in time, is much less common. It is safe to say that no one has planned for, and few have even imagined a scenario with the loss of hundreds or even thousands of nodes across all the critical national infrastructures simultaneously. That, however, is *precisely* the circumstance that would be created by an EMP attack scenario. In an EMP attack scenario, the immediate impact is expected to affect the different infrastructures simultaneously through multiple electronic component disruptions and failures over a wide geographical area.

The report of the Commission is divided into an examination of several key areas that might be affected by an EMP event. I have taken key excerpts from each of the areas to share with you in the following part of this chapter. The most important area that would be affected by an EMP bomb would be the electric power grid. The greatest attention of the report from the commission was dedicated to the power grid aspect of the problem. The reason for this is that, should such an attack happen, the other key systems in our society would also fail as they need electricity to function.

1. THE ELECTRIC POWER GRID

Essentially every aspect of American society requires electrical power to function. Continued electrical support is necessary for sustaining water supplies, production and distribution of food, fuel, communications and everything else that is a part of our economy.

For most Americans, production of goods and services and most of life's activities stop during a power outage. Not only is it impossible to perform many of everyday domestic and workplace tasks, but also people must divert their time to dealing with the consequences of having no electricity. No infrastructure, other than electric power has the potential for nearly complete collapse in the event of a sufficiently robust EMP attack.

Today the existing electrical system at peak demand periods increasingly operates at or near reliability limits of its physical capacity. Therefore, a relatively modest upset to the system can cause functional collapse. As the system grows in complexity and interdependence, restoration from collapse or loss of significant portions of the system becomes exceedingly difficult.

Should the electrical power system be lost for any substantial period of time, the Commission believes that the consequences are likely to be catastrophic to civilian society. Machines will stop, transportation and communication will be severely restricted; heating, cooling and lighting will cease; food and water supplies will be interrupted; and many people may die. "Substantial period" is not quantifiable, but generally, outages that last for a week or more and affect large geographic regions without sufficient support from outside the outage area would qualify.

This strategy leaves us ill prepared to respond effectively to an EMP attack that would potentially result in damage to vast numbers of components nearly simultaneously over an unprecedented geographic scale. The magnitude of an EMP event varies with the type of design and yield of the weapon, as well as its placement. The Commission has concluded that even a relatively modest to small yield weapon of particular characteristics, using design and fabrication information already disseminated through licit and illicit means can produce a potentially devastating E1 field strength over very large geographical regions.

A key issue for the Commission in assessing the impact of such a disruption to the nation's electrical system was not only the unprecedented widespread nature of the outage (e.g. the cascading effects from even one or two relatively small weapons exploded in optimum location in space would almost certainly shut down an entire interconnected electrical power system, perhaps affecting as much as 70% or possibly more of the United States, all in an instant) but more significantly, widespread damage may well adversely impact the time to recover and thus have a potentially catastrophic impact.

After a few days, what little production that does take place would be offset by accumulating loss of perishables, collapse of business, loss of the financial systems and dislocation of the work force. The consequences of lack of food, heat (or air conditioning), water, waste disposal, medical, police, fire fighting support and effective civil authority would threaten society itself.

All production for these large transformers used in the United States is currently offshore. Delivery time for these items under benign circumstances is typically one to two years. There are about 2,000 such transformers rated at or above 345 kVk in the United States. Delivery of a new large transformer ordered today is nearly 3 years, including both manufacturing and transportation. An event damaging several of these transformers at once means it may extend delivery time to well beyond current time frames as production is taxed.

Power plants, particularly newer ones, are highly sophisticated, very high speed machines and improper shutdown can damage or destroy any of the many critical components and can even cause a catastrophic failure. Nuclear plants are an exception due to the nature of their protection schemes. Proper shutdown depends on synchronized operation of multiple controllers and switches. For example, coal intake and exhaust turbines must operate together or else explosion or implosion of the furnace may occur. Power plant survivability depends on a great many protective systems creating multiple pathways to plant damage and failure. Restoration of some damage can be very long-term, certainly months and in some instances years. The loss of generation of any size itself would contribute to system-wide collapse and certainly would limit restoration.

It does not take many damaged plants, out of the many hundreds, to seriously impact the system operation and the ability to restore service. The fact that all power plants exposed to E1 EMP will be illuminated simultaneously (within one power cycle) making the situation extremely serious.

Generation start–up for most plants requires power from another source to drive pumps, fans, safety systems, fuel delivery and so on. In the case of EMP, large geographic areas of the electrical system will be down and there may be no existing system operating on the periphery for the generation and loads to be incrementally added with ease.

Protective and safety systems have to be carefully checked out before start-up or greater loss might occur. Repair of furnaces, boilers, turbines, blades, bearings and other heavy high value and long lead-time equipment would be limited by production and transportation availability once at-site spares are exhausted. While some spare components are at each site and sometimes in spare parts pools domestically, these would not cover very large high value items in most cases, so external sources would be needed. Often supply from an external source can take many weeks or several months in the best of times, and sometimes a year or more, if only one plant is seeking repair. With multiple plants affected at the same time, let alone considering infrastructure impediments, restoration time would certainly become protracted.

If the voice communications were completely interrupted, it would be difficult, but still reasonably possible to successfully continue operations, provided there were no significant system disruptions. However in the case of an EMP event with multiple simultaneous disruptions, continued operation is not possible. Restoration without some form of communication is also not possible. Communication is clearly critical to the path of restoration.

E1 is likely to disrupt and perhaps damage protective relays, not uniformly but in statistically very significant numbers. Left unprotected, as would likely result from E1 damage or degradation to the protective relays and the high value assets would likely suffer damage or the transient currents produced during the system collapse.

The harmonics cause transformers case heating and over currents in capacitors potentially resulting in fires.

The principal effect of EMP would be E1 induced arcing across the insulators that separate the power lines from the supporting wood or metal poles. The arcing can damage the insulator itself and in some cases result in pole-mounted transformer explosions. Damage to large numbers of insulators and pole mounted transformers could also result in a shortage of replacement parts.

The important effect of the loss of load in the EMP scenario is that it happens simultaneously. Thus it represents a substantial upset to the entire grid, causing the frequency to spin up and protective relays to open on generation and can by itself result in a cascading failure and blackout of the entire NERC region. Similarly, any consumer or industrial electrical device that is shut down or damaged by EMP contributes to the load loss and further drives the system to collapse. The Commission has concluded that the electrical system within the NERC region so disrupted will collapse with near certainty.

The intermediate time EMP, or E2 (E2 is an increased surge of damaging current that would follow the lesser E1 power surge), is similar in frequency regime to lightning, but vastly more widespread, like thousands to millions of simultaneous lightning strikes.

Adequate numbers of trained and experienced personnel will be a serious problem even if they could all be contacted and could make themselves available. Several substations tripping nearly simultaneously would lead itself to system collapse.

All of these collapsed mechanisms acting simultaneously provide the unambiguous conclusion that electrical power system collapse for the NERC region largely impacted by the EMP weapon is inevitable in the event of attack using even a relatively low-yield device of particular characteristics.

During Hurricane Katrina the blackout caused gas stations to cease operating paralyzing transportation and greatly impeding evacuation efforts. The Katrina blackout, which affected the region for weeks and lasted for months in some localities, so severely impeded recovery efforts that even 3 years later New Orleans and its vicinity is still far from being fully recovered.

A power generation facility may trip because a surge of current is unexpectedly presented through a fault from a particular load. Yet a substantial portion of the system may well be rendered out of service as the disruption triggers a series of cascading failures, each instigating the next failure. In the case of an EMP attack, elements within many critical facility components are likely to be damaged or disrupted simultaneously over a relatively broad geographic area, thus creating an almost certain cascading collapse of the remaining elements.

Skilled labor for a massive and diverse repair effort is not currently available if allocated over a large geographic area with great numbers of components and devices to check and repair where necessary. This scope of damage could cover perhaps 70% or possibly more of the continental United States as well as a significant part of Canada's population. This is far too large to bring in the limited skilled labor from very distant points outside the affected area in any reasonable time.

Other infrastructures would be similarly impacted simultaneously with the electrical system such as transportation, communication, and even water and food to sustain crews. The ability to find and get spare parts and components or purchase services would be severely hampered by lack of normal financial systems in addition to communication transportation, and other factors. The Hurricane Katrina blackout caused precisely such problems.

Expert judgment and rational extrapolation of models and predictive tools suggest that restoration to even a diminished but workable state of electrical service could well take many weeks, with some probability of it taking months and perhaps more than a year at many locations; at that point, society as we know it couldn't exist within large regions of the nation. The larger the affected area the stronger the field strength from the attack, the longer will be the time to recover. Restoration to our current standard of electric power cost and reliability would almost certainly take years with severe impact on the economy and all that it entails.

The electrical system must be protected against the consequences of an EMP event to the extent reasonably possible. The level of vulnerability and extreme consequence combine to invite an EMP attack. The reduction of our vulnerability to attack and the resulting consequences reduce the probability of attack. It is also clear the Cold War type of deterrence through mutual assured destruction is not an effective threat against many of the potential protagonists.

2. TELECOMMUNICATIONS

The major elements of the civilian telecommunication network are electronic systems with circuit boards, integrated circuit chips, and cable connections such as routers that switch and transport information between users of the network (e.g. transport phone

213

calls). Like the equipment that generates demand on the network, these electronics have an inherent vulnerability to EMP threats.

The Commission sponsored testing and analytical efforts that led to the conclusion that an EMP attack would disrupt or damage a functionally significant fraction of the electronic circuits in the nation's civilian telecommunications systems in the geographic region exposed to EMP. Extended power outages will exacerbate attempts to repair damage and lead to fuel shortages that end up taking network capacity off-line.

The situation becomes more serious if the power outages are long term and widespread. In such cases, the likely loss of major telecommunications facilities would significantly reduce NS/EP services. A majority of residential telephones today depend on power from local central offices, which would be lost once the backup power at these offices is depleted. Other residential telephones also require commercial power to function. Thus, citizen ability to access 911 call centers would be a major concern in an extended power outage situation.

Hurricane Katrina in August 2005 damaged cell phone towers and radio antennas. The prolonged blackout resulting from Katrina exhausted the fuel supplies of backup generators servicing emergency communications. Consequently, emergency communications for police, emergency services and rescue efforts failed. Significantly, these same nodes, so critical to emergency communications—cell phone towers and radio antennas—are vulnerable to an EMP attack. A protracted blackout resulting from an EMP attack would also exhaust fuel supplies for emergency generators just as occurred during Hurricane Katrina.

Public telecommunication networks can successfully handle a local power outage or short term outage, such as the August 14, 2003 Northeast blackout. However, a major concern exists with outage durations that range in weeks or months. The widespread collapse of the electric grid due to an EMP event would lead to cascading effects on interdependent infrastructures as happened during the Katrina blackout.

3. BANKING AND FINANCE

Today, most significant transactions are performed and recorded electronically; however, the ability to carry out these transactions is highly dependent on other elements of the national infrastructure. According to the President's National Security Telecommunications Advisory Committee (NSTAC), "The financial services industry has evolved to a point where it would be impossible to operate without the efficiencies of information technology and networks."

The increasing dependence of the United States on an electronic economy, so beneficial to the management and creation of wealth, also increases U.S. vulnerability to an electromagnetic pulse (EMP) attack. Because financial markets are highly interdependent, a wide-scale disruption of core clearing and settlement processes would have an immediate systemic effect on critical financial markets.

Virtually all transactions involving banks and other financial institutions happen electronically. Virtually all record keeping of financial transactions are stored electronically. Just as paper money has replaced precious metals, so an electronic economy has replaced the paper one. The electronic technologies that are the foundation of the financial infrastructure are potentially vulnerable to EMP. These systems also are potentially vulnerable to EMP indirectly through other critical infrastructures, such as the power grid and telecommunications.

EMP effects propagate at the speed of light and would cover a broad geographic area. Such an attack potentially could achieve the NAS criteria for financial infrastructure catastrophic "simultaneous destruction of all data backup and backup facilities in all locations." An EMP would probably not erase data stored on magnetic tape. However, by shutting down power grids and damaging or disrupting data retrieval systems, EMP could deny access to essential records stored on tapes and compact discs. Financial operations could not tolerate the kind of disruptions or mass systemic destruction likely to follow an EMP attack. Disruption of these systems would force consumers to revert to a cash economy.

The Katrina blackout, comparable to a small EMP attack, disrupted normal business life for months and resulted in a staggering economic loss that is still an enormous drain on the national economy. The financial network is highly dependent on power and telecommunications for normal operations. Widespread power outages would shut down the network, and all financial activity would cease until power was restored.

An EMP attack that disrupts the financial services industry would in effect stop the operation of the U.S. economy. Business transactions that create wealth and jobs could not be performed. Loans for corporate capitalization and for private purposes, such as buying homes and automobiles could not be made. Wealth recorded electronically in bank databases could become inaccessible overnight. Credit, debit, and ATM cards would be useless.

In the immediate aftermath of an EMP attack, banks would find it very difficult to operate and provide the public with the liquidity they require to survive; that is to buy food, water, gas or other essential supplies and services. An EMP attack that damages the power grid or electronic data retrieval systems would render banking transactions virtually impossible as a practical or legal matter.

A survey by Commission staff on natural and man made disasters found no case in which banks, bereft of their electronic systems because of blackout, reopened their doors and did business by hand. Unless banks have well prepared contingency plans in place to revert to paper and handwritten transactions in advance it is very doubtful that bank managers would have the capability.

A related NAS study concludes that an attack that destroys only electronic records would be "catastrophic and irreversible." Data and essential records are useless if inaccessible. According to the NAS, "Irrecoverable loss of critical operating data and essential records on a large scale would likely result in catastrophic and irreversible damage to U.S. society.

4. PETROLEUM AND NATURAL GAS

The United States economy is dependent on the availability of energy. All of these energy resources were delivered from their points of production or ports of entry to users for further distribution points through the national pipeline system.

Control system components with low voltage and current requirements, such as integrated circuits, digital computers, and digital circuitry, are ubiquitous in the U.S. commercial petroleum and natural gas infrastructures, and EMP caused failures can induce dangerous system malfunctions resulting in fires or explosions.

The pipeline system consists of more than 300,000 miles of interstate and intrastate transmission lines and an additional 1.8 million miles of smaller distribution lines that move gas closer to cities and individual homes and businesses.

The infrastructure described in the previous section is dependent on the continuous operation of a wide variety of electrical components; pumps to extract fuel from wells and manage its movement through pipelines, electrically driven systems to process materials in refineries, transportation systems to deliver fuels to users from storage sites, point-of-sale electronics to process transactions to retail customers, and so on, all of which represent potential points of vulnerability to an EMP pulse.

Pumping facilities that produce thousands of horsepower of energy and metering facilities that measure thousands of barrels per hour are routinely operated remotely via these systems. They can be properly operated only by using extremely reliable communications systems. The control aspect may include controls to a well pump to increase or decrease output or to shut it down altogether.

The principal electronic components of a SCADA system are most vulnerable to an EMP attack. They are found in all the major subsystems of the SCADA installation. If the SCADA system for an oil pipeline is inoperative due to the effects of an EMP event, it is the opinion of a number of former pipeline personnel that operations would have to be shut down. A petroleum pipeline failure can be catastrophic. Leaking oil could contaminate water supplies and cause disastrous fires. U.S. refineries are critically dependent on the computers and integrated circuitry associated with process control, which are vulnerable to EMP effects.

The petroleum and natural gas infrastructures are critically dependent on the availability of assured electric power from the national grid, as well as all the other critical national infrastructures, including food and emergency services that sustain the personnel manning these infrastructures. In turn, all these infrastructures rely on the availability of fuels provided by the petroleum and natural gas sector.

5. TRANSPORTATION INFRASTRUCTURE

Railroad Control Centers have no specific electromagnetic protection. Some buildings require chilled water for continuing computer operations. The buildings are interconnected by a fiber-optic ring and telephone lines. None of this equipment has specific EMP protection, and there is no data on the EMP vulnerability of this equipment. It is important to note that computer failure or total loss of power in the locomotives could cause loss of electrical control for the brakes.

Today, cities typically have a food supply of only several days available on grocery shelves for their customers. Replenishment of that food supply depends on a continuous flow of trucks from food processing centers to food distribution centers to warehouses and to grocery stores and restaurants. If urban food supply flow is substantially interrupted for an extended period of time, hunger and mass evacuation, and even starvation and anarchy could result.

Trucks also deliver other essentials. Fuel delivered to metropolitan areas through pipelines is not accessible to the public until it is distributed by tanker trucks to gas stations. Garbage removal, utility repair operations, fire equipment and numerous other services are delivered using specially outfitted trucks. Nearly 80% of all manufactured goods at some point in the chain, from manufacturer to consumer are transported by truck. An EMP attack will certainly immediately disable a portion of the 130 million cars and 90 million trucks in operation in the United States. Vehicles disabled while operating on the road can be expected to cause accidents. Vehicles need fuel and service stations need electricity to power pumps.

The potential EMP vulnerability of automobiles derives from the use of builtin electronics that support multiple automotive functions. Modern automobiles have as many as 100 microprocessors that control virtually all functions.

6. FOOD INFRASTRUCTURE

A high-altitude electromagnetic pulse (EMP) attack can damage or disrupt the infrastructure that supplies food to the population of the United States. The food infrastructure depends critically for its operation on electricity and on other infrastructures that rely on electricity. An EMP attack could disrupt, damage, or destroy these systems which are necessary in making, processing and distributing food

Agriculture for growing all major crops requires large quantities of water, usually supplied through irrigation or other artificial means using electric pumps, valves and other machinery to draw or redirect water from aquifers, aqueducts and reservoirs. Tractors and farm equipment for plowing, planting, tending, and harvesting crops have electronic ignition systems and other electronic components. Farm machinery runs on gasoline and petroleum products supplied by pipelines, pumps, and transportation systems that run on electricity or that depend on electronic components. Fertilizers and insecticides that make possible high yields from croplands are manufactured and applied through means containing various electronic components. Egg farms and poultry farms typically sustain dense populations in carefully controlled environments using automated feeding, watering and air conditioning systems. Dairy farms rely heavily on electrically powered equipment for milking cows and for making other dairy products. These are just a few examples of how modern food production depends on electrical equipment and the electric power grid which are both potentially vulnerable to EMP.

Food processing also requires electricity. Cleaning, sorting, packaging and canning of all kinds of agricultural products are performed by electrically powered machinery. Butchering, cleaning, and packaging of poultry, pork, beef, fish and other meat products also are typically automated operations, done on electrically driven processing lines. An EMP attack could render inoperable the electric equipment and automated systems that are ubiquitous and indispensable to the modern food processing industry.

Food distribution also depends heavily on electricity. Vast quantities of vegetables, fruits, and meats are stored in warehouses where they are preserved by refrigeration systems, ready for distribution to supermarkets. Refrigerated trucks and trains are the main means of moving perishable foods to market; therefore, food distribution also has a critical dependence on the infrastructure for ground transportation. Ground transportation relies on the electric grid that powers electric trains; runs pipelines and pumping stations for gasoline and powers signal lights, street lights, switching tracks and other electronic equipment for regulating traffic on roads and rails.

Because supermarkets typically carry only enough food to supply local populations for one to three days and need to be re-supplied continually from regional warehouses, transportation and distribution of food to supermarkets may be the weakest link in the food infrastructure in the event of an EMP attack. The trend toward modernization of supermarkets may exacerbate this problem by deliberately reducing the amount of food stored in supermarkets and regional warehouses in favor of a new "just-in-time" food distribution system. The new system relies on electronic databases to keep track of supermarket inventories so that they can be replaced with fresh foods exactly when needed, greatly reducing the need for large stocks of warehouse foods.

The electric power grid on which the food infrastructure depends has been component tested and evaluated against EMP, and it's known to be vulnerable. Moreover, power grid blackouts induced by storms and mechanical failures on numerous occasions have caused massive failure of supermarket refrigeration systems and impeded transportation and distribution of food. This has resulted in spoilage of perishable foods and caused food shortages lasting days or sometimes weeks. These storm-and-accident-induced blackouts of the power grid are not likely to have consequences as severe or as geographically widespread for the food infrastructure as an EMP attack would.

In the face of some natural disasters like Hurricane Andrew in 1991, federal, state and local emergency services combined have sometimes been hard pressed to provide the endangered populations with food. Fortunately, there are few known instances of actual food starvation fatalities in the United States. In such localized emergencies as Hurricane Andrew, neighboring areas of the disaster area are usually able to provide needed emergency services (food, water, fire and medical services) in a timely fashion.

In the case of Hurricane Andrew, for example, although the area of the damage was relatively small, the level of damage was extraordinary and many people were affected. Consequently, emergency services were brought in not just from neighboring states, but from many *distant* states. For example, electric transformers were brought in from other states to help rebuild the local power grid. The net result was a nationwide shortage of transformers for one year until replacements could be produced from overseas suppliers, who needed six months to build new transformers.

Yet an EMP attack potentially could disrupt or collapse the food infrastructure over a large region encompassing many cities for a protracted period of weeks, months, or even longer. Widespread damage of the infrastructures would impede the ability of undamaged fringe areas to aid in recovery. Therefore it is highly possible that the recovery time would be very slow and the amount of human suffering great, including loss of life.

Because the United States is a food superpower with relatively few farmers, technology is no longer a convenience. It is indispensable to the farmers who must feed the nation's population and much of the rest of the world.

In 1900, 39% of the U.S. population (about 30 million people) lived on farms; today, that percentage has plummeted to less than 2% (only about 4.5 million people). The United States no longer has a large labor force skilled in farming that could be mobilized in an emergency. The transformation of the United States from a nation of farmers to a nation in which less than 2% of the population is able to feed the other 98% is made possible only by technology. Crippling that technology would be injurious to the food infrastructure with its security depending on the characteristics of an EMP attack.

The food processing industry is an obvious technological choke-point in the U.S. food infrastructure. Food processing of vegetables, fruits and all kinds of meat is a highly automated assembly-line operation, largely driven by electric power. An EMP attack that damages this machinery or blacks out the power grid would stop food processing. The work force in the food processing industry is sized and trained to run a largely automated system. In the event of an attack that stops the machines from running, personnel would not be sufficiently numerous or knowledgeable to process food the old fashioned way, by hand. Depending on climate, most foods that are not refrigerated would begin to spoil in a few hours or days.

Finally, the distribution system is probably the most vulnerable technological chokepoint in the U.S. food infrastructure.

Regional warehouses are probably the United States' best near-term defense against a food shortage because of the enormous quantities of foodstuffs stored there. For example, one typical warehouse in New York City received daily deliveries of food from more than 20 tractor-trailers and redistributes to market more than 480,000 pounds of food. The warehouse is larger than several football fields, occupying more than 100,000 square feet. Packaged, canned and fresh foods are stored in palletized stacks 35 feet high. Enormous refrigerators preserve vegetables, fruits and meats and the entire facility is temperature controlled.

However, regional warehouses potentially are vulnerable to an attack that collapses the power grid and causes refrigeration and temperature controls to fail. Moreover, the large quantities of food kept in regional warehouses will do little to alleviate a crisis if it cannot be distributed to the population promptly. Distribution depends largely on trucks and a functioning transportation system.

An EMP attack that disrupts the food infrastructure could pose a threat to life, industrial activity and social order. Absolute deprivation of food, on average, will greatly diminish a person's capacity for physical work within a few days. After four to five days without food the average person will suffer from impaired judgment and have difficulty performing simple intellectual tasks. After 2 weeks without food, the average person will be virtually incapacitated. Death typically results after one or two months without food.

A natural disaster or deliberate attack that makes food less available, or more expensive would place at least America's poor, 316 million people at grave risk. They would have the least food stockpiled at home and be the first to need food supplies. A work force preoccupied with finding food would be unable to perform its normal jobs. Social order likely would decay if a food shortage were protracted. A government that cannot supply the population with enough food to preserve health and life could face anarchy.

In the event of a crisis, often merely in the event of bad weather, supermarket shelves are quickly stripped as some people begin to hoard food. The ability to promptly replenish supermarket food supplies becomes imperative in order to avoid mass hunger.

An EMP attack that damages the power grid and denies electricity to warehouses or that directly damages refrigeration and temperature control systems could destroy most of the 30-day regional perishable food supply. Blackouts also have disrupted transportation systems and impeded the replenishment of local food supplies.

Hurricane Katrina caused a protracted blackout in New Orleans and the coastal region destroying the food supply. Flooding, downed trees and washed out bridges paralyzed transportation. But the Katrina blackout by itself was sufficient to stop transportation and prevent rapid replenishment and repair of the food infrastructure because gas stations could not operate without electric power.

An EMP attack could also paralyze transportation of food by rendering gas pumps inoperable, causing vehicles to fail and blacking out traffic lights, resulting in massive traffic jams. Hurricane Katrina's destruction of the food supply was a major contributing factor to the necessity of mass evacuation of New Orleans and the coastal population. Because many evacuees never returned, the protracted disruption of the food infrastructure, which lasted weeks and in some localities months while the electric power grid was being restored, was a major factor contributing to permanently reducing the population of New Orleans and coastal Louisiana. Hurricane Katrina's effect on the food infrastructure is comparable to what can be expected from a small EMP attack.

Inn September 1999Hurricane Floyd in September 1999 put more than 200 supermarkets out of operation in North Carolina. Protracted blackouts caused massive food spoilage despite emergency efforts taken before the storm to preserve perishable goods in freezers. Floyd blackouts also impeded replenishment of some supermarkets by inducing traffic signal failures that contributed to massive traffic jams.

An ice storm blacked out the Washington, D.C. area in January 1999. Warm food, potentially a survival issue in the freezing winter conditions, was not available in most people's homes because electric ovens no longer worked.

In addition, most gas-powered ovens would not work because those built since the mid 1980's have electronic ignition and cannot be lit with a match.

Food poisoning became a real threat when a storm affected the power grid. The embattled people of Montreal were unable to use stoves. They could not eat food that had been kept too long in refrigerators that no longer worked.

Hurricane Andrew in August 1992 laid waste to 165 square miles in South Florida and left 3.3 million homes and businesses without electricity. Andrew's aftermath posed an immediate threat to life in South Florida, in part, because of damage to the food infrastructure. Most grocery stores had been destroyed.

Andrew's blackout of the power grid made the crisis over food, water and shelter worse by severing communications between relief workers and victims. Without power, there was an almost complete collapse of communications—no telephones, radio or television. Consequently, many people were unaware of relief efforts or of where to go for help. Had Hurricane Andrew damaged a larger area, it is likely that undamaged fringe areas would have been less capable of coming to the rescue, resulting in a significant loss of life.

Compared to blackouts, an EMP attack could inflict damage over a wider geographic area and damage a much wider array of equipment; consequently, recovery of the food infrastructure from EMP is likely to be much more complicated and more protracted.

Federal, state and local agencies combined would find it difficult to cope immediately, or even over a protracted period of days or weeks, following an EMP attack that causes the food infrastructure to fail across a broad geographic area encompassing one or more states. Infrastructure failure at the level of food distribution because of disruption of the transportation system, as is likely during an EMP attack, could bring on food shortage affecting the general population is as little as 24 hours.

Yet an EMP attack could so damage the food infrastructure that millions of people would be at risk. Federal, state and local agencies combined would find it difficult to cope immediately or even over a protracted period of days or weeks following an EMP attack that caused the food infrastructure to fail across a broad geographic area encompassing one or more states.

The United States is a food superpower. Of the world's 183 nations, only a few are net exporters of grain. The United States, Canada, Australia and Argentina supply over 80% of the net cereal grains exported worldwide—the United States alone providing more than half. A collapse of the food infrastructure in America would cause the potential of worldwide starvation.

7. WATER INFRASTRUCTURE

Water and its system of supply is a vital infrastructure. High-altitude electromagnetic pulse EMP can damage or disrupt the infrastructure that supplies water to the population, agriculture, and industry of the United States.

By making water move uphill, the gravity pump has made possible the construction and growth of cities and towns in locations that in previous centuries would have been impossible. Skyscrapers and high-rise buildings, which would be impractical, are dependent on a gravity-fed water system made possible by the electric pump.

Electrically driven pumps, valves, filters, and a wide variety of other electrical machinery are indispensable for the purification of water for drinking and industrial purposes and for delivering water to consumers. An EMP attack could degrade or damage these systems, affecting the delivery of water to a very large geographical region.

Electrical machinery is also indispensable to the removal and treatment of wastewater. An EMP attack that degraded the processes for removing and treating wastewater could quickly cause public health problems over a wide area.

The electric power grid provides the energy that runs the water infrastructure. An EMP attack that disrupts or collapses the power grid would disrupt or stop the operation of the SCADA'S and electrical machinery in the water infrastructure.

Federal, state and local emergency services, faced with the failure of the water infrastructure in a single large city, would be hard pressed to provide the population with the minimum water requirements necessary to sustain life over a time frame longer than a few days. An EMP attack could disrupt the water infrastructure over a large geographic area encompassing many cities for a protracted period or even months.

Electrically driven pumps, valves, filters and a wide variety of other machinery and control mechanisms purify and deliver water to consumers and remove wastewater. An EMP attack could damage or destroy these systems, cutting off the water supply or poisoning the water supply with chemicals and pathogens from wastewater.

High-lift and low-lift pumps are ubiquitous throughout the infrastructure for purifying and delivering water and removing wastewater. Water cannot be purified or delivered nor sewage removal be treated if these systems are damaged or destroyed. Paddle flocculates and other types of mixers are the primary means of chlorination and other chemical purification. If these systems cease functioning, water cannot be purified and likely would remain hazardous. Denial of water can cause death in three to four days, depending on the climate and level of activity.

Resupplying local stores with water would be difficult in the aftermath of an EMP attack that disrupts transportation systems, a likely condition if all critical infrastructures were disrupted.

People are likely to resort to drinking from lakes, streams, ponds and other sources of surface water. Most surface water, especially in urban areas is contaminated with wastes and pathogens and could cause serious illness if consumed.

Boiling water for purification would be difficult in the absence of electricity. Even most modern gas stoves require electricity for ignition and cannot be lighted by a match. In any event, gas also may not be available to light the stoves.

Most industrial processes require large quantities of water and would cease if the water infrastructure failed.

Demoralization and deterioration of social order can be expected to deepen if a water shortage is protracted. Anarchy will certainly loom if government cannot supply the population with enough water to preserve health and life.

Federal, state, and local governments do not have the collective capability, if the water infrastructure fails over a large area to supply enough water to the civilian population to preserve life.

Storm-induced blackouts of the electric grid have demonstrated that in the absence of electric power, the water infrastructure will fail.

Montreal officials feared not only a shortage of drinking water, but also an inadequate supply of water for fighting fires.

8. EMERGENCY SERVICES

Emergency services are essential to the preservation of law and order, maintenance of public health and safety and protection of property. Americans have come to rely on prompt and effective delivery of fire, police, rescue and emergency medical services through local government systems.

An EMP attack will adversely affect emergency services' ability to accomplish these objectives in two distinct ways: by increasing the demand for services and by decreasing the ability to deliver them.

The demand for assistance will increase greatly in the event of an EMP attack. The possibility of fire caused by electrical arcing resulting from an EMP attack cannot be ruled out. Fires indirectly caused by an EMP attack, principally because of people being careless with candles used for emergency lighting or with alternative heating sources during power blackouts, are also a concern.

If electric power is interrupted for any period of time, people at home who depend on oxygen concentrators, respirators, aspirators and other life–sustaining equipment that require electric power will need to find alternative solutions quickly.

If power is out for more than several days, people dependent on dialysis machines, nebulizers and other life-supporting medical devices also will be at risk. Finally, inability to replenish home supplies of medicines will eventually lead still more people to depend on emergency services.

If looting or other forms of civil disorder break out, it is likely that local police services will be overwhelmed.

On the other hand, when the failure of police and emergency services becomes protracted, the lawless element of society may emerge. For example, Hurricane Katrina, in August 2005, damaged cell phone towers and radio antennas that were crucial to the operation of emergency communications. Consequently, government, police and emergency services were severely impacted in their ability to communicate with the public and with each other. Looting, violence and other criminal activities were serious problems in the aftermath of Katrina.

Some equipment needed to perform emergency services will be temporarily upset or directly damaged by an EMP attack, resulting in diminished capabilities.

Computers are essential to normal PSAP operations. Computer failures can be expected at relatively low EMP field levels of 3 to 6 kilovolts per meter (kV/m). At higher field levels, additional failures are likely in computers, routers, network switches and keyboards embedded in the computer-aided dispatch, public safety radio, and mobile data communications equipment.

9. SPACE SYSTEMS

Commercial satellites support many significant services for the Federal Government including communications, remote sensing, weather forecasting and imaging. The national security and Homeland Security use satellites for critical activities including backup communications, emergency response services, and continuity of operations during emergencies. GPS and military uses are factors that are necessary for our military superiority.

The identical problems that an EMP bomb poses for electronics here on earth will be problems for the destruction of our satellites in orbit. This would be catastrophic for our way of life. I will comment no further on this threat as it would simply be repetitious.

The complete text of the report of the Commission can be seen on the web at www.empcommission.org/does/empc_exec_rpt.pdf

CONCLUDING THOUGHTS

It was tragic, that after the Commission completed its work, the Department of Homeland Security decided to classify its contents.

But after about 5 years the report was released and is summarized in this chapter. The effect of classifying the report those years was to keep the public without knowledge of the threat of an EMP. That fact, in turn, has delayed any effort to address the problem. The reason given for classifying the report of the Commission was to avoid handing terrorists a "cookbook" on how to disrupt the grid.[25]

> Dr. Graham warned that it will not be just civilians at risk from an EMP event. Given our armed forces' reliance on critical national infrastructures (e.g. electric power, telecommunications, food and water), a cascading failure of these infrastructures could seriously jeopardize our military's ability to execute its missions in support of our national security. Projection of military power from air bases and seaports requires electricity, fuel, food and water. The coordination of military operations depends on telecommunications and information systems that are also indispensable to society as a whole. Within the U.S. these assets are in most cases obtained by the military from our critical national infrastructures.[26]

So the EMP threat from a nation that is really weak could literally destroy a super power; thus, you have the potential fulfillment of an important end time prophecy declared by the prophet Joel thousands of years ago. Joel 3:10: "Beat your plowshares into swords and your pruning hooks into spears; Let the weak say, 'I am strong.'"

To sum up this section, allow me to quote various people with intelligence information that serve as a fitting understanding of the problem of an EMP attack. In *Town Hall Magazine*, Peter Brookes explains it in simple terms with the following words:

> All modern electrical conveniences we take for granted on a day-to-day basis in the 21st century go kaput—without an obvious explanation. And as a result, modern life as we know it comes to a virtual standstill. Moreover, in the blink of an eye, U.S.

military forces within line-of-sight of the EMP—up to this moment the world's most potent, computerized, and capable forces—is now practically out of business. One estimate suggests a major EMP attack would push American society back 100 years technologically.[27]

In a recent video before EMPACT America's EMP conference, Newt Gingrich, who is a senior fellow at the American Enterprise Institute, said that an EMP attack is the greatest strategic threat we face, because without adequate preparation, its impact would be so horrifying that we would basically lose our civilization in a matter of seconds.

Dr. William Graham, the chairman of the committee appointed by President Clinton said, "If there were an EMP attack, the impact would be something you might imagine life to be like around the 1800's, but with several times the population we had in those days and without the ability to support and sustain all these people. Starvation would be a distinct possibility. Life would be even more primitive than the 1800's since back then many more were in the farming business.[28]

According to the *WND News Agency* the Department of Homeland Security told Congress that life in the United States would be unsustainable after an EMP attack:[29]

At its core are information technology and networks without which the industry cannot operate. That is to say, when the power goes out, our money for all intents and purposes disappears and becomes unreachable until the lights go back on. And not just the small amounts of cash we have saved in our local bank, but our investments.

So today we have to assume that an EMP attack on the U.S. financial infrastructure could achieve the simultaneous destruction of all data backups and backup facilities in all locations. Wealth, recorded electronically in bank databases could become inaccessible overnight. Credit, debit, and ATM cards could become useless.[30]

Maloof made this keen observation in his book on the result of an EMP attack on America:

> Prior to his death in September 2000, retired U.S. Army Lieutenant General Robert L. Schweitzer pointed out that 90% of our military communications now pass over civilian networks. If an electromagnetic pulse takes out the telephone systems, we are in deep trouble because our military and non-military nets are virtually inseparable. It is almost equally impossible to distinguish between the U.S. national telecommunication network and the global one. It is finally becoming possible to do what Sun Tzu wrote about 2000 years ago: to conquer an enemy without fighting. The paradigm of war may well be changing. If you can take out the civilian economic infrastructure of a nation, then that nation—in addition to not being able to function internally cannot deploy its military by air or sea, or supply them with any real effectiveness—if at all.[31]

CYBER ATTACKS

Another way in which weak nations can cause catastrophic damage to a powerful nation is through cyber attacks on high-voltage transformers. "They are difficult to move, custom built and take years to replace under normal circumstances. These transformers are no longer made in the United States. They rely on electronics, sensors and telecommunications which are linked to the outside and are not secure." [32]

Following is a lengthy article from *Blaze Magazine* that helps us understand how incredible the problem of cyber attacks has become:

> In pleading with Congress Wednesday against automatic defense budget cuts, Defense Secretary Leon Panetta also warned of another crippling situation like Pearl Harbor. It won't come in the form of bombers and torpedo planes though, but as hackers and worms of the cyber variety with the ability to cripple U.S. infrastructure.
>
> *CNS News* reports Paretta saying that those with the capability to launch a cyber attack would be able to "paralyze" the United States. Sen. Lindsey Graham (R-S.C.) asked Panetta to clarify. "You said something that just kind of went over everybody's head, I think, that there's a Pearl Harbor in the making here. You're talking about shutting down financial systems, releasing chemicals from chemical plants, releasing water from dams, shutting down power systems that can affect the very survival of the nation. What's the likelihood in the next five years that one of these major events will occur?" To this Panetta responded simply by saying that the "technological capability" to send our country into a mode like that of Pearl Harbor in a surprise attack is already available *now*. Panetta's references to "the next Pearl Harbor" echo sentiments he shared last year with regard to cyber-attacks, according to *CNS News*.
>
> In June, 2011, while being confirmed Defense Secretary, Panetta said to the panel, "The next Pearl Harbor we confront could very well be a cyber attack that cripples our power systems, our grid, our security systems, our financial systems, and our government

systems." Those in the United States—both the government and private industry—are already the targets of thousands of attacks per day, according to Panetta. With that, he notes the importance of improving safety of systems in not only the defense sector but the private sector as well.

The Pentagon faces cuts of about $500 billion in projected spending over ten years on top of the $492 billion that President Obama and Congressional Republicans already agreed to in last summer's deficit cutting budget. Dempsy said cuts would mean fewer troops, the possible cancellation of major weapons and the disruption of operations around the world.[33]

Ron Rhodes has written a book, which he called *Cyber Meltdown*. I will give samples of what his outstanding research has produced so you can get a picture as to the dangerous future that such attacks pose to America. The book was published by Harvest House Publishers and can be purchased at most bible book stores. I would recommend you get a copy of the book, as it is a true eye-opener to a very alarming future.

Rhodes shares the following shocking insights, which should serve to enlighten you on this subject, and give you a small glimpse of what is contained in the book. Only by reading the entire book can you get the full picture. Rhodes reveals that the number of security events per month has shot up to 1.8 billion. Over 13 million computer attacks are launched each day against the Senate Security Operations Center. Not a moment passes that is free of attack.

Richard Clarke, former antiterrorism czar to President Bill Clinton and George W. Bush, warns that through cyber attacks great damage can be done to the very infrastructure of America. He tells that there would be computer shutdowns in the Pentagon with defense networks grinding to a halt. Computer systems that control air traffic would collapse and infrastructure attacks could cause refinery fires and explosions in various cities. He warns of chemical plants exploding and releasing lethal clouds of chlorine gas into the air. He talks of major gas pipelines exploding in cities, freight train derailments, blackouts over large areas taking place in just a few minutes without a single terrorist or soldier ever appearing in this country.

U.S. cyber experts have discovered that computer hackers from Russia and/or China have successfully planted software in the U.S. electricity grid infrastructure. These logic bombs could be activated from a remote location to sabotage the electric system at a later date.

One way of shutting down a computer system used by a bank, the military or any other agency is to overload the system with thousands of messages at the same time. This is often accomplished by putting an information site with useful information on the Internet that many people would have an interest in. When you click on such a site, the person who posted it has installed a software code that installs into your computer without your knowing that it happened. There is not an indication that anything unusual is going on, but it gives the hacker the ability to use your computer when it is turned on. In this way, your computer becomes a robot for the hacker. At a point in time, he can send tens of thousands of messages to a computer system which he wants to shut down. He has unlimited numbers of computers he can use to do his evil work of destruction without the owners of the computers even knowing that their computers were used in the attack.

As a result of the ability of the hacker to use this method, U.S. government websites were receiving about a million hits per second. As a result the websites became temporarily unavailable. The servers shut down.

It is reported that China has produced routers for computer use that have codes installed in them which give them the ability to destroy the computer systems in which they are installed. The thing that makes users of such devices purchase them is because they are ridiculously cheap. Some of the buyers of these routers are the U.S. Pentagon, the Marine Corps and the Air Force. Imagine being a pilot in a warfare situation and suddenly the Chinese push a button and it creates damage to make the aircraft incapable of delivering its weapons. Perhaps it could even cause a mechanical problem that would cause the airplane to crash. What then? It seems stupid for American defense systems to be purchased from our enemies who are out to destroy us. We seem to be putting ourselves at risk in incalculable ways.

Software has been developed that can break into computers that control machinery at the heart of industry, allowing an attacker to assume control of critical systems such as pumps, motors, alarms and valves. It could, technically, make factory boilers explode, destroy gas pipelines or even cause a nuclear plant to malfunction. In other words, there are computer worms that can activate a sequence that causes the industrial process to self-destruct. Such computer worms can cause generators to shred themselves, high-tension power-transmission lines to burn, gas pipelines to explode and much more. Electrical generators on our own soil could be shut down by a foreign country through cyber attacks. Our own tests prove it. The implantation of this software in government network systems is called a *logic bomb,* which is malware or a computer code that contains instructions that can erase the data on a computer network that causes it to shut down. Once this logic bomb activates, a computer becomes a useless piece of hardware until it is wiped clean and software reinstalled. Then, after all of the work is completed what would stop the hacker from repeating his attack? Cyber experts are warning the government about Chinese and Russian penetrations in our country's electric grids, which depend on the Internet to function.

One of the problems with cyber crime is that an expert hacker can cover his tracks in such a way that no one knows for sure where the hacker came from.

There you have it! A country with a weaker and smaller army could have a team of a hundred talented computer hackers who could render great cyber damage to any country in the world. Therefore, many smaller nations may be able to inflict cyber damage on the United States that is equal to the United States' ability to inflict cyber harm on them. The United States may actually suffer more harm from such attacks because of its greater dependence on cyberspace. This could be a means of fulfilling the prophet's vision that in the end time weaker nations could claim they are powerful, when in reality, they are not. Joel 3:10, "Beat your plowshares into swords And your pruning hooks into spears; Let the weak say, 'I am strong.'"

Imagine a world where other countries can hack in our systems to plant a defective code in the product you are designing for the military, so it will not work during a future crisis. Imagine hackers planting logic bombs in the electricity grid and Internet backbones to shut them down as a strike against the military's command-and-control structure. One reason why many U.S. officials sense vulnerability is that our own cyber geniuses have discovered hard evidence that logic bombs and trapdoors have already been planted in U.S. networks. *They are already there.*

All of the above information about cyber attacks is a short review of material contained in the book, *Cyber Meltdown* by Ron Rhodes. The above does not even represent the tip of the iceberg of information and understanding to be found in this important and well-written work. I recommend that you purchase a copy of this book so that you can see and understand the entire chilling information for yourself. It is truly incredible and gives a formidable warning to prepare for such things.

CHAPTER 10

MODERN INVENTIONS IN PROPHECY

While the Bible is not a book of science, it is correct when it speaks about the subject of science. So-called scientists living during Bible times scoffed at the scientific statements the Bible made. Long ago, in Old Testament times, God spoke about scientific issues not yet discovered by men. The last two centuries have proven such Bible statements to be accurate, and the scientific guesses of scientists living in Old Testament times were wrong with what they believed contradicted what the Bible taught.

We have seen a similar situation in *our* day. Things stated as fact in the Bible thousands of years ago, were scoffed at by so-called scientists. Yet, scientific achievements that have taken place in our lifetime have shown the Bible to be accurate regarding these matters. Before getting into the signs of the times as they relate to the prediction of modern inventions, allow me to share with you a few of the multitudes of biblical scientific statements made before our time that were recently discovered to be accurate.

Isaiah 40:22 says: "It is He who sits above the circle of the earth, And its inhabitants are like grasshoppers, who stretches out the heavens like a curtain, and spreads them out like a tent to dwell in." The Hebrew word "KHUG" translated *circle* means roundness; thus, in this verse we find that the writers of Scripture knew the world was round. Until 322 BC all archaeological finds declared the earth to be flat. But in 322 BC Aristotle wondered if it couldn't be round because of the way ships disappeared. The idea was ruled out by the Romans. They continued to believe the earth was flat. Even in 1492 AD, "when Columbus sailed the ocean blue," people thought he would fall off the edge of the flat world.

In the day Job lived, most people believed the earth was supported by foundations. Here are a few of the tales that have come down to us through the ancients:

The Egyptians believed the earth was supported by five great pillars, one on each corner and one in the middle. I can understand that had the earth been flat someone could have peered over the corners and seen the four corner pillars. But what about the pillar in the middle?

The Greeks had this legend: Atlas stood with his head bowed bearing the earth on his neck and shoulders. I wonder what supported Atlas?

The Hindus ancient explanation was that the earth was balanced on the back of a giant elephant. The elephant is standing on the back of a large turtle and the turtle is swimming in a huge cosmic sea.

While people were dreaming up theories like that, Job wrote, in Job 26:7: "He stretches out the north over empty space; He hangs the earth on nothing." This is exactly what modern science believes today! All ancient scientists believed the earth was rigidly supported and all movement was in the heavens. It wasn't until 1687 AD that Sir Isaac Newton, with the telescope, proved the earth was, in fact, hung on *nothing*.

Next, I would have you note Job 38:7 where we learn that stars emit sound: "The morning stars sang together." Psalm 19:1-3 also gives information on this subject: "The heavens declare the glory of God; and the firmament shows His handiwork. Day unto day utters speech, and night unto night reveals knowledge. There is no speech nor language where their voice is not heard." The Hebrew word for sang is "ranan." That word pertains to the emitting of a loud shriek, shrill sound or noise. Again, science didn't catch up with this biblical scientific fact until World War II when we invented radar to detect German aircraft and submarines.

In February, 1942 radar received a loud noise so extreme that it couldn't be operated. At first it was thought that the Germans had developed some sort of a cramming device, but the source of the noise was found to be a sunspot. This discovery gave birth to the radio telescope. While the natural ear cannot hear the sounds, the radio telescope can! It has always been said this was Job's imagination for the stars cannot sing—or can they?

Light, color and sound are all fundamentally the same. There are waves of rays pulsating across our universe. Some reach the eye as light or color while others hit the ear as sound. There are rays of color so slow that you can't see them. These rays are grouped from infrared on down. There are rays of color so short and fast that you can't see them. This group are called ultra violet and up.

Exactly as there are light and color rays that do not reach the eye, so there are sound waves that do not reach the ear. Recent experiments have convinced scientists that every ray of light has a tonal value as well. The light of the sun, or any other star, carrying light through space carries with it a note of sound. So Job was scientifically correct when he said the stars sing—for where light is sound will accompany it.

How did Job know this thousands of years before men of science knew it? Men of science discovered this through advanced scientific instruments that were not available in Job's time. How did Job know? He knew because God told him.

Furthermore, the first book of the Bible teaches that all seas lie in one bed. Please note Genesis 1:9-10: "Then God said, Let the waters under the heavens be gathered together into one place, and let the dry land appear; and it was so. And God called the dry land Earth, and the gathering together of the waters He called Seas. And God saw that it was good."

The words "one place" in Genesis 1:9 is today what we would, call one bed. He states that the waters were called seas, plural—that is, more than one body of water, and all oceans lie in one bed. Thus he revealed that he understood that there was more than one body of water in this common bed. Yet, this fact was not known until the compass and improved sailing vessels made possible the trips of Magellan and Columbus. These exploratory trips established that a ship can sail around the world because all seas are in one bed. The discoveries of these men led to establishing the fact that all large bodies of salt water are inter-joined.

Another interesting scientific fact that Job knew about is seen in Job 38:16: "Have you entered the springs of the sea? Or have you walked in search of the depths?" Scientific facts are also spoken of this subject in 2 Samuel 22:16: "Then the channels of the sea were seen, The foundations of the world were uncovered, at the rebuke of the LORD, at the blast of the breath of His nostrils." The word "channels" means canyons. The word "search" that Job used can also be translated canyons. It wasn't until 1873 that scientists even knew there were canyons in the sea. As a result of echo sounding, developed in World War II, we now know the bottom of the sea has mountain ranges. Another recent discovery along the lines of oceanography was the discovery of springs in the oceans.

Moses spoke of the flood in Genesis 7:11 and Genesis 8:2: "In the six hundredth year of Noah's life, in the second month, the seventeenth day of the month, on that day all the fountains of the great deep were broken up, and the windows of heaven were opened. The fountains of the deep and the windows of heaven were also stopped, and the rain from heaven was restrained." Science knew absolutely nothing about this subject until 1930. It was then a deep sea diving expedition was conducted by the National Geographic Society. They found fresh water welling up in the ocean. As a result of this expedition, scientific investigation was made, and it was discovered that what the Bible had declared thousands of years ago was true.

Still another example of scientific information in the Bible, relative to the oceans, is seen in the words written atop all pilot charts used in the U.S. Navy. The charts state: "Founded upon the researches made and data collected by. Lt. M.S. Maury, U.S. Navy." This is the man who in 1855 AD discovered that the oceans have roads in them. Upon discovering them he charted sea lanes and currents. Yet, thousands of years before Mr. Maury, the Bible told us in Psalm 8:8: "The birds of the air, and the fish of the sea that pass through the paths of the seas." The Hebrew word "paths" carries the literal meaning of customary roads. Thus, David knew there were roads or customary paths in the sea and that life passed through these roads.

Even the birds of the air follow these roads as the fish of the sea are in them. Since Maury's discovery of the paths of the sea, fisherman have learned that schools of fish are frequently found passing through them in search of the food these currents carry with them.

There are many areas of scientific truth that were revealed in the Bible long before human scientists discovered them. In the field of oceanography note Job 36:27-28 where we are told: "For He draws up drops of water, which distill as rain from the mist, which the clouds drop down and pour abundantly on man." The Hebrew and the English definition of the word *distill* is to have small moisture droplets of steam or vapor collect into water droplets large enough to fall, to purify or to take out the impure part.

In this regard, Ecclesiastes 1:7 has this to say: "All the rivers run into the sea, yet the sea is not full; To the place from which the rivers come, There they return again." Thus, we can positively conclude that the Bible writers knew about the basic mechanics of the water vapor cycle. That is, drops of water are drawn up into the sky forming vapor clouds. They then distill into rain and then return to the rivers, which empty into the oceans continuing the cycle. It was not until the 17th century AD that the thermometer and barometer were invented which scientifically proved these thousands of year old statements from the Bible.

The Bible also speaks about air circulation in Ecclesiastes 1:6: "The wind goes toward the south, and turns around to the north; The wind whirls about continually, And comes again on its circuit." Job 28:24-25 gives further insight into this matter: "For He looks to the ends of the earth, And sees under the whole heavens to establish a weight for the wind, And apportion the waters by measure." These writers of God's Word knew thousands of years before men discovered it that the wind had weight, and the wind has a continuing circuit. It wasn't until 1643 AD with Torricelli's invention of the barometer that it was discovered that the wind had weight.

In 1820, the idea of a weather map came into focus, but it was not until 1940 that a basic pattern for air circulation was discovered. Now we talk about "low pressure centers" and "high pressure centers" which the Bible casually told us about before instruments of precision made it scientific fact. God's Word is full of scientific facts that no one knew about for thousands of years after the Bible declared them. In a moment we will see the same thing in regards to man's more recent modern inventions that the Bible predicted.

Genesis 1:20 tells us: "Then God said, Let the waters abound with an abundance of living creatures, and let birds fly above the earth across the face of the firmament of the heavens." Remember, waters are above and below the earth and this water is present in rain. Thus did Moses realize that there are swarms of living miniature animals that multiply rapidly in the oceans. In 1676, a scientist caught a drop of rain and put it under his microscope. He couldn't believe his eyes and put it this way, "There are little animals in this rain water." Thus again, it was not until the invention of the microscope that man could see "waters abounding with an abundance of living creatures." You catch a drop of rain and put it under a powerful microscope and you will see waters abounding with swarms of rapidly multiplying creatures, so science has now proven that every drop of water has colonies of life. Yet, without the microscope, Moses knew that.

Now, having seen how God addressed matters of science in the Bible thousands of years before scientists discovered them through instruments of precision, we see that the writers of the Bible were inspired of God.

As God, in the past, has revealed the things discussed above, and what He said, has now been proven true, so God has spoken about scientific achievements that are presently being invented. We call these things "signs of the times" because God predicted them thousands of years ago, and they are being developed today before our very eyes.

In my book, *The End Time Clock is Ticking*, there is a chapter called, "Things Are Different Now." The purpose of that chapter was not to go into detail about identifying the signs of the times. The real purpose was to refute the common notion that nothing has changed. We are being told that all things continue today as they have since the beginning of time—that there is nothing new happening! There are not *really* any signs of the times. I concluded that book with a brief summary of several things that are happening now which have never before happened in history. Some of those things mentioned are presented here as signs of the times. This is not repetition from the previous book in the sense that we are repeating certain signs of the times. They are presented here in their appropriate place as I identify and number the signs.

SIGN # 44 AN INCREASE IN KNOWLEDGE

Daniel 12:4 states: "But you, Daniel, shut up the words, and seal the book until the time of the end; many shall run to and fro, and *knowledge shall increase.*" Did you know that 80% of all scientists who have ever lived from Adam and Eve to our day are alive right now on planet earth? For nearly 6,000 years men were going along with virtually no startling increase in knowledge. At the turn of the 19th century things started to happen. Since World War II and the establishment of Israel as a nation, things have *really* been happening. We are now being told that the total store of man's knowledge doubles every two years.

When you look at what is on the drawing boards for the future, you may say, "That's fantastic." But who in 1945, at the conclusion of World War II, could have even imagined that we could go from coast to coast in this country in four hours? Who could have guessed that polio would be eliminated or that the miracle drugs we have today would exist? Things we take for granted such as tubeless tires, power steering, air conditioning, refrigerators, dish washers, electric can openers and garbage disposals were unknown during World War II. Who would have thought that laundry would be washed and dried by push buttons, that there would be a television set in every home, that hundreds of scientific breakthroughs would be a common thing? Who could have guessed it?

Now what of the future? There is talk about the ability to grow hair on bald heads. We already have a method of conveying speech to paper by just speaking to a computer. An unbreakable electric bulb is in the making. We now have talking books and newspapers to save eyestrain. And for the ladies, there's the possibility of nylon stockings that will not run—even if a nail were poked through them, and on and on it goes with the things that will soon be on the market. We are indeed in the midst of a knowledge explosion just as God's Word said there would be in the last days!

I want to use this sign—the exponential growth in knowledge—as a kick off for various modern inventions that were predicted in the Bible thousands of years ago. It is *only* in our lifetime that we are seeing an incredible rapid increase in knowledge. That explosive growth of knowledge is proof positive this sign in Daniel 12:4 is relevant.

If you look at history, you'll see that every generation built modestly on the knowledge of the previous generation, but the gains were slow. The apostle Paul, for example, sailed roughly in the same type of ships that carried Columbus to America 1,500 years later. Compare that with how we have gone from the Wright Brothers to space shuttles in 50 years.

Between Adam and Christ, it's estimated that the total store of human knowledge doubled. Then it doubled again from Christ to 1750, again from 1750 to 1900. It doubled again from 1900 to 1950. Do you see how the time it takes to double gets shorter and shorter? We are now dealing with exponential growth. It took 4,000 years to double in the beginning. Then it took only 1,700 years to double, then 150 years, then 50 years. Then the total storehouse of knowledge double doubled again between 1950 and 1960. That was only 10 years.

In our generation, the knowledge explosion has become exponential. It's believed that the total storehouse of man's knowledge now doubles in less than two years. Looking back at our month work program story again, it's like the month of January was the history of the world, and you just happen to be alive on the 31st day. Imagine what kind of increases and awesome spectacular things will develop as our knowledge increases in the future.

A couple of recent inventions that are mind-boggling will illustrate how far we have come in inventing unbelievable things. I'll allow the following article about DARPA speak for itself. "DARPA is developing technologies that could someday allow drones, flying overhead, to "see" below the earth's surface and identify areas that have underground tunnels." That is truly incredible.[1]

Another equally remarkable story tells us that the army has developed a weapon that shoots a "smart bullet" which can fire over barriers and down into trenches. The rifle fires bullets that are radio-controlled. "The XM25 rifle uses bullets that are programmed to explode when they travel a set distance allowing enemies to be targeted no matter where they are hiding. When the ammunition exploded, it would explode with the force of a hand grenade above the enemy." [2]

I was "blown away" when I saw a video on the Internet that was played at the Sony Corporation annual shareholder meeting in 2013. The video gave stunning information on what is unbelievable information on the incredible increase in all fields on knowledge presently going on. One of the spectacular things about the video is how rapidly it's all happening. Listed below are a few of the things contained in the video that relate to exponential increase in knowledge and rapid change in lifestyle and the way we do things:

- Ten of the most important jobs today (2013) did not exist in 2004.
- Today's college students are studying for jobs that do not presently exist, but will exist by the time they graduate.
- One in eight couples married last year met online.
- Over 200 million people use My Space.
- There are 31 billion searches on Google every month. In 2006 there only 2.6 billion monthly searches.
- The number of text messages sent *every day* exceeds the total population of the planet.
- In 1984, there were 1,000 Internet devices—in 1992 there were two million—in 2008, there were one billion such devises.
- One week of information in the *New York Times* contains more information than a person would be exposed to in his entire life in the eighteenth century.
- Four exabytes of information will be generated this year. That is more than the previous five thousand years.
- The amount of technical information doubles every two years.
- For students starting a technical four-year degree—one-half of what they learn in their first year of study will be outdated by the third year in study.
- The Japanese Computer Company ITT have invented a computer capable of pushing 14 trillion bytes of information per second. It's constantly tripling that number every six months. It is expected to continue to do so for the next twenty years.

SIGN # 45 THE ATOMIC BOMB

The Bible declares:

> Alas for the day! For the day of the LORD is at hand;
> It shall come as destruction from the Almighty. Is not
> the food cut off before our eyes, joy and gladness
> from the house of our God? The seed shrivels under
> the clods, storehouses are in shambles; barns are
> broken down for the grain has withered. How the ani-
> mals groan! The herds of cattle are restless because
> they have no pasture. Even the flocks of sheep suffer
> punishment. O LORD, to You I cry out for fire has
> devoured the open pastures, and a flame has burned
> all the trees of the field. Joel 1:15-19

This is a perfect description of what an atomic bomb will do.
Speaking of the Antichrist, Revelation 6:4 says: "Another horse,
fiery red, went out, and it was granted to the one who sat on it to
take peace from the earth, and that people should kill one another,
and there was given to him a *great* sword." The sword was the main
weapon of warfare in ancient days, but here it says that unto this
end time ruler was given "a *great* sword." This would be a weapon
greater than any that has ever existed in any other time.

Scattered throughout Scripture are references to men on the
battlefield burning alive while they are still standing on their feet.
Take for example, Isaiah 24 which says:

> The earth mourns and fades away. The world lan-
> guishes and fades away. The haughty people of the
> earth languish. The earth is also defiled under its
> inhabitants, because they have transgressed the laws,
> changed the ordinance, broken the everlasting cov-
> enant. Therefore the curse has devoured the earth,
> and those who dwell in it are desolate. Therefore the
> inhabitants of the earth are burned, and few men are
> left (Isaiah 24:4-6).

Add Isaiah 13 to the passage in Isaiah 24, and you have a picture of an end time battle that is horrific:

> The noise of a multitude in the mountains, like that of many people! A tumultuous noise of the kingdoms of nations gathered together! The LORD of hosts musters the army for battle. They come from a far country, from the end of heaven. The LORD and His weapons of indignation to destroy the whole land (Isaiah 13:4-6).

Nuclear warheads now deployed on missiles currently have the capacity to produce a holocaust of fire that can kill every human being on the face of the earth. Note the type of results the weapons used in Isaiah 13:8 produce: "And they will be afraid. Pangs and sorrows will take hold of them. They will be in pain as a woman in childbirth. They will be amazed at one another. Their faces will be like flames." Further note that this battle is in the end time. Isaiah 13:6 tells us: "Wail for the day of the LORD is at hand! It will come as destruction from the Almighty."

Note please, that while it's said that the destruction comes from the hand of the Almighty, it clearly states that various nations are involved. Thus, we may conclude that this and other like Bible prophecies where it states that the Lord does thus and so could mean that He is using nations to exact His judgment.

Pertaining to the same judgment, Joel 1:15 says: "Alas for the day! For the day of the LORD is at hand; It shall come as destruction from the Almighty." Note the descriptiveness of atomic warfare in Joel 1:19: "O LORD, to You I cry out for fire has devoured the open pastures, and a flame has burned all the trees of the field." Then Joel 2 gives us the following information about this battle:

> "Blow the trumpet in Zion, and sound an alarm in My holy mountain! Let all the inhabitants of the land tremble for the day of the LORD is coming, for it is at hand. A day of darkness and gloominess, a day of clouds and thick darkness like the morning clouds

spread over the mountains. A people come, great and
strong, the like of whom has never been nor will there
ever be any such after them, Even for many successive
generations. A fire devours before them, and behind
them a flame burns. The land is like the Garden of
Eden before them, and behind them a desolate wilder-
ness. Surely nothing shall escape them (Joel 2:1-3).

Here we learn that the opposing forces will be of such strength, as
far as their war-making ability is concerned, that there never was any
like it before in history nor shall anything ever be like it again. This
alone tells me that the United States and/or Russia will be involved.
When in all history have there been any like these two nations?

Then note in Joel 2:3 we have a description of what nuclear
warfare would be like. In nuclear warfare many die from the initial
blast. After the blast, many die from the resulting fire. It says the fire
devours before and fire devours after the blast. Furthermore, what
type of warfare other than atomic warfare could burn up all the pastures and trees, etc. as is stated in Joel 1:19? Then in Joel 2:3 what
else could make total desolation, such as is described, other than
today's weapons? Notice also that *nothing* shall escape them, not
just no one, but *nothing*! When in the history of any warfare has that
ever happened? Only atomic warfare can create such circumstances.

Note another insight in Joel 2:5: "With a noise like chariots over
mountaintops they leap, Like the noise of a flaming fire that devours
the stubble, Like a strong people set in battle array." What a description of the roaring and devouring fire of an atomic blast.

Then Joel 2:6 clinches it with the following words: "Before their
face the people shall be much pained: all faces shall gather blackness." The Hebrew word translated "blackness" is a word denoting
a blackness caused by a flame or fire. Again, I would remind you of
the description of Isaiah 13:8 where it says: "Their faces shall be as
flames." The actual beginning of this prophecy is Joel 1:13 where
the Jews have already returned to their ancient land and have rebuilt
the temple. In a TV documentary on Hiroshima, one man not near
the blast zone met a man who had been near the blast zone whose
face was completely black as a result of the atomic detonation.

Now, if you will take note of Ezekiel 38:21-22, you will see the great description of the results of the battle spoken of there. Let's look at this carefully and take one detail of this battle at a time: "And I will bring him to judgment with pestilence and bloodshed. I will rain down on him, on his troops, and on the many peoples who are with him, flooding rain, great hailstones, fire, and brimstone" (Ezekiel 38:22).

The first word I call your attention to is the word "hailstones." Atomic tests in the Pacific Ocean indicate there is not only an intense fireball plus beta and gamma rays which are very destructive, but there are also great hailstones. Large dents in the armor plating on the surface of ships located in the test area were noted. At first this seemed a mystery, but films and other data compiled at the time of the tests indicated that the tremendous air turbulence caused by the blasts resulted in the formation of hailstones of very large proportions. It was determined that huge hailstones were the cause of the dents in the armor plating of these ships.

Scientific data? It verifies Bible prophecies. What was the cause of the unusual hail? It was the movements of extreme cold fronts caused from the vacuum created by the blast. That freak weather phenomena associated with atomic bomb blasts will be discussed later in greater detail. But suffice to say, a part of the result of large atomic and hydrogen bombs is huge sized hailstones weighing many dozens of pounds.

The next term in Ezekiel 38:22 we'll examine is easier to understand than the rest, and that's the term "fire". It's utterly impossible to describe the immensity of the heat produced in a hydrogen bomb explosion. Words are totally inadequate. On August 6, 1945, the first atomic bomb was dropped on Hiroshima Japan. The second atomic weapon was a plutonium material bomb dropped on Nagasaki on August 9, 1945. This bomb was a simpler form than the uranium (U-235) bomb, which exploded over Hiroshima. The heat blast alone caused the greatest number of deaths. It is no small wonder, when you consider the force and intensity of that blast, that the temperature at the center of the blast momentarily reached, a temperature hotter than the sun. After the blast, President Truman stated "The force from which the sun draws its power has been loosed against those who brought war on the Far East."

The effect of the "primitive" Hiroshima bomb was classified as a "nominal" 20-kiloton explosion. It obliterated but a four square mile area, yet its blast effect was so intense that 50,000 people were killed and 55,000 more were wounded and 200,000 people were left homeless. A subsequent report from the scientists at Kyushu Imperial University classified the effects of the bomb on the human body under three headings: (1) Instant death, (2) Symptoms like those of dysentery followed by death, (3) Throat ulcers, bleeding gums, falling hair and eventual death.

Japanese newsmen reporting the Nagasaki bomb effects stated that persons were paralyzed ten miles from the explosion center; others with only minute wounds eventually died. Those bombs were like toys compared to today's bombs. We have gone from kiloton to megaton bombs.

In 1963, the Russians exploded a 57 megaton bomb over Siberia. Instead of the "nominal" explosive power of 20,000 tons of TNT like the Hiroshima bomb, the Russian bomb had the explosive power of 57,000,000 tons of TNT, and there is no limit to the explosive capability of hydrogen bombs.

In 1953, President Eisenhower decided to let the American people see a motion picture of what its most terrifying weapon, the hydrogen bomb, could do. The motion picture depicts the test of a hydrogen weapon in the Pacific in November 1952. In the climax of the blast a whole island disappeared. It was transmuted into deadly vapor and ash. Since then, however, this explosion has been dwarfed by the even larger thermonuclear blast, which surprised even the controlling scientists. Its effects flared beyond the control boundaries and the fallout of radioactive ash burned natives of the Pacific islands and fisherman many miles away. Nothing more really needs to be said. No better description of a hydrogen bomb blast can be given than to state that it causes great fires that consume everything so that as Joel 1:19 says, *nothing* shall escape.

The next term seen in Ezekiel 38:22 is the word "brimstone". Bible dictionaries list brimstone as being sulphur like that found on the shores of the Dead Sea in the area once called Sodom.

Unrelated. as it may seem to the subject at hand, my mind goes back to the Egyptian use of Russian nerve gas on Yemen in 1967.

When poisonous gas used in warfare is released, as people die there is blood coming out of their bodily openings. This, I suggest, relates to two other descriptions of this battle in Ezekiel 38:22.

Note in that verse the words pestilence and blood. All of the things mentioned in this verse are the results of hydrogen bombs. A Tribulation passage in Revelation 8:7 uses the mixture of the same things. It says: "And hail and fire followed hail mingled with blood."

The term "pestilence" in Ezekiel 38:22 could be related to the same thing. There is no question but that present scientific warfare has the capability of producing a fulfillment of this word "pestilence."

The next thing to notice from the descriptions of Ezekiel 38:22 is the term "overflowing rain". Several years ago Russia exploded a 100 megaton force bomb in the atmosphere. Though it was thousands of miles away, the explosion dropped the Mississippi River level by two feet. Years ago, when America was still testing hydrogen bombs underground in the Nevada desert, they discovered that it caused great inrushes of cold air, even though the tests were underground. In other words, for days after the tests, it was found that the aftermath of H-bomb explosions is violent weather patterns. They asked a frightening question: "What would happen in the far greater 'in-rush' of Arctic high-pressure cold fronts if the explosions were above the surface of the ground?"

Now consider the fact that Ezekiel, Joel, and Isaiah never knew anything about atomic bombs. How better could they describe nuclear warfare than what we have just read? I'd say that the stage has been set for these end time prophecies to be fulfilled. There has never been a generation in the history of this planet that had the capacity to do the things mentioned in these prophecies. We have that capacity today.

In Matthew 24:21-22, we are told that "except the days be shortened during the Tribulation that no flesh would be saved." Read carefully the full text in Matthew 24:21-22: "For then there will be great tribulation, such as has not been since the beginning of the world until this time, no, nor ever shall be. And unless those days were shortened, no flesh would be saved; but for the elect's sake those days will be shortened."

Before showing how this verse relates to the atomic bomb in prophecy, allow me to share with you a fact that has confused many that have studied this verse. The Bible tells us that the Tribulation will last exactly seven years. The Bible even gives the exact number of days. Therefore, it is asked "How can that be if the days are to be shortened?"

This is explained to us in Revelation 8:12: "Then the fourth angel sounded: And a third of the sun was struck, a third of the moon, and a third of the stars, so that a third of them were darkened. A third of the day did not shine, and likewise the night." This event takes place in the early part of the Tribulation.

The Greek tense and action of the word employed here shows us that this situation is to be continuous — not temporary. In other words, when this event takes place, the sun, moon and stars will not shine for one third of the amount of time that they had normally shone. What could that possibly mean? It means that from that point forward, there would be 16-hour days rather than 24-hour days. In other words, the length of the day will be cut by one third, exactly as the verse says it will be.

Now, what is a day? Is it not one complete period of darkness and light? Presently, and throughout history, our days have been 24 hours each. However, at this point in the Tribulation, and for the duration of the Tribulation, the days will be 16 hours each. It is plainly stated that exactly one-third of the light period and one-third of the dark period will no longer exist. That amount of time will be eliminated permanently for the remainder of the Tribulation.

Thus, the *number* of days will not be shortened, but the *length* of each day will be shortened. This is so because the length of each day is reduced by one third. If I had candy in the form of lollipops and I had one hundred of them and I said, "Except these lollipops would be *shortened* you can't have any of them", what would I mean? Would you take some of them away so that there would remain only 90 for example? No indeed. The intention of the statement is that each one would be shortened so that there are still 100 of them, but each one is now shorter than what it originally was. This is *exactly* what Matthew 24:22 says.

That verse does not say that the *number* of days will be less. It says the *days* will be shortened. Certainly nothing can be more obvious than that! So, it's not a matter of having less daylight hours and more darkness hours or vise-versa.

You see, the Bible predicted that the Tribulation would last exactly 7 years, but nowhere did God say there had to be 24-hour days. Let me give you some verses from the Old Testament that predicted this very thing. In these verses we are also given the scientific reason why the days will be shortened. From the book of Isaiah:

> From the ends of the earth we have heard songs: "Glory to the righteous!" But I said, "I am ruined, ruined! Woe to me! The treacherous dealers have dealt treacherously. Indeed, the treacherous dealers have dealt very treacherously. Fear and the pit and the snare are upon you, O inhabitant of the earth, and it shall be that he who flees from the noise of the fear shall fall into the pit, and he who comes up from the midst of the pit shall be caught in the snare. For the windows from on high are open, and the foundations of the earth are shaken. The earth is violently broken. The earth is split open. The earth is shaken exceedingly. The earth shall reel to and fro like a drunkard, And shall totter like a hut; Its transgression shall be heavy upon it, And it will fall, and not rise again (Isaiah 24:16-20).

When it speaks of the *foundation of the earth*, it's talking about its axis, which has remained stable since the flood of Noah's day. Here the earth's foundation (axis) is shaken during the Tribulation. This cannot refer to an earthquake but is explaining the fourth trumpet of Revelation 8:12. The Hebrew word *dissolved* should be translated by the English word *disorientated*. Isaiah 24:20 explains this event. Have you ever seen a man who is drunk try to walk? He doesn't do well, does he? He reels to and fro and doesn't walk as he should. Well, that's how the earth is going to be when this event takes place. Why? It's because something causes the earth to move on its axis. It's not going to revolve as it once did.

Now note with me how Matthew 24:21-22 relates to the matter of atomic warfare in the last days. It clearly states that unless the days of the Tribulation are shortened, no human life would remain on earth. It would be difficult to see how over seven billion people around the world could all be killed in a short period of time using swords, spears and other weapons used by the ancients when these words were written. In Ezekiel 38-39 we see that unusual weapons are used in the end times and that these weapons will provide Israel with their energy needs for seven years.

Then further note from Ezekiel's prophecy that they will not begin to bury the dead for seven months after they die. This is clearly and emphatically seen in Ezekiel 39.

> They will set apart men regularly employed, with the help of a search party, to pass through the land and bury those bodies remaining on the ground, in order to cleanse it. At the end of seven months they will make a search. The search party will pass through the land; and when anyone sees a man's bone, he shall set up a marker by it, till the buriers have buried it in the Valley of Hamon Gog (Ezekiel 39:14-15),

For seven months they will search out the land to identify where the dead bodies are and then they will take another seven months to bury them. The point of this passage is that the people who search out the land and identify where the dead bodies are do not touch any of the bodies. That job is reserved for those who actually bury the dead. The reason for this is because in a nuclear war only those properly clothed and trained will be able to successfully deal with the contaminates without harm to themselves.

Another passage that describes something that happens in a nuclear explosion is found in Zechariah 14:12: "And this shall be the plague with which the LORD will strike all the people who fought against Jerusalem: Their flesh shall dissolve while they stand on their feet, Their eyes shall dissolve in their sockets, And their tongues shall dissolve in their mouths." This is a perfect description of the result of a neutron bomb blast.

Well does Grant Jeffrey describe a neutron bomb in Zechariah 14:12 as he says" "The prophets description that "the flesh shall consume away" describes the terrible effect of neutron bombs, which use gamma rays that destroy the flesh of their victims while vaporizing bones. Only the victim's skeleton remains and nearby buildings and equipment are undamaged.'"[3]

Joel Rosenberg, who has had contact with high-ranking government officials of many countries, said that he got the following concerns from Frank Gaffney who served as the Assistant Secretary of Defense in the Reagan administration and is now head of the Center for Security Policy. I quote him:

> Frank told me that Iran worried him for several reasons, and not just because of its nuclear program. "First, Iran now has the capability of firing a Scud missile off the back of a commercial container ship, making it possible to deliver a nuclear warhead into the U.S. without having an ICBM. Second, Iran is working on building an electromagnetic pulse bomb, which could detonate over an American, European or Israeli city, fry all electronics and communications and render a country virtually defenseless."[4]

You might want to look up information like this on the Internet. It will surprise you as to how the descriptions of nuclear warfare fit perfectly the verses quoted above where the Bible tells us about the end time wars.

SIGN # 46 WEAPONS OF MODERN WARFARE

Ezekiel 39:9 states: "Then those who dwell in the cities of Israel will go out and set on fire and burn the weapons, both the shields and bucklers, the bows and arrows, the javelins and spears; and they will make fires with them for seven years."

People used to laugh at this prophecy, but they don't laugh any more. They would say, how is it possible to burn a tank and other modern weapons of war? A Dutch improvement of a wood material has developed an item called Lingostone. It is said to be harder than steel. Reports have it that the Soviets are making tanks out of this material, thus cutting production costs and giving them the ability to avoid anti-tank weapons that zero in on metal.

The advantages of using this material is obvious—it's cheaper than using metal. To lose one in battle is not too costly. It avoids sophisticated weapons of warfare, and it's stronger than an all-metal tank. Lingostone burns like coal in a furnace. So, there you have one type of weapon being manufactured that does burn like Ezekiel claims weapons of that day will burn.

Furthermore, with nuclear reactors providing much of the energy in the world at an ever-increasing rate, this burning of Russian weapons could also refer to the nuclear fuel that she brings with her in her weapons at this battle. What's more, we have learned that nuclear power plants, such as are on our nuclear submarines will burn out in seven years. That's why the submarines must be brought back into port and refueled every seven years.

Isn't that remarkable that seven years is the identical number of years that Israel will use fuel from Russian weapons? Furthermore, could this be a clue that this battle will therefore take place at the time of the rapture or before it? Another main source of fuel is oil and gas, and a huge invading army such as the one described here in Ezekiel 38-39 would have to have huge amounts of fuel with them.

Another startling fact about atomic warfare is the result that people could not live in the areas affected by the atomic blasts because of radiation. The same thing could be said about anthrax and other types of contamination from the ground. There are many scriptures that tell us a day is coming when men will not be able to live where they once lived. I list a few of them below.

> "And Babylon, the glory of kingdoms, the beauty of the Chaldeans' pride, Will be as when God overthrew Sodom and Gomorrah. It will never be inhabited, Nor will it be settled from generation to generation; Nor will the Arabian pitch tents there, Nor will the shepherds make their sheepfolds there" (Isaiah 13:19,20).

"I will also make it a possession for the porcupine, And marshes of muddy water; I will sweep it with the broom of destruction, says the LORD of hosts" (Isaiah 14:23).

"Because of the wrath of the LORD she shall not be inhabited, but she shall be wholly desolate. Everyone who goes by Babylon shall be horrified and hiss at all her plagues" (Jeremiah 50:13).

"Come against her from the farthest border; Open her storehouses; cast her up as heaps of ruins, And destroy her utterly; Let nothing of her be left" (Jeremiah 50:26).

"Therefore the wild desert beasts shall dwell there with the jackals, And the ostriches shall dwell in it. It shall be inhabited no more forever, nor shall it be dwelt in from generation to generation" (Jeremiah 50:39).

"They shall not take from you a stone for a corner nor a stone for a foundation, but you shall be desolate forever," says the LORD" (Jeremiah 51:26).

"And the land will tremble and sorrow; for every purpose of the LORD shall be performed against Babylon, to make the land of Babylon a desolation without inhabitant" (Jeremiah 51:29)

"Babylon shall become a heap, A dwelling place for jackals, An astonishment and a hissing, without an inhabitant" (Jeremiah 51:37).

Nothing like this has ever happened in world history where no one could live in a land after a war, and none of the building material would ever be used again. In Isaiah 13:19 (quoted above) God says the destruction will be like the destruction when He overthrew

Sodom and Gomorrah. And how was that? It was unexpected, sudden and quick.

How will it be in the Tribulation? The answer to that question is that what happened to Sodom and Gomorrah will happen in the Tribulation. Revelation 18:17 tells us how quickly it will start and be over with: "For in one hour such great riches came to nothing. Every shipmaster, all who travel by ship, sailors, and as many as trade on the sea, stood at a distance".

What but atomic warfare could destroy a city or a country in one hour with such devastation that no one is left and no one can dwell in that land for decades to come? The Bible is awesome in its predictions of the future. It is always specifically accurate and shocking. Really, only those living when these things happen can possibly understand the prophecies that foretold them.

When the United States tested its atomic weapons on islands in the Pacific, they claimed those islands could not be inhabited for 40 years because of the anthrax and radioactive contamination of the land. Is it any wonder that God said that in the end of time Egypt could not be inhabited for 40 years? Ezekiel 29:12 states, "I will make the land of Egypt desolate in the midst of the countries that are desolate; and among the cities that are laid waste, her cities shall be desolate forty years; and I will scatter the Egyptians among the nations and disperse them throughout the countries."

The idea of end time atomic warfare was put in a remarkable biblical perspective in the *Lamplighter Magazine*. Following is a summation of that article:

> It should be evident that what we are talking about is a weapon unparalleled in human history; a weapon with the capacity to obliterate huge cities in seconds. This is a scenario that perfectly fits with the kind of swift, mass destruction spoken of in the book of Revelation. Indeed, considering the widespread death predicted by John, it would be hard for us to imagine anything other than a nuclear holocaust, which could come close to producing such carnage.

The poisoning of the waters (Revelation 8:11), the severe reduction in visibility (Revelation 8:12), the death of much of the earth's vegetation (Revelation 8:7), malignant sores (Revelation 16:2), the end of ocean life (Revelation 16:3), and the inability of the atmosphere to block out harmful ultraviolet rays resulting in severe burns (Revelation16:8) are all expected results of nuclear war. The implications of these prophecies are not pretty—the earth has an appointment with a devastation which shall be horrible beyond imagination.

Amazingly, predictions by secular writers parallel the horrific visions of John in nearly every major detail. Contrast the words of secular writer Jonathan Schnell author of the book, *The Fate of the Earth* (1970) with what the Bible says as he describes the consequences of a nuclear war:

- "Bearing in mind that the possible consequences of the detonations of thousands of megatons of nuclear explosives include the extinction of many ocean species." Revelation 16:3 states: "And every living creature in the sea died."
- "A significant decrease in photosynthesis in plants around the world; the scalding and killing of many crops." Revelation 8:7 tells us: "And a third of the trees were burned up and all green grass was burned up."
- "The increase in rates of cancer and mutation around the world." Revelation 16:2 states: "And a foul and loathsome sore came upon the men who had the mark of the beast."
- "The attendant risk of global epidemics." Luke 21:11 states: "And there will be great earthquakes in various places, and famines and pestilences."
- "The possible poisoning of all vertebrates by sharply increased levels of vitamin D in their skin as a result of increased ultraviolet light." Revelation 16:8 states: "The fourth angel poured out his bowl on the sun and power was

given to him to scorch men with fire. And men were scorched with great heat."

- "And the outright slaughter of all targeted continents of most human beings and other living things by the initial nuclear radiation, the fireballs, the thermal pulses, and blast waves, the mass fires, and the fallout from the explosions." Revelation 9:18 states: "By these three plagues a third of mankind was killed—by the fire and the smoke and the brimstone."

- "Considering that these consequences will all interact with one another in unknown ways and furthermore are in all likelihood an incomplete list, one must conclude that a full scale nuclear holocaust could lead to the extinction of mankind." Matthew 24:22 states: "And unless those days were shortened, no flesh would be saved; but for the elect's sake those days will be shortened."[5]

In addition to the possibility of atomic warfare, other horrendous weapons have been developed and are already in the war arsenal. For example, a book on the subject tells of a weapon called the *particle-beam weapon*. Of that weapon we are told, "A tank based particle-beam weapon is similar to a flamethrower but tremendously more destructive. This weapon shoots its target with what appears to be focused lightening bolts. The tank targeted a bus and three automobiles filled with Iraqi insurgents. The bus melted into a mass of molten metal to approximately the size of a Volkswagen Beetle. The bodies of the insurgents had shrunk to less than 18 inches in height."[6]

SIGN # 47 THE INVENTION OF THE SMART BOMB

Jeremiah 50:9 brings before us a most interesting insight to post-World War II military technology when it states "For behold, I will raise and cause to come up against Babylon an assembly of great nations from the north country, and they shall array themselves against her; from there she shall be captured. Their arrows shall be like those of an expert warrior; none shall return in vain."

The word *expert* in the verse means "wise" or "guidance." In other words, the weapon that they use will have wisdom in and of itself. Then notice the words, *like those of an expert warrior.* Again this refers to the weapon that is shot by the army that is in the fight. In other words, this verse clearly says that the wisdom and guidance is in the *arrow* itself—*not* in the warrior.

No one had this technology even as recently as the Vietnam War. This is an incredible statement of Bible prophecy that no one on earth from Adam until recently could ever have dreamed of. Yet the Bible predicted this modern weaponry millenniums ago. That is amazing.

Because of the wisdom being in the weapon itself indicates that once it's fired, it will go successfully to its target; therefore, *none shall return in vein* as Jeremiah 50:9 predicted.

SIGN # 48 THE AUTOMOBILE

Nahum 2:4 states: "The chariots rage in the streets, They jostle one another in the broad roads; They seem like torches, They run like lightning." What ever existed in history since Adam and Eve to the present day could Nahum 2:4 be talking about other than the modern day automobile? This sign hardly needs comment, but Nahum tells us that in the end time there would be cars, and then he gives us the best description of a car that you can find anywhere:

- The "chariot" was what the ancients used for transportation. Their chariots were pulled by horses. In our day, our "chariots" are our cars pulled by *horsepower.*
- The "jostling against one another" is speaking of the accidents that happen in a car.
- The "broad ways" are the freeways and wide roads built especially for cars. Back in the ancient world, all roads were narrow since they had no cars.
- The phrase, "they shall seem like torches" is an obvious reference to the headlights of cars.
- Then he says, "They shall run like lightning." This needs no comment at all. I have one car where the speedometer goes up to 120 MPH.

261

SIGN # 49 TELEVISION

Did you know that Revelation 11 predicted satellite television? How else would it be possible for all the nations of the world to see the following scene taking place in Jerusalem, *while* it is taking place. unless there were satellite TV?:

> Then those from the peoples, tribes, tongues, and nations will see their dead bodies three-and-a-half days, and not allow their dead bodies to be put into graves. And those who dwell on the earth will rejoice over them, make merry, and send gifts to one another, because these two prophets tormented those who dwell on the earth. Now after the three-and-a-half days, the breath of life from God entered them and they stood on their feet, and great fear fell on those who saw them (Revelation 11:9-11).

SIGN # 50 MODERN MECHANICAL MIRACLES

In Revelation 13:15, we read about talking robots: "He was granted power to give breath to the image of the beast, that the image of the beast should both speak and cause as many as would not worship the image of the beast to be killed." Not many years ago people laughed at the idea of a robot that could talk, but they aren't laughing today.

From time to time, *Science News Letter* carries feature stories about the field of cybernetics. Let me share some of what is happening in this exciting field. A robot was introduced to the American Psychologist Association some time ago. The robot showed human-like characteristics.

The psychologists learned that this robot could learn from experience. The robot could actually behave like a human in that it could express emotions such as love, hate, fear and anger. The robot could recognize what it confronted and respond with a proper emotion.

Still another machine can reproduce itself making a better version of itself each time a new model was made. One developer of cybernetics told of the following experiment. He said, "When the robot's battery would run down, I would flash a light and blow a whistle. Recognizing that the light is a source of power, the robot would get up and come toward the light. When it was rejuvenated it would go into the corner and sit down. This was repeated and finally there was no light, only the whistle and the robot still came."

Thus, these machines feature some of the characteristics of the human brain. The robots of today govern themselves and seek their goals free from several possibilities. A true cybernetic does more than take orders. It corrects it's own mistakes and reacts to external stimuli. Does that sound shocking to you? It shouldn't! Two thousand years ago Revelation 13:15 predicted such things would be.

One machine currently being worked on, when hooked to the scalp of a human being and using EEG waves will be able to read that person's mind. In many shopping malls, there are computers that will talk to you. You ask the computer a question, it will respond with the appropriate answer.

SIGN # 51 ISRAEL'S ANTI-BALLISTIC SYSTEM IS CALLED ARROW

A word that is used that seems old fashioned is the word "arrow." In speaking of the Gog invasion of Israel in Ezekiel 39, we read these words:

> Then I will knock the bow out of your left hand, and cause the arrows to fall out of your right hand. Then those who dwell in the cities of Israel will go out and set on fire and burn the weapons, both the shields and bucklers, the bows and arrows, the javelins and spears; and they will make fires with them for seven years (Ezekiel 39:3,9).

This is obviously a prophecy of end time events. Israel has an anti- ballistic missile system that moves ten times faster than the speed of sound. This system is called the "Arrow Anti Ballistic Missile System." Here we see the very terms used in the Old

Testament to describe the end time weapons use the actual names given to the latest military hardware.

SIGN # 52 THE EXISTENCE OF PARATROOPERS

The Bible also spoke of paratroopers thousands of years before they existed: "You will ascend, coming like a storm, covering the land like a cloud, you and all your troops and many peoples with you" (Ezekiel 38:9).

Not long ago Russian paratroopers did an experiment and the news account said, "They came down like a cloud." Paratroopers, one of the most vital parts of our fighting forces today, came into existence as a method of warfare in our lifetime. Before World War II there was no such thing as men jumping out of airplanes by parachute in warfare. Thus, what Ezekiel says here could take place tonight, but it could not have taken place before I was born. Consequently, this gives us another reason why these are the last days.

CHAPTER 11

HOW TO PREPARE FOR THE COMING OF THE LORD

Man is incurably religious. Wherever man is found, you will find some sort of religion. As a result there are thousands of religions in today's world, and that number is growing constantly. But there is only one Bible, and the Bible teaches there is only one way of salvation and that's by personal faith in Jesus Christ. Jesus claimed this while He was here on earth, in John 14:6 where it says, "Jesus said to him, I am *the* way, *the* truth, and *the* life. No one comes to the Father except through Me."

Peter verifies this in Acts 4:12 when he said, "Nor is there salvation in any other, for there is no other name under heaven given among men by which we must be saved." The people to whom Peter spoke these words were very religious—in fact—more religious than most people.

In this verse, and many others, the Bible sharply distinguishes between religion and being saved. Strictly speaking Christianity is not a religion at all—it's a relationship to a person—Jesus Christ. Being religious does not make one a Christian any more than going into a garage makes one a car. The very first syllable of the word Christian is *Christ*. If you don't have Christ, you're not a Christian. It's my purpose in this final chapter to explain to you what it means to have Christ. This is the declaration of 1 John 5:12, "He who has the Son has life; he who does not have the Son of God does not have life."

Now religion teaches salvation by works, human merit and the observation of ordinances. The Bible teaches salvation through the sacrifice of another.

The ancient Egyptians had religion—so did the Babylonians and the multitudes of Jesus' day—but none of them had salvation. The word religion in the original Greek means to frighten, to bewail or be troubled. The basic meaning, therefore, of the word religion is a ceremonial service caused by fears and troubles. It's man's effort— his frantic effort—to find relief from his fears, his troubles and his conscience.

Contrast this with the message of salvation, which results in peace and assurance. Christianity and religion have nothing in common. Religion promotes doubt. Faith in Christ promotes assurance. In every instance when the Bible speaks of the concept of religion it's associated with a hallow formalism that God rejects. It's a lie of Satan to have men religious without salvation. He gets them satisfied with their own works so that they will feel that they do not need the work of Christ.

Someone has said, "There are only two religions—the done one and the doing one. The Bible abounds with examples of these two conflicting ideas. God says the work of salvation is *done* while Satan says salvation is by *doing*! The case of our first parents is a beautiful example of this. After they had sinned, we read this of them in Genesis 3:7, "Then the eyes of both of them were opened, and they knew that they were naked; and they sewed fig leaves together and made themselves coverings." In this situation—instead of turning to God, they turned to religion. Religion, of course, is you manufacturing your own so-called good works to gain the approbation of God. That's what we have in Genesis 3:7. Instead of crying out to God for mercy, they tried to cover their sins with the work of their own hands. This first act of our original parents is perpetuated in all of their offspring.

Man instinctively feels and knows that he needs a covering, but he seeks that covering by the work of his own hands. Adam and Eve were no doubt religious and sincere, but their fig leave aprons would not do. So, when the Lord came into the garden they hid themselves and sought to hide from the only one that could save them. Their religion had failed and they needed something more. This something more is what God will to reveal to them. What God revealed is summed up in many Bible verses in the New Testament. Let me share a few them with you.

- John 3:16, "For God so loved the world that He gave His only begotten Son, that whoever believes in Him should not perish but have everlasting life."
- John 1:29, The next day John saw Jesus coming toward him, and said, Behold! The Lamb of God who takes away the sin of the world!"
- Further, the angel said to Mary in Matthew 1:21, "And she will bring forth a Son, and you shall call His name JESUS, for He will save His people from their sins."
- Jesus declared this as the only way of salvation in John 10:8, "All who ever came before Me are thieves and robbers, but the sheep did not hear them.
- The apostle Paul added his thoughts to this in, Galatians 1:8, "But even if we, or an angel from heaven, preach any other gospel to you than what we have preached to you, let him be accursed." The verses above present God's way of salvation. Many may think that there is another way to heaven, but they are wrong, for Proverbs 14:12 declares, "There is a way that seems right to a man, but its end is the way of death."

Each person needs to ask himself, "Am I religious or am I saved?"

Now, you may ask, "How does Genesis 3:21 sum up in simply, easily-understood language how I can have assurance of a relationship with God that produces for me a salvation that I cannot produce myself??" Let me refresh your memory by quoting the verse again. Gen 3:21: "Also for Adam and his wife the LORD God made tunics of skin, and clothed them." God took an animal—probably a lamb—and He slayed it before their eyes and clothed them with the garment of the slain beast.

The word translated "coat" here is literally long robe—it completely covered them. Notice the striking contrasts. Adam's work was:

1. The work of his own hands
2. A bloodless effort at atonement
3. A wholly inadequate covering

God's provision was.

1. A gift, which God Himself provided.
2. The death of an innocent substitute.
3. Produced by the shedding of innocent blood
4. A complete covering

Notice Adam had nothing to do with its preparation. God had created and then killed the animal all by Himself. Adam and Eve simply watched the Lord do what He did. The lamb had to die in order to give up his skin to cover the first sinners. In others words, the sacrifice was an innocent animal which had to die in the place of the guilty sinner.

What a tremendous prophetic picture of the one of whom John the Baptist spoke of when he said in John 1:29: "The next day John saw Jesus coming toward him, and said, Behold! The Lamb of God who takes away the sin of the world!" In this first sacrifice shared in Genesis 3:21, God lays down the one and *only* condition of all acceptable sacrifice. Anything short of this is only "fig leaves" in the sight of God.

We meet the subject of this sacrifice and offering again in Genesis 4:3: "And in the process of time it came to pass that Cain brought an offering of the fruit of the ground to the LORD."

Now, Adam and Eve obviously taught their sons about bringing a sacrifice to the Lord, otherwise how they have know about sacrifice at all. Foolish Cain refused God's way and brought a sacrifice of the fruit of the field, which was the fruit of his own labor. It did not involve the shedding of blood and the death of an innocent substitute.

There can be no doubt that Cain was sincere and that he brought a marvelously beautiful sacrifice, but God would have nothing to do with it. He rejected it even though Cain probably brought of the best that he was capable of producing. Apparently Cain was very conscious of his duty toward God. Note further that He *brought this gift to God.* Cain was not an atheist. He brought his offering *to the Lord.* He was a worshipper of God. But with all of his religion and willingness to sacrifice, he was still rejected by God. On the other hand, God accepted the sacrifice of Cain's brother Abel.

Cain refused to come God's way! The inviolable rule of acceptable sacrifice had been laid down in Genesis 3:21. It was here that God rejected the self-efforts of Cain's father and ordered instead a bloody sacrifice of an innocent victim that could properly typify His own Son. God taught them there that fig leaves—the work of man's own hand—is totally unacceptable to God.

Abel believed the Word of God and brought a lamb which was accepted by God. We are told this in Genesis 4:4-5: "Abel also brought of the firstborn of his flock and of their fat. And the LORD respected Abel and his offering, but He did not respect Cain and his offering. And Cain was very angry, and his countenance fell." So, even though Cain was religious and worshipped God—still he was *lost!*

The lesson from Genesis 3 is very clear. Allow me to lay it out for you by way of summary:

- First, like Adam we have all sinned.
- Second, like Adam, having violated Gods demands, we deserve the judgment of God.
- Third, the best effort of our own effort to satisfy God's justice falls short. The Bible teaches, "All have sinned and come short of the glory of God" (Romans 3 23).
- Fourth, to be forgiven by God and have our way to heaven provided, we must accept the sacrifice of God's son in shedding His blood for sins by His death on the cross of Calvary. That's what Adam did, and that's what everyone who wants to go to heaven must do.

SCRIPTURE REFERENCES

SIGNS OF THE TIMES LISTING

SIGNS IN BOOK ONE

Sign # 1 The Rebirth of the Nation of Israel

Sign # 2 Israel Became a Nation in a Single Day

Sign # 3 The Timing of the Regathering of Israel

Sign # 4 The Great Depression Occurred Just before Israel Became a Nation

Sign # 5 Palestine Would Be a Land of Desolation

Sign # 6 The Jewish People Would Get Control Over the Holy Land Jerusalem.

Sign # 7 Jewish People Would Return to Israel From All Over the World

Sign # 8 The Budding of the Fig Tree

Sign # 9 Russia Reluctance to Allow Jewish People to Immigrate to Israel

Sign # 10 The Division of the Land of Palestine Between Arabs and Jewish People

Sign # 11 The Return of the Yemenite Jews to Israel

Sign # 12 Jewish People Would Purchase Land for Money

Sign # 13 The Jewish People Returned in Unbelief

Sign # 14 Israel Would be a United Nation

Sign # 15 The Dry Bones of Israel

Sign # 16 Israel Would Have a Great Army

Sign # 17 Suffering of the Jewish People as They Traveled to the Holy Land by Ship

Sign # 18 The Arab Reaction to the Return of the Jewish People

Sign # 19 The Forceful Removal of Jewish People from Their Homes in Arab Countries.

Sign # 20 Arabs Will be Forced Out of the Land of Israel

Sign # 21 The Jewish People Would Return to Israel on Airplanes

Sign # 22 Bible Prophecies About Jerusalem are Coming to Pass

Sign # 23 Jerusalem is in the Hands of the Jewish People

Sign # 24 Jerusalem is a Problem to the Nations of the World

Sign # 25 Half the City of Jerusalem Would be a Special Problem In the End Time

Sign # 26 The Boundaries of the New City of Jerusalem

Sign # 27 Jerusalem is Again the Capital of Israel

Sign # 28 A Population Explosion of Jerusalem

Sign # 29 End Time Jerusalem: A City Without Walls

Sign # 30 Two Nations Would Claim a Right to the Holy Land

Sign # 31 The Palestinians Would Claim Jewish Scared Places As their Own

Sign # 32 The Building up of Zion

Sign # 33 The Rebuilding of Waste Cities

Sign # 34 Israel's Highway Building Program

Sign # 35 There Would be a Road Called "The Way of Holiness"

Sign # 36 The Harbor at Haifa

Sign # 37 The Discovery of Oil and Gas in Israel

Sign # 38 The Building of the City of Tel Aviv

Sign # 39 Israel's Cities Have Become Fortified

Sign # 40 There is an Airport in the Land that Once Belonged to the Philistines

Sign # 41 The planting of Trees in the Desert

Sign # 42 The Planting of the Myrtle Tree

Sign # 43 The Forests of Israel

Sign # 44 The Reforestation of Israel

Sign # 45 Prophecies Concerning the Husbandry of the Soil

Sign # 46 Israel is a Major Producer of Wheat

Sign # 47 The Processing of Oils and Fat in the Holy Land

Sign # 48 The Increase of Rainfall in Israel

Sign # 49 The Mountains of Lebanon's Snow Helps the Deserts of to Bloom

Sign # 50 Sheep Herding is Now a Vital Industry in Israel

Sign # 51 The Streams Breaking Out in the Desert
Sign # 52 The Waters of Aravah
Sign # 53 The Desert Will Bloom Like a Rose
Sign # 54 The Sea Water Would become Fresh Water
Sign # 55 The Fruit and Vegetable Production of Israel
Sign # 56 Israel Is an Exporter of Food to Other Nations
Sign # 57 The Large Fields of Pasture in Israel
Sign # 58 Israel Farmers Would be Prosperous
Sign # 59 The Abundance of the Dead Sea
Sign # 60 The Industrial Wealth of Israel
Sign # 61 Israel's Merchant Fleet
Sign # 62 Gentile Nations Giving Their Wealth to Israel
Sign # 63 Germany Has Given Much for the Suffering Caused Before and During World War II
Sign # 64 The Finding of Rich Ore Deposits in the Holy Land
Sign # 65 The Iraq Oil Pipeline to the Mediterranean Sea
Sign # 66 There Are Current Efforts That Will Lead To the Rebuilding of the Temple
Sign # 67 The Temple Mount Will be Shared By Jews and Arabs
Sign # 68 The Stage is Being Established for the Antichrist to Take Over the Temple When It's Rebuilt
Sign # 69 The Discovery of the Blue Dye that is Needed for the Making of the Garments of the Priesthood.
Sign # 70 The Present Day Effort At Finding a Red Heifer
Sign # 71 The Making of Objects to be Used in Temple Worship
Sign # 72 The Establishment of Who the True Rabbi Are
Sign # 73 The Training of Priests to Serve in the Rebuilt Temple
Sign # 74 The Discovery of Anointing Oil at Qumran
Sign # 75 The Reinstitution of Harps
Sign # 76 The Making of Specific Clothing to be Worn by Temple Priests
Sign # 77 The Remaking of Temple Furnishings
Sign # 78 The Building of the Sacrificial Alter
Sign # 79 The Desire of the Arabs to Cut Israel Off From Being a Nation
Sign # 80 The Senseless Murder of Jewish People
Sign # 81 Anti-Semitism

Sign # 82 The Use of Modern Technology to Kill Jewish People and Destroy the State of Israel

Sign # 83 The Specific Hatred of Muslims Toward Jews

Sign # 84 The Dead Sea is Dividing Into Two Seas

Sign # 85 Lebanon Has Become an Enemy of Israel

Sign # 86 The Golden Gate of Jerusalem is Still Closed

Sign # 87 England Was the First to Transport Jews to the Holy Land in Sea-Going vessels

Sign # 88 The Revival of the Hebrew Language

Sign # 89 The Re-establishment of the Jewish Sanhedrin

Sign # 90 Israel's Old Estates are Better Now Than They Were in the Beginning

Sign # 91 Praise Will Come to the Jewish People in Lands Where They Have Been Put to Shame

Sign # 92 The Prophecies Concerning Israel's Holy Places

Sign # 93 Israel Giving Land to the Arabs

Sign # 94 The Desolation of the land East of the Dead Sea

Sign # 95 The Increase of Animal Life in the Holy Land

Sign # 96 The Book of Jonah Gives a Symbolic Picture of Israel's History

Sign # 97 God's Miraculous Way of Keeping Israel in the L:and

Sign # 98 In the End, Israel Would be the Center of World Attention

Sign # 99 Israel's Stamps of Prophecy

Sign # 100 The Covenant of Death That Israel Will Sign

Sign # 101 The Coming War Muslims Between Israel and it's is Building Today

Sign # 102 The Reason Provided for Russia's Invasion of Israel

Sign # 103 All of the Nations of the World will Come Against Israel

Sign # 104 In the End, Israel Stands Alone

Sign # 105 The Restoration of Petra

Sign # 106 The Discovery of an earthquake Fault in Israel

Sign # 107 In the end Israel Will See Three nations Come Against Them

Sign # 108 The Burning of Weapons of War

Sign # 109 The Coming Persecution of West Bank Settlers

SIGNS IN BOOK TWO

Sign # 1 The League of Arab States Being Formed Today
Sign # 2 The Rebuilding of Moab and Amnon.
Sign # 3 The Suez Canal
Sign # 4 The Revolution in Iran
Sign # 5 The Potential Destruction of Egypt
Sign # 6 Damascus Will Be Made a Desolation
Sign # 7 Lebanon Will Be Destroyed
Sign # 8 Egypt Is Again Ruled by Egyptian Rulers
Sign # 9 The Six Day War
Sign # 10 The Arabs Possess the Ancient High Places
Sign # 11 The Drying Up of the Nile River
Sign # 12 Egypt's Fear of Israel
Sign # 13 The Hebrew Language Would be Spoken in Egypt
Sign # 14 The Highway From Egypt to Syria
Sign # 15 Libya Taking Its Place in Prophecy
Sign # 16 God's Judgment on Iran
Sign # 17 Jewish People Driven Out of Gaza
Sign # 18 Radical Islam
Sign # 19 Muslim Inner and Outer Rings
Sign # 20 The Inner Ring of Muslim Nations
Sign # 21 Israel's Iron Dome Missile Defense System
Sign # 22 I Will Bless, I Will Curse
Sign # 23 The Coalition of the Gog-Magog War
Sign # 24 Persia (Iran) is Moving into Russia's Orbit
Sign # 25 Ethiopia Will be Part of the Russian Coalition
Sign # 26 Libya is Moves Into Their Prophetic Position
Sign # 27 Gomer Moves Into Her Prophetic Place
Sign # 28 Togarmah (Turkey) Lining Up With Russia and Iran
Sign # 29 The Rise of Communism
Sign # 30 Possible Russian Invasion of Israel
Sign # 31 Russia's Allies Lining Up With Her.
Sign # 32 Russia Will Be A Protector of Arab Nations
Sign # 33 The timing For the Russian Invasion
Sign # 34 Israel Invade by Airplanes
Sign # 35 Four World Powers Will Unite for the purpose of

Forcing Israel to Give Up Land to the Arabs.
Sign # 36 The Prediction of Modern Cities
Sign # 37 The Reasons For the Russian Invasion
Sign # 38 The Inability of Western Nations to Help
Sign # 39 Russia's Supply of Horses
Sign # 40 The Fall of the Soviet Union
Sign # 41 In the End Time Russia sill have a mighty army
Sign # 42 Why God is Against Russia
Sign # 43 The Atheism of Russia
Sign # 44 Egypt Will Be Part of the Coalition seeking to Destroy Israel.
Sign # 45 An Increase of Ravenous Birds in Israel
Sign # 46 The Alignment of Nations
Sign # 47 The Catholic Church and the Revived Roman Empire
Sign # 48 The Revival of the Old Roman Empire
Sign # 49 The Movement Toward World Government
Sign # 50 Buying and Selling Through a Numbering System
Sign # 51 A World Court
Sign # 52 A World Religion is Developing
Sign # 53 The Coming New World Economic Order
Sign # 54 The Drying Up of the Euphrates River
Sign # 55 The Highway From the East
Sign # 56 An Army of 200 Million Men
Sign # 57 China's Interest in the Middle East

SIGNS IN BOOK THREE

Sign # 1 False Christs
Sign # 2 Insubordination
Sign # 3 Individualism
Sign # 4 Sensationalism
Sign # 5 Confusion
Sign # 6 Lawlessness
Sign # 7 False Prophets
Sign # 8 Wars That Are More Frequent and Intense
Sign # 9 Rumors of Wars
Sign # 10 Ethnic Wars
Sign # 11 Wars of Kingdom Against Kingdom

Sign # 12 Famines

Sign # 13 Pestilence

Sign # 14 Earthquakes

Sign # 15 Unusual Weather Patterns

Sign # 16 Persecution of Christians

Sign # 17 Hatred of Christians

Sign # 18 Apostasy Will Develop As a Result of the Persecution

Sign # 19 Believers Will Betray One Another

Sign # 20 People Will Hate One Another

Sign # 21 A Day of Traitors

Sign # 22 An Explosion of Cults

Sign # 23 Iniquity Will Abound

Sign # 24 Lawlessness Will Increase

Sign # 25 Love Will Diminish

Sign # 26 The Gospel Will Be Preached Around the World

Sign # 27 Christians Will Not Think the Return of Christ is Immanent

Sign # 28 People Will Make Fantastic Claims as They Perform Signs
and Wonders

Sign # 29 The Population Explosion

Sign # 30 The Earth Will Be Filled With Violence

Sign # 31 The Imagination of Men will Be Evil Continuously

Sign # 32 Men Will Not Fear God

Sign # 33 Gluttony

Sign # 34 Government Corruption

Sign # 35 Homosexuality

Sign # 36 An Age of Pride

Sign # 37 Idleness

Sign # 38 Tsunamis

Sign # 39 Revolution and Insurrection in Many Countries

Sign # 40 Terrorism

Sign # 41 Signs in the Heavens

Sign # 42 People Will Have Heart Failure For Fear of What They
Believe is Coming to Earth

Sign # 43 The Weak Will Say They Are Strong

Sign # 44 An Increase in Knowledge

Sign # 45 The Atomic Bomb

Sign # 46 Weapons of Modern Warfare

Sign # 47 The Invention of the Smart Bomb
Sign # 48 The Automobile
Sign # 49 Television
Sign # 50 Modern Mechanical Miracles
Sign # 51 Israel's Anti-Ballistic Missile called "The Arrow"
Sign # 52 The Existence of Paratroopers

APPENDIX

BIOGRAPHIES OF MEMBERS ON THE COMMISSION APPOINTED BY PRESIDENT BILL CLINTON TO INVESTIGATE THE EFFECT THAT AN EMP EVENT WOULD HAVE ON THE U.S.A.

Dr. William R. Graham, chairman of the commission.

He is the retired Chairman of the Board and Chief Executive Officer of National Security Research Ins., a Washington based company that conducted technical operational and policy research and analysis related to U.S. national security. He currently serves as a member of the Department of Defense's Defense Science Board and the National Academies Board on Army Science and Technology. In the recent past, he has served as a member of several high level study groups, including the Department of Defense Transformation Study Group the Commission to Assess United States National Security Space Management and Organization, and the Commission to Assess the Ballistic Missile Threat to the United States. From 1986-89 Dr. Graham was the director of the White House Office of Science and Technology Policy, while serving concurrently as Science Advisor to President Reagan, Chairman of the Federal Joint Telecommunications Resources Board, and a member of the President's Arms Control Experts Group.

Dr. John S. Foster, Jr.

He is Chairman of the Board of GKN Aerospace Transparency Systems and consultant to Northrop Grumman Corporation, Technology Strategies & Alliances, Sikorsky Aircraft Corp., Intellectual Ventures, Lawrence Livermore National Lab, Ninesigma, and Defense Group. He retired from TRW as Vice President, Science and Technology, in 1988 and continued to serve on the Board of Directors of TRW from 1988 to 1994. Dr. Foster was Director of Defense Research and Engineering for the Department of Defense from 1965-1973, serving under both Democratic and Republican administrations. In other distinguished service, he has been on the Air Force Scientific Advisory Board, the Army Scientific Advisory Panel and the Ballistic Missile Defense Advisory Committee, Advanced Research Projects Agency. Until 1965, he was a panel consultant to the President's Science Advisory Committee, and from 1973-1990 he was a member of the President's Foreign Intelligence Advisory Board. He is a member of the Defense Science Board, which he chaired from January 1990 to June 1993. From 1952-1962, Dr. Foster was with Lawrence Livermore National Laboratory, where he began as a Division Leader in experimental physics, became Associate Director in 1958, and became Director of LLNL and Associate Director of the Lawrence Berkeley National Laboratory in 1961.

Dr. Earl Gjelde

He is the President and Chief Executive Officer of Summit Power Group Inc., and several affiliated companies, primary participants in the development of over 5,000 megawatts of natural gas fired electric and wind generating plants within the United States. He has served on the boards of EPRI and the U.S. Energy Association among others. He has held a number of U.S.A. government posts, serving as President George H. Walker Bush's Under Secretary and Chief Operating Officer of the U.S. Department of the Interior (1989) and serving President Ronald Reagan as Under Secretary and Chief Operating Officer of the U.S. Department of the Interior (1985-1988), the Counselor to the Secretary and Chief Operating Officer of the U.S. Department of Energy (1982-1985); and Deputy Administrator, Power Manager and Chief Operating Officer of the Bonneville Power Administration. While in the Reagan Administration, he served concurrently as Special Envoy to China (1987), Deputy Chief of Mission for the U.S.-Japan Science and Technology Treaty (1987 –1988), and Counselor for Policy to the Director of the National Critical Materials Council (1986-1988). Prior to 1980, he was a Principal Officer to the Bonneville Power Administration.

Dr. Robert J. Hermann

He is a Senior Partner of Global Technology Partners, LLC, a consulting firm that focuses on technology, defense aerospace, and related businesses worldwide. In 1998, Dr. Hermann retired from United Technologies Corporation (UTC), where he was Senior Vice President, Science and Technology. Prior to joining UTC in 1982, Dr. Hermann served 20 years with the National Security Agency with assignments in research development, operations, and NATO. In 1977, he was appointed Principal Deputy Assistant Secretary of Defense for Communications, Command, Control, and Intelligence. In 1979, he was named Assistant Secretary of the Air Force for Research, Development and Logistics and concurrently was Director of the National Reconnaissance Office

Mr. Henry (Hank) M. Kluepfel

Mr. Kluepfel is a Vice President for Corporate Development at SAIC. He is the company's leading cyberspace security advisor to the President's National Security Telecommunications Advisory Committee and the Network Reliability and Interoperability Council. Mr. Kluepfel is widely recognized for his 30 plus years of experience in security technology research, design, tools, forensics, risk reduction, education, and awareness, and he is the author of industry's de facto standard security base guideline for the Signaling System Number 7 (SS7) networks connecting and controlling the world's public telecommunications networks. In past affiliations with Telcordia Technologies (formerly Bellcore), AT&T, BellSouth and Bell Labs, he led industry efforts to protect, detect, contain and mitigate electronic and physical instructions and led the industry's understanding of the need to balance technical, legal, and policy based countermeasures to the then emerging hacker threat. He is recognized as a Certified Protection Professional by the American Society of Industrial Security and is a Senior Member of the Institute of Electrical and Electronics Engineers.

Gerald Richard L. Lawson, USAF (Ret.)

He is Chairman of Energy, Environment and Security Group, Ltd., and former President and CEO of the National Mining Association. He also serves as Vice Chairman of the Atlantic Council of the U.S., Chairman of the Energy Policy Committee of the U.S. Energy Association; Chairman of the United States delegation of the World Mining Congress; and Chairman of the International Committee for Coal Research. Active duty positions included serving as Military Assistant to the President; Commander, 8th Air Force; Chief of Staff, Supreme Headquarters Allied Powers Europe; Director for Plans and Policy, Joint Chiefs of Staff; Deputy Director of Operations, Headquarters U.S. Air Force; and Deputy Commander in Chief, U.S. European Command.

Dr. Gordon K. Soper

Dr. Soper is employed by Defense Group Incorporated. There, he has held various senior positions where he was responsible for broad direction of corporate goals relating to company support of government customers in areas of countering the proliferation of weapons of mass destruction, nuclear weapons effects and development of new business areas and growth of technical staff. He provides senior level technical support on a range of task areas to the Defense Threat Reduction Agency (DTRA) and to a series of Special Programs for the Office of the Secretary of Defense and the White House Military Office. Previously, Dr. Soper was Principal Deputy to the Assistant to the Secretary of Defense for Nuclear, Chemical and Biological Defense Programs; Director, Office of Strategic and Theater Nuclear Forces Command and Communications (C3) of the Office of the Assistant Secretary of Defense (C31); Associate Director for Engineering and Technology Chief Scientist at the Defense Communications Agency (now DISA); and held various leadership positions at the Defense Nuclear Agency (now DTRA).

Dr. Lowell L. Wood, Jr.

He is a scientist-technologist who has contributed to technical aspects of national defense, especially defense against missile attack, as well as to controlled thermonuclear fusion, laser science and applications, optical and underwater communications, very high performance computing and digital computer-based physical modeling, ultra high power electromagnetic systems, space exploration and climate stabilization geophysics. Wood, obtained his Ph.D. in astrophysics and planetary and space physics at UCLA in 1965, following receipt of bachelor's degrees in chemistry and math in 1962. He has held faculty and professional research staff appointments at the University of California (from which he retired after more than four decades in 2006) and is a Research Fellow at the Hoover Institution at Stanford University. He has advised the U.S. Government in many capacities, and has received a number of awards and honors from both government and professional bodies. Wood is the author, co-author or editor of more than 200 unclassified technical papers and books and more than 300 classified publications, and is named as an inventor on more than 200 patents and patents-pending.

Dr. Joan B. Woodard

She is Executive Vice President and Deputy Laboratories Director for Nuclear Weapons at Sandia National Laboratories. Sandia's role is to provide engineering support and design to the Nation's nuclear weapons stockpile, provide our customers with research, development and testing services, and manufacture specialized non-nuclear products and components for national defense and security applications. The laboratories enable safe and secure deterrence through science, engineering, and management excellence. Prior to her current assignment, Dr. Woodard served as Executive Vice President and Deputy Director, responsible for Sandia's programs, operations, staff and facilities: developing policy and assuring implementation; and strategic planning. Her Sandia history began in 1974, and she rose through the ranks to become the Director of the Environmental Programs Center and the Director of the Product Realization Weapon Components Center; Vice President of the Energy & Environment Division and Vice President of the Energy Information and Infrastructure Technologies Division. Joan has been elected to the Phi Kappa Phi Honor Society and has served on numerous external panels and boards, including the Air Force Scientific Advisory Board, the National Academy of Sciences' Study on Science and Technology for Countering Terrorism, the Secretary of Energy's Nuclear Energy Research Advisory Council, the Congressional Commission on Electromagnetic Pulse, and the Intelligence Science Board. She has received many honors, including the Upward Mobility Award from the Society of Women Engineers and was named as "One of Twenty Women to Watch in the New Millennium" by the Albuquerque Journal. She also received the Spirit of Achievement Award from National Jewish Hospital.

END NOTES

INTRODUCTION

1. Adapted from Josephus: *War of the Jews*; Book Vi, Chapters IV & V)
2. *Lamplighter Magazine,* January-February, 2008, p.5

ABOUT MATTHEW 24

1. Derek Prince, *Prophetic Guide to the End Times*, Page 54. Chosen Books, Grand rapids, Michigan
2. Ibid. Page 54

CHAPTER 2 FALSE CHRISTS AND FALSE PROPHETS

1. *Time Magazine*, February 20, 1989
2. Ed Hindson, *Foreshadows of Wrath and Redemption*, pp.39-40 (Harvest House Publishers, Eugene, OR, 1999)
3. Ibid., pp. 41-42

CHAPTER 3 WARS AND RUMORS OF WAR

1. Derek Prince, *Prophetic Guide to the End Times*, p. 53 (Chosen Publications, Grand Rapids, MI 2008)
2. 3/6/20
3. http://www.frontpagemagazine.com/
4. The *Lamplighter Magazine*, September – October 2008, p. 16.

CHAPTER 4 FAMINES

1. http://agriculture.imva.info
2. http://www.theaustrailian.com.au
3. *Los Angeles Times*, July 21, 2011
4. *Los Angeles Times*, January 1, 2012.
5. http://www.theaustrailian.com.au
6. http://www.prisonplanet.com
7. http://www.prisonplanet.com
8. *Los Angeles Times*, April 26, 2010.
9. *Voice of Evangelism Magazine*, June-July, 2009.
10. *Los Angeles Times*, August 4, 2011,
11. Ibid
12. *Los Angeles Times*, August 20, 2011.
13. Ibid.
14. *Time Magazine* of April 7, 2008
15. http://www.telegraph.co.uk/
16. http://www..telegraph.co.uk/earth/8359076/
    us-farmers-fear-of-the-return-of-the- dust-bowl-days
17. *Los Angeles Times* home section, April 26, 2007 p. 1.
18. *Los Angeles Times*, June 10, 2007, p. 1.
19. Ibid.
20. *Denver Post*, August 5, 2012, Page B1.
21. http://www.telegraph.co.uk/science/science/science-
    news/7980954/bee decline
22. Midnight Call Magazine, November, 1996
23. *Los Angeles Times*, July, 14 2008.
24. *Los Angeles Times*, January 26, 2009
25. *Los Angeles Times,* December 22, 2008
26. *Los Angeles Times*, August 30, 2011
27. Ibid.
28. http://www.telegraph.couk/earth/8359076/US-farmersd-fear-
    the-return-of-the-dust-bowl.html
29. *Los Angeles Times*, December 12, 2011
30. *Midnight Call Magazine*, June 2012
31. *Los Angeles Times*, March 6, 2011
32. *Los Angeles Times*, March 26, 2011

33. http://business.financialpost.com/2011/06/29/ global-agriculture-suppy-keeps- worsening
34. Ibid.
35. http://theeconomiccollapseblog.com
36. Ibid.
37. http://www.theaustrailian.com.au
38. *Houston Chronicle*, May 31, 2012
39. *Los Angeles Times*, August 23 2012, Page A6.
40. *Time Magazine*, January 30, 2012
41. http://www./telegraph.co.uk/
42. *Midnight Call Magazine*, April 2011, page 37
43. http://theeconomiccollapseblog.com
44. Ibid.
45. Ibid.
46. *Los Angeles Times*, November 26, 2008.
47. *Los Angeles Times*.
48. *Los Angeles Times*, August 3, 2008
49. *Wall Street Journal*, January 9,
50. *Los Angeles Times*, November 16, 2010
51. Ibid
52. *Los Angeles Times*, March 1, 2013, D-10
53. *Los Angeles Times*, April 30, 2013, p. AA1

CHAPTER 5 PESTILENCES

1. http://www.prophectnewswatch.com/July/10/2009
2. *Associated Press*, March 16, 2009.
3. *Lamplighter Magazine*, May-June, 2005, p. 17.
4. The *Midnight Call Magazine*, November, 1996.
5. *Associated Press*: 3/16/2009 8:55 AM
6. http://www.washintonpost.com/wpdyn/content/article/2010/10/11ar2010101104518.html?wprss=rssnation
7. http://www.washingtonpost.com/blog/2011/01/dead-birds-dead-fish-turn-up_a.html
8. *Los Angeles Times*, January 6, 2011,
9. *Contra Costa CA Times,* March 8, 2011
10. *Los Angeles Times*, March 9, 2011.

11. *Los Angeles Times*, October 17, 2007 front page.
12. *Los Angeles Times*.
13. Ibid.
14. The *Washington Post* (issue unknown)
15. *USA Today*, March 6, 2013
16. Unknown Source
17. The *Hal Lindsay Television Report,* June 7, 2013
18. The *Los Angeles Times*, June 30, 2013

CHAPTER 6 NATURE WILL BE UNSTABLE

1. http://earthquake.usgs.gov/earthquake/equarchives/yer/eqstats.php
2. *NaturalNews*.com, January 5, 2008.
3. *AFP news*, March 13, 2011.
4. *Prophecy in the News Magazine*, August, 2005, p. 28.
5. *Los Angeles Times*, October 28, 2010.
6. *Joel Rosenberg Newsletter*, December 20, 2010.
7. http://www.examiner.com/
8. Ibid.
9. *Newsweek magazine*, March 28, 2011.
10, *Lamplighter Magazine*, May-June, 2011, Page 18.
11. *Los Angeles Times,* April 28, 2011.
12. *Los Angeles Times*, April 18, 2011.
13. *Los Angeles Times*, August 4, 2011.

CHAPTER 7 THE PERSECUTION AND HATRED OF CHRISTIANS

1. *Times of London*, August 3, 2009.
2. *Readers Digest*, August, 1997.
3. http:/www.wnd.com/
4. The *Voice of the Martyrs* e-mail, January 9, 2009.
5. http:/www.telegraph.co.uk
6. *The Voice of the Martyrs Newsletter*, October 2010.
7. *The Voice of the Martyrs Newsletter*, December 11, 2008.
8. *Israel My Glory Magazine* November/December, 2008.
9. *Prophecy News Watch*, December 11, 2008.

10. *Los Angeles Times*, March 9, 2010.
11. *The Voice of the Martyrs Newsletter*. August, 2010.
12. Brad O'Leary, *America's War On Christianity* (Washington, D.C. World Net Daily Press 2010) pp. 14-15
13. Ibid. p.27
14. Ibid. p.29
15. Ibid. p.31
16. http:/www.jeremiahproject.com/prophecy/discrimination.html
17. http://archive.newsmax.com/archives/articles/2003/10/2/102405.shtml
18. http://www.andrewwklavan.com/2010/02/19/me-atonenewsnow/
19. Internet article quoted in *Prophecy in the News Magazine*, March 2007, Pp. 38.
20. www.contact@afa.net
21. wttp://www.christianpost.com/news/gropwing-intolerance-for Christianity-in-u.s.
22. Ibid.
23. *Washington Times* Newspaper, May 15, 2002.
24. The *Legal Alert* newsletter magazines of the Christian Law Association.
25. The *Legal Alert*, published by the Christian Law Association, December, 2004.
26. Ibid.
27. Brad O'Leary, *America's war on Christianity* (Washington, D.C. World Net Daily Press 2010) p.34
28. Ibid. p.63
29. Ibid. p.69
30. Ibid. p.75
31. *Los Angeles Times*, April 16, 2010.
32. http:/www.washiungtomtimes.com/
33. *Pacific Justice Institute* press release, March 9, 2009.
34. www.*OneNewsNow*, March 6, 2009.
35. http://archive.newsmax.com/archives/articles/2003/9/30/254824.shtml
36. www. *OneNewsNow*, March 3, 2010.
37. *Friends of Israel Magazine*, June 2010.

38. *Pacific Justice Institute* letter at the end of 2009.
39. http;?www.wnd.com/
40. http:/www.visiontoamerica.org/articles/
muslim-students-want-to-take-over-christian-college
41. http:/www.dailymail.co.uk, December 4, 2009.
42. OneNewsNow.com, August 19, 2009.
43. *Israel My Glory Magazine*, January/February, 2010.
44. http://archive.newsmax.com/archives/articles/2003/9/30/1548
24.shtml
45. http://www.jeremiahproject.com/prophecy/discrimination.htl
46. http://www.toddstarnes.com/2010/10/-christian-roommate-ad-is-civil-rights-violation
47. James Newton as quoted in Lamplighter Magazine, November-December, 2010, p. 11.
48. *Lamplighter magazine*, March-April 2005, p. 11.
49. *Christian Law magazine.*
50. http:/www.Christian.org.uk/
51. Christian Examiner, February 2009, p. 18.
52. *Columbus, Ohio Dispatch* December 17, 2004.
53. info@ prophecy newswatch.com May 30, 2008.
54. *Legal Alert* newsletter, November, 2008.
55. The *Lamplighter Magazine*, July-August. 2009.
56. *Christian Law Magazine*; Article from several publications of their magazine.
57. http://www.jeremiahprojecy,com/prophecy.warxian1.html
58. http://www.wnd.com/2013/03/lesbian-mary-mother-of-god/
59. Strong's number 4624
60. Roberet Liebi, *Are we Really Living in the Last days?* (Germany, Christlicher Medienvertrich Hagedorn Publishers) P. 289

CHAPTER 8 MISCELLANEOUS SIGNS FROM THE GOSPELS

1. http://cbsnews.com
2. As reported in the *Lamplighter Magazine*, March-April 2005
3. Unknown source

4. AFA Journal, June 2011, p. 6
5. *Los Angeles Times*, September 13, 2012, p. A-16
6. *Whistleblower Magazine*, September 2005, p.15
7. *Los Angeles Times*, January 2,2103, p. D-1
8. http://townhall.com
9. Ibid. P.2
10. *Strong's dictionary* # 4535
11. *Strong's Dictionary* #181
12. *Strong's Dictionary* #5400
13. Roberet Liebi, *Are we Really Living in the Last days?* (Germany, Christlicher Medienvertrich Hagedorn Publishers) Pages 310-311.

CHAPTER 9 THE WEAK
WILL SAY THEY ARE STRONG

1. *Los Angeles Times*, November 2, 1989
2. *Time Magazine*, January 1990
3. http:www,worldtribune.com/worldtribune/05/ front2453711.9284722223.htlm
4. http:www.khouse.org/articles/2005/585/
5. http://hawaiifreepress.com/ArticlesMain/tabid/56.articleType/ ArticleView/articeld/4861/The-Threat-to-US-Security.aspx
6. http://www.personalliberty.com/conservativepolitics/ organizations-corporate-media-growing-wise-to-emp-threat/
7. http://www.familysecuritymatters.org/publications/id.5801/ pub_detail.asp
8. http://www.cbn.com/cbnnews/us/2011/november/ Intel-Shows-Iran-Nuke-Attack-on-US-Easy/as/EMP
9. http://en.wikipedia.org/wiki/Electromagnetic_pulse
10. http://www.time.com/time/nation/ article/0,8599,1976224.00.html
11. http://www.familysecuritymatters.org/publications/id.5801/ pub_detaial.asp
12. http://www.khouse,org/articles/2005/585/.
13. http://hawaiifreepress.com/ArticlesMain/tabid/56.articleType/ ArticleView/articeld/4861/The-Threat-to-US-Security.aspx

14. http://www.shtfplan.com/emergency-preparedness/emp-threat-within-one-year-9-out-of-10-americans-would-be=-dead_05042010
15. F. Michael Maloof, *A Nation Forsaken,* (Washington, D.C.,WND Books, 2013) P. 82
16. Ibid. P. 19.
17. Ibid. P. 27-28
18. http://www.biblepophecyblog.com/2012/07/iran-leader-we-must-prepare-for-end.html>utm.source-feedburnedr&utm*me-dium=email&utm*_campaign=feed%3A+BibleProphecy-Bog+%28Bible+Prophecy+Blog%29
19. http://www.newsmax.com/nresfront/irannuclearplan/2008/07/29/id/324724
20. http://www.onesecondafter.com/pb/wp_d10e87d9wp_d102=e87d9.html
21. F. Michael Maloof, *A Nation Forsaken*, (Washington,D.C., WND Books, 2013) P. 115
22. Ibid. P. 116
23. Ibid. P. 109
24. Ibid. P. 85
25. http://www.nytimes.com/2012/11/15/science/earth/electronics/electricity-industry-is-urged-to-gird-against-terrorist-attacks.html?_r=3&
26. F. Michael Maloof, A Nation Forsaken, (Washington, D.C., *WND Books*, 2013) P. 79
27 .http://townhall.com/tipsheet/christfield/2010/07/30/uipdatweds_emp_threat_how_our_enemies_could_knock-out-everything
28. http://www.wnd.com/2011/11/370917/
29. http://www.wnd.com/2012/09/congress-told-u-s-life-unsustainable-after-emp/
30. F. Michael Maloof, *A Nation Forsaken,* (Washington, D.C., *WND Books*, 2013), P. 71
31. Ibid. P. 108
32. http://www.wnd.com/2012/11/u-s-electrical-grid-inherent-ly-vulnerable/?cat_orig=us

33. **http://cnsnews.com/news/article/less-50-us-households-now-led-married-couples-says-census-**
34. http://www.theblaze.com/stories/defense-secretary-cyberattacks-have-the-potential-for-another-pearl-harbor/

CHAPTER 10: MODERN INVENTIONS IN PROPHECY

1. http://www.alternet.org, January 31, 2011,
2. http://www.dailymailco.uk/sciencetech/article-1334114/new-us-army-rifles-use-radio-controlled-smart-bullets
3. Grant Jeffrey, *Shadow Government* (Colorado Springs, Colorado, Waterbrook Press, 2007) p. 86.
4. Joel Rosenberg, *Epicenter* (Carol Stream, Illinois, Tyndale Publishers, Inc., 2006) p. 234.
5. http://www.lamblion.com/articles/articles/tribulation5.php
6. Grant Jeffrey, *Shadow Government* (Colorado Springs, Colorado, Waterbrook Press, 2007) p. 90.